The Trial of Man

The Trial of Man

*Christianity and Judgment
in the World of Shakespeare*

Craig Bernthal

ISI BOOKS
2003

Cataloging-in-Publication Data

Bernthal, Craig
    The trial of man: Christianity and judgment in the world of Shakespeare / Craig Bernthal — 1st ed. — Wilmington, DE: ISI Books, 2003

    p. / cm.

    ISBN 1-932236-03-1
    1. Shakespeare, William, 1536–1616 — Knowledge — Law.
    2. Shakespeare, William, 1536–1616 — Criticism and interpretation. 3. Shakespeare, William, 1536–1616 — Characters — Judges. 4. Justice, Administration of — History.

    PR3028 .B47 2003   2003102916
    822.33—dc21   CIP

Interior design by Kara Beer

Printed in the United States

ISI Books
the imprint of the
Intercollegiate Studies Institute
P. O. Box 4431 • 3901 Centerville Road
Wilmington, Del. 19807
www.isibooks.org

For Gail, my north star

TABLE OF CONTENTS

ACKNOWLEDGMENTS

I am deeply grateful to Bruce Thornton, who encouraged me to write this book and whose scholarly energy continues to be an inspiration. Thanks to my colleagues for reading the manuscript and for their unflagging support: Bruce, David Borofka, Connie and John Hales, Steve Yarbrough, and Liza Wieland. Thanks also to my fine editor at ISI, Jeremy Beer, and to Luis Costa, Dean of Arts and Humanities at California State University, Fresno, who supported this project in more ways than one. And thanks most of all to Gail, my persevering re-reader, bulwark, and love.

I know my state, both full of shame and scorn,
Conceived in sin, and unto labour born,
Standing with fear, and must with horror fall,
And destined unto judgment, after all.

Ben Jonson, "To Heaven"

INTRODUCTION

God and the Courts

I practiced trial law for five years, but nothing I encountered during that time was more eye-opening than the "Rule 9" internship I did after my second year in law school. In Washington state, Admission to Practice Rule 9 authorizes law students who have completed two years of study to work in the office of a prosecuting attorney and try misdemeanor cases in district court. I worked for the Snohomish County Prosecutor for four months in the summer of 1977. After a one-week orientation, in which I saw one speeding trial, I was on my own with a daily load of district court cases.

I learned quickly that each judge ran his courtroom in a different way, and each seemed to have a different idea of what criminal procedure and the law of evidence required. There were rules in the district courts—sometimes at odds with what the law actually said—that had not filtered down to law schools, and I spent the summer learning them the hard way, eliciting snarls from judges and, sometimes, peals of laughter. I was a tinhorn with nothing but knowledge that came out of books, and that not under the best command. In district court, given the penny-ante nature of what was at stake for most defendants, appeals were usually more expensive than they were worth. This gave judges a certain latitude, both with regard to courtroom procedure and the application of law. For instance, I once heard a district court judge announce in a civil case—to the stupefaction of the plaintiff's attorney, who was trying to collect a small debt—that a certain statute requiring punitive interest did not apply in *his* court.

One of the judges I faced weekly particularly favored an inquisitorial rather than an adversarial approach to trial. He liked to take over for both attorneys, questioning the witnesses and even cross-examining them, until he decided he had enough facts to make a decision. He thought that attorneys were superfluous at best, and damned obstacles to the truth at worst. He couldn't dismiss attorneys from his court, but he would have liked to. He would have cleared his docket by noon instead of three o'clock.

Reading through Shakespeare's plays, which contain well over thirty trial scenes, one could conclude that Shakespeare also thought attorneys dispensable. In all of his plays, there is only one appearance by a lawyer. In that instance, the lawyer represents only himself, and it turns out he has a fool for a client. (We will get to him in the first chapter.) Unlike today's courtroom dramatists, Shakespeare was primarily interested in judgment, not the fencing between lawyers that takes place in courtroom thrillers like *Anatomy of a Murder*, Judge John Voelker's excellent novel and the granddaddy of today's huge crop of pale offspring. Shakespeare's courtroom dramas focus on the judge and parties "unrepresented by counsel." This is a bit surprising, since the amount of litigation in England grew by leaps and bounds during Shakespeare's lifetime, and the number of lawyers with it. The absence of lawyers in his plays might be accounted for by their absence in the most dramatic cases: treason trials especially and criminal trials in general. (Our right to certain procedural protections, such as the right to counsel, were absent in Elizabethan and Jacobean criminal courts.)

What cannot be accounted for by reference to the practice of Shakespeare's day is the absence of juries in his plays. The jury system was well established, particularly in criminal matters, and the English were proud of it. Yet Shakespeare presents not even one jury; he is not interested in how twelve people arrive at judgments of fact, but in how one judge, given God-like responsibility without God-like powers, finally decides the facts and declares a verdict. Judgment is the archetypal situation for Shakespeare, the one event that every human being will have to face, on one or both sides of the grave. In the final judgment there will be no lawyers, juries, or witnesses, and Shakespeare, the poet of the universal, concentrates on that scene. The tension in Shakespeare's trial scenes pulses between the judge, the accused, and often the accuser. Shakespeare asks: Given humanity's limited resources, doubtful morality, and the opacity of even the recent past, how can the most well-intentioned judge arrive at the truth in any contested matter? How can judges ever be completely sure of the correctness of their verdicts? (Of course, knowing the virtual impossibility of this, we do not require absolute certainty in any determination of fact. Triers of fact, judge or jury, make their determinations by a preponderance of the evidence in civil cases and beyond a reasonable doubt in criminal cases.) Even if a judge is fortunate enough to determine accurately the relevant facts in any particular case, the problem of justice remains. What punishments should be meted out? What fines should be levied, damages awarded, remedies applied? Even if judges had perfect knowledge and a perfect sense of justice, could we devise a system that was free from corruption? And Shakespeare also broaches the broader political question: How does the health of the body politic affect the judicial system, and vice versa?

Shakespeare puts these questions and more to his audience, and they give us no less trouble than they did Shakespeare's contemporaries. Today, even conservatives are thinking twice about supporting the death penalty, given the significant potential for mistake and the impossibility of unexecuting someone. Since 1975, eighty-seven inmates have walked off death rows across the nation because wrongful convictions have been established.[1] Mistaken identity is sometimes established, newly discovered exculpatory evidence is presented, or DNA tests lead to exoneration (in eight cases, as of this writing). Concerning even-handed justice, there is no doubt that black or Hispanic criminals generally get longer jail sentences than whites convicted for committing the same crimes. And what about cases of judicial corruption? Although such cases rarely come to light, judges have been convicted of taking bribes and there is no reason to believe that any judicial system will ever exist in which all the judges are spotless.[2] These problems, very much with us today, are all examined by Shakespeare and his audience, though from a very different perspective than ours, for Shakespeare's society was profoundly Christian, while ours is thoroughly secular. If we are going to understand law and judgment in Shakespeare's plays—and thus to a large degree, Shakespeare himself—we have to understand the historical context in which Shakespeare wrote, and we must start by examining Christianity's relationship to the law in Renaissance England and how it affected people's beliefs about law and judgment.

The Theological Foundations of English Law

Christianity furnished the single most powerful and pervasive frame of reference for the English of the sixteenth and seventeenth centuries. The Bible was *the* central piece of cultural equipment for making sense of the world and evaluating it, and it was also the most influential source of language, providing a vast number of maxims and stories, which the English used extensively in the form of allusions and analogies. Shakespeare's plays are pervaded by references to the Bible partly because it was such an important part of an Englishman's working vocabulary.

Shakespeare lived in a Europe wracked with the religious controversies of the Reformation. Tudor and Stuart policy, foreign and domestic, was inextricably bound up with these controversies, making religion a continual subject of discussion in Renaissance England. Educated English citizens understood religious arguments in detail, and by today's standards, possessed an impressive grasp of theology. As Roland Mushat Frye notes, "Approximately half of the books published in England between the inception of printing and the parliamentary revolution bore explicitly religious titles, and religious ideas figured prominently or pervasively in many if not most of the others."[3] Church attendance was mandatory in Shakespeare's day, as was chapel attendance for students going to Oxford and Cambridge. Anglican priests were required yearly to read, Sunday by Sunday, the sermons contained in the official *Homilies Appointed to Be Read in Churches,*[4] encouraging a homogeneity of belief—and also giving the government a way to indoctrinate its citizens. English grammar school students had the regular assignment of attending service on Sunday and summarizing the sermon (in Latin, of course) for school on Monday.

The people of Elizabethan and Jacobean England believed that man's will and perceptions had been corrupted by the fall of Adam and Eve, and as the result of this original sin, man had a natural inclination toward evil. Good and evil were clearly distinguishable, but evil was, superficially, easier, more attractive, and more compelling than the good. As a result, a person often chose to commit sinful acts, and sinning, as Hamlet tells Gertrude, becomes addictive. The more one chose evil, the easier it became to choose, the heart became hardened, and small sins led to large ones. Since the health of the commonwealth depended on the spiritual health of its citizens, any kind of debauchery or loose moral behavior was seen as a threat to the community, one that necessitated communal action. Thus, the law played a major role in the constant battle against sin, preserving the spiritual health of the individual and the body politic. Law was as much a religious as a civil institution, and this sharply differentiates the Elizabethan judicial system from ours.

The prevailing theory of law in our time is that the law is rational, utilitarian, and secular. Legislators create rules to accomplish policy objectives. Laws are the instruments used to promote the finite, material interests of particular groups and individuals. Judges, in reaching decisions, use legal precedents to solve problems, not to propound universal truths or to make the will of God explicit. Laws are evaluated not with respect to any universal standard of right and wrong, but by workability. In evaluating a law, the question our legislators ask is whether it accomplishes the policy objectives that it was designed to promote. For us, this means the law is never final, because policy is never final. Laws are continually revised, and if a judge is overruled by a higher court or, in effect, by the legislature, this may only indicate that people have decided to institute new policy: thus, at one point, a federal income tax is unconstitutional (*Pollock v. Farmer's Loan and Trust Co.* [1895]) because it violates the constitutional provision requiring that a direct tax be apportioned among the states on the basis of population, but at another point, income taxes become constitutional (in 1912 the Sixteenth Amendment to the Constitution was passed). Sometimes the Supreme Court decides that the time for new policy has come, as in *Roe v. Wade* (1973), where the court discovered a hitherto unrecognized constitutional right to an abortion during the first trimester of a pregnancy, a limited right during the second, and an extremely limited right during the third. However you feel about *Roe v. Wade* as policy, the decision was certainly a remarkable "find" in the Constitution.

Modern positivist jurisprudence, the author of which is the utilitarian Jeremy Bentham, sees law as the rational creation of the state for its own ends. Bentham's idea of law's origin and purpose would have seemed strange to the jurists of Renaissance England. They understood that God was the source of law. The state, in fact, was subordinate to the law of God and created for the benefit of that law. The state did not create law, according to the Christian view, but merely discovered it, gave expression to it, enforced and guarded it. Most law developed over the centuries as custom, an organic product of God's creation. Elizabethan legislators and jurists are more comparable to modern physicists than they are to modern members of their own profession, for like physicists, they sought the universal and immutable.

In England, these ideas are given their most influential expression by the fifteenth-century political theorist, Sir John Fortescue, in *On the Laws and Governance of England*. Fortescue encourages a hypothetical prince to study law because:

> All laws that are promulgated by man are decreed
> by God. For, since the Apostle says, "All power is
> from the Lord God," laws established by man, who
> receives power to this end from God, are also
> formulated by God. . . . By this you are taught that to
> learn the laws, even though human ones, is to learn
> laws that are sacred and decreed of God, the study of
> which does not lack the blessing of divine
> encouragement.[5]

Fortescue argues that all men want happiness—which must include virtue—and that justice makes people happy. But since original sin has destroyed man's desire to be virtuous, the discovery of law comes to us through divine grace:

> As Pariensis says . . . "The fundamental appetite of
> man for virtue is so vitiated by original sin, that to
> him the works of vice savour sweet and those of virtue
> bitter." Wherefore that some give themselves to love
> and pursuit of virtues is a gift of divine goodness, not
> derived from human merit. Are not, then, the laws
> which, guided and directed by grace, accomplish all
> these effects worthy to be studied with all
> application?[6]

A set of metaphors was developed to show how God's grace, as law, flowed through the country. Descriptions of England as a "body politic" find the eventual sustenance of that body in a hierarchal chain that ran from the lowliest Englishman to the king, and from the king to God. In *De Republica Anglorum* (1565), Sir Thomas Smith used the metaphor of the body politic to describe the king's relationship to the judicial system as follows: "the prince is the life, the head and the authority of all things that be done in the realm of England," adding "this head doth distribute his authority and power to the rest of the members for the government of his realme, and the commonwealth of the politique bodie of England in choosing the election of the chiefe officers and magistrates and in the administration of justice."[7]

William Hughes, in "The Diversity of Courts and Their Jurisdictions" (1642), stated that the king was the "fountain of justice."[8] This metaphor was more generally applied in Sir Francis Bacon's 1612 essay "Of Judicature," where he used it to describe the continuing effect of bad judicial decisions: "One foul sentence doth more hurt than many foul examples, for these do but corrupt the stream, the other corrupteth the fountain."[9] Bacon used the same idea in a 1617 speech to the judges and justices of the peace of England, in which he stressed that itinerant justices—the assize judges who toured each circuit in England twice a year—were more likely to be disinterested and free from local prejudice than justices of the peace who resided where they held court:

> The six circuits of England are like the four rivers in Paradise. They go to water the whole kingdom, and pass through the whole land to the distributing of justice for a man's life, his goods, and his freehold, and do justice from the greatest to the groom. Where justice is local and not itinerant, there judges are subject to be affected and infected with the conditions and humours of the country where they are, but justices itinerant in their circuits, they preserve the laws pure, and are not led by affections. . . . This manner of justices itinerant carrieth with it the majesty of the King to the people and the love of the people to the King; for the Judges in their circuits are sent *a latere Regis* to feel the pulse of the subject and to cure his disease.[10]

Ironically, in the 1621 proceeding in Parliament to impeach Lord Chancellor Bacon, the chief justice of the realm,

for taking bribes, Sir Robert Phelps turned the fountain metaphor against Bacon, accusing him of muddying the stream
nearest the source, since Bacon, as chief justice, was closest
to the king. If the fountains of justice were muddy, how could
the streams—the justices of the peace and circuit court
judges—be pure?[11]

Though the king was the fountain from which the judges,
as vessels, distributed justice throughout the body politic, God
was the acknowledged source of the fountain. In his
Archeion, William Lambarde flatly states: "It is the office of
the King to deliver Justice," and at the end of the book he
explains from whom the delivery is being made:

> Now therefore, as God is highly to be thanked, that
> these *Flowers* of *Justice* are thus *delivered forth* and
> *Dispersed* abroad: So is *hee* also heartily to bee prayed
> unto, that those which *occupie* the *place* of *Justice* by
> them, may so behave themselves as it may appeare
> that they doe not *exercise* the *judgments* of man, but
> of *God himselfe*, the *chief justice* of the *World* for so
> shall the good be *succoured*, and the *evill suppressed*,
> so shall the *judges* themselves be well *acquitted*, so
> shall her *Majestie* be duly served, and *God himselfe*
> honoured aright.[12]

Thus, the administration and enforcement of law in Renaissance England was embedded in a politico-theological
framework in which the laws themselves, and trials and verdicts in the most mundane of cases, had national and cosmo-
logical significance. This was reflected also in court ritual.
For instance, at the border of the first county they entered,
circuit judges were met by trumpeters and the sheriff's bailiff,
and as they neared the first town where trials would take
place—the "assize" town—they were met by the sheriff himself, local officers, and representatives of the local gentry. The

parade into town included pikemen and liverymen, specially clothed for the occasion. The judge was greeted with music, bells, and sometimes a Latin oration. The judge then went to his lodgings, where he met with the local gentry to learn the state of the county and to get a sense of the cases he was about to hear. The next stop after this was the church, where the local minister read prayers and the sheriff's chaplain delivered a sermon. These sermons were long, usually forty to fifty pages, though the prizewinner is probably William Pemberton's sermon at the Hertford assizes in 1615: it went 108 pages. With this spiritual boost, the judge was ready to hear cases throughout his circuit, which would comprise five or six counties.[13]

Trials were the occasions in which human judges applied laws, the instruments of God's grace, to the resolution of human conflict and the accomplishment of justice. Courtrooms were the sites where temporal and spiritual authority met, and judges, to do God's will on earth, attempted to disentangle the truth from satanic deception. In keeping with this, criminal trials were displayed to the public as morality plays, illustrating divine principles about the discovery of sin, punishment, grace, and repentance. Trials and executions were presented to the public in such a way as to reinforce Christian doctrine. Trials reminded Christians that they were faced with the same choice between good and evil as their forebears Adam and Eve, and that, like their original parents, they would be held accountable for their decisions. Criminals who repented on the scaffold, who showed "a broken and contrite heart," and thus gave evidence of having accepted God's grace, were said to have "died well." They could look forward to forgiveness and a place in heaven. Each of these conversions affirmed Christian beliefs and legitimated the state as God's servant.

This, of course, represents the ideal functioning of the

system, but Englishmen realized, and Shakespeare takes it as his fundamental premise, that people fall far short of what God wants them to be. The human condition, steeped in original sin, affected the judicial system as well as the men who appeared before it. Poor kingship could lead to unfair adjudication and unfair adjudication could undermine the king. Likewise, corruption in the judicial system, for whatever reason, could arouse the wrath of God, whose displeasure might then be visited on the kingdom in rebellion and anarchy. Trials, therefore, did not merely decide the fate of individual criminal defendants or settle the claims of civil litigants, but provided microcosmic readings of the kingdom's health and its conformity with cosmic patterns of order, which were simply manifestations of God's will.

The fairness with which a trial was conducted indicated as much about the health of the body politic as the result. The ethical foundation of trial rested on principles of due process and the rule of law: the conviction that judicial proceedings would be conducted by a set of rules that were known beforehand and bound all participants. In his *History of the World*, Sir Walter Raleigh distinguished monarchy from tyranny solely on the basis of the manner in which judges administered the law:

> The most ancient, most generall, and most approved [form of government] was the Government of one ruling by just Lawes, called *Monarchy*, to which *Tyranny* is opposed, being also a sole and absolute Rule, exercised according to the *will* of the Commander, without respect or observation of the Lawes of God or Men. For a lawful *Prince* or *Magistrate* (said Aristotle) is the Keeper of Right and Equity, and of this condition ought every magistrate to be, according to the rule of God's word: *Judges and Officers shalt thou make thee in thy cities and these shall judge.*[14]

The citizens of Renaissance England believed the primary function of the government was to dispense justice. Good government was equated with fairness in the courts, and that meant judges had to evenhandedly apply the same rules to everyone. For the English, "the rule of law" was no empty piece of rhetoric, but something they regarded as the cornerstone of their judicial system and the birthright of every citizen; it was what distinguished their country from most others in Europe. In France or Spain, the people might be subject to the capricious whims of their rulers, but not in England, where the same laws bound everyone, including the monarch. That the rule of law was of divine origin was established by reference to Deuteronomy 17:18–20, which directed the king of Israel to read the law every day of his life, to revere it, to keep it, "and to not consider himself better than his brothers and turn from the law to the right or to the left."

The idea that human law is the manifestation of natural law, the *jus naturale*, which has its ultimate origin in the mind of God, was maintained with vigor in England until the end of the eighteenth century. Edmund Burke was its last great advocate. "All human laws are, properly speaking, only declaratory," he said. And although the laws enacted by men were likely to be imperfect manifestations of God's will, human beings had the duty to declare the law of God as accurately as they could. Burke and Fortescue would have understood each other perfectly, for Burke also thought that judges worked in service to God. Burke wrote, "Religion is so far, in my opinion, from being out of the province of a Christian magistrate, that it is, and it ought to be, not only his care, but the principle thing in his care; and its object the supreme good, the ultimate end and object of man himself."[15]

Judgment Day

In Elizabethan and Jacobean England, Judgment Day and a person's day in court served as analogs for each other and also functioned together, since an earthly criminal judgment, which led the defendant to repentance, prepared the way for a more successful judgment in the hereafter. Since most criminals who were judged guilty left quite soon for other realms, divine judgment often followed hard upon the human. In this spiritual shuttle from one jurisdiction to another, human judges and executioners simply completed the first of a two-step process. And even though the wicked might escape the judgment of human courts, God's judgment might overtake them before they died. Richard Hooker, the Church of England's greatest theologian, colorfully described this possibility in a sixteenth-century funeral sermon:

> The judgments of God do not always follow crimes as thunder doth lightning, but sometimes the space of many ages comes between. When the sun hath shined fair the space of six days upon their tabernacle, we know not what clouds the seventh may bring. And when their punishment doth come, let them make their account in the greatness of their sufferings to pay the interest of that respect which hath been given them. Or if they chance to escape clearly in this world, which they seldom do; in the day when the heavens shall shrivel as a scroll and the mountains move as frightened men out of their places, what cave shall receive them? what mountains or rock shall they get by entreaty to fall on them? what covert to hide them from that wrath, which they shall neither be able to abide or avoid?[16]

Shakespeare and his countrymen were surrounded by an iconography of the last judgment that had developed in Europe over centuries. The most famous of all its depictions, Michaelangelo's, had its thematic counterparts on the chancels of many English churches. (For example, the chancel arch in St. Peters Church, Wenhasten, Suffolk, shows the dead rising from the earth to meet their maker.) In the early sixteenth century, books with woodcuts illustrating the dance of death and the fifteen signs preceding Doomsday entered England. The *Queen Elizabeth Prayer Book*, which appeared in five editions during Shakespeare's lifetime, contained a depiction of the dance of death and the last judgment. Mystery play cycles, which Shakespeare may have seen in his childhood, all ended with the last judgment.

The centrality of final judgment in the English Renaissance mind is demonstrated by a great body of art, sermons, poetry, and also drama. Christopher Marlowe's *Doctor Faustus* (ca. 1589) provides an early example of how the English morality play's concern with divine judgment worked its way into the popular theater of the Renaissance. Doctor Faustus, discontent with his university studies, longs to have the powers of a god. He sells his soul to the devil, signing it away in blood, for twenty-four years of supernatural power and knowledge, but what he gets in return is only a spectacular bag of tricks, which he uses to do little more than amaze people and play practical jokes. The meanness of Faustus's character is demonstrated by the paltry ways he uses his power and the pleasure that it gives him. The play is a countdown toward judgment for Faustus, and Marlowe adapts the medieval morality play, which also builds to judgment, to tell Faustus's story. Like the morality play, *Faustus* shows the forces of good and evil (in the forms of a good and a bad angel) contending for Faustus's soul; the play has the traditional parade of the seven deadly sins, and a spiritual counselor in the character of an "Old Man," who tries to save Faustus.

But unlike the morality play, in which Everyman is always saved, Faustus is damned, though the Old Man and
Faustus's good angel try to save him. The Old Man tells Faustus
to leave that "damned art" which has the power to charm his
soul to hell; Faustus can still change directions. "Yet, yet thou
hast an amiable soul, / If sin by custom not grow into nature."
In other words, constant rejection of grace, constant persis-
tence in the same sin, so that sinning grows into one's very
nature, inures the heart to any incursion of grace. The result
is damnation. Faustus, moved by the Old Man's words, is attempting to repent when up pops Mephistophilis, his demonic
tempter, who threatens to "piecemeal tear" Faustus's flesh if
he goes any further. Faustus abjectly caves in to the threat
and his cowardice does him in. On the eve of his damnation, it
is too late for Faustus to repent. His good angel tells him:

> Hadst thou affected sweet divinity,
> Hell, or the devil, had had no power on thee,
> Hadst thou kept on that way, Faustus, behold
> In what resplendent glory thou hadst sat
> In yonder throne, like those bright shining saints,
>   And triumphed over hell.[17]

(5.2.106–11)

Faustus sees Christ's blood streaming in the firmament and
cries out "One drop would save my soul, half a drop," but it is
too late, and a horde of devils drags Faustus to hell. *Doctor
Faustus* develops two religious themes prominent in English
Renaissance literature: that a villain can so harden his heart
that he puts himself beyond redemption, and that cowardice
is often the deadly enemy of repentance. Shakespeare illustrates the same themes in a scene from *Hamlet,* where Claudius
tries to repent.

Having secretly murdered his brother in order to become

king and to take his brother's wife, Claudius is haunted by the knowledge that there will be a final, inescapable judgment. Plagued by his conscience, and knowing that he faces hell, Claudius would like to repent, but cannot. In a scene that owes a lot to *Doctor Faustus,* Claudius finds that he has cut himself off from God:

> O, my offence is rank, it smells to heaven;
> It hath the primal eldest curse upon't,—
> A brother's murder. Pray can I not,
> Though inclination be as sharp as will,
> My stronger guilt defeats my strong intent,
> And, like a man to double business bound,
> I stand in pause where I shall first begin,
> And both neglect. What if this cursed hand
> Were thicker than itself with brother's blood,
> Is there not rain enough in the sweet heavens
> To wash it white as snow? Whereto serves mercy
> But to confront the visage of offence?
> And what's in prayer but this twofold force,
> To be forestalled ere we come to fall,
> Or pardoned being down? Then I'll look up.
> My fault is past—but O, what form of prayer
> Can serve my turn? 'Forgive me my foul murder?'
> That cannot be, since I am still possess'd
> Of those effects for which I did the murder—
> My crown, mine own ambition, and my queen.
> May one be pardon'd and retain th'offence?
> In the corrupted currents of this world
> Offence's gilded hand may shove by justice,
> And oft 'tis seen the wicked prize itself
> Buys out the law. But 'tis not so above.
> There is no shuffling, there the action lies
> In his true nature, and we ourselves compelled
> Even to the teeth and forehead of our faults
> To give in evidence.

$$(3.3.36–64)^{18}$$

This speech pulls in the core of the New Testament: grace, repentance, forgiveness, and judgment. Claudius is in the position of Cain. Part of him is desperate for forgiveness, and he would like to repent, but then he would have to confess his crimes, not only to God, but to Denmark. Additionally, Claudius clings to the fruits of the murder: his kingship and his brother's wife. Neither can he give up his motive for the murder, his own ambition. Like many people in the Bible, Claudius is bound to "double business," and he comes to the essential human crux, as defined in the Old Testament and the Gospels: the choice between God and the things of this world. Though the rich young man of Matthew 19:16–28 has not committed Claudius's crimes, he and Claudius face essentially the same choice. The young man can give away everything he has to follow Christ, or he can clutch his possessions. Like Claudius, he opts to keep the immediate safety his possessions provide, eliciting the following comment by Jesus to his disciples: "Verily I say unto you, That a rich man shall hardly enter into the kingdom of heaven. And again I say unto you, It is easier for a camel to go through the eye of a needle, than for a rich man to enter into the kingdom of God." The phrase "to double business bound" describes Claudius's psychological condition, suspended between the desire to repent and the fear to do so, but it also alludes to the law of agency: an honest servant or agent cannot let his own business conflict with his master's. The same metaphor is used in Luke 16:13, a verse that Shakespeare possibly had in mind when writing Claudius's speech: "No servant can serve two masters: for either he will hate the one, and love the other; or else he will hold to the one, and despise the other. Ye cannot serve God and mammon."

What makes Claudius's situation so agonizing is that he cannot repent, which means he will not be forgiven, and will face judgment, like Hamlet's father, with all his sins upon his head. Claudius needs God's help, in the form of grace, to even begin to repent, but as Marlowe's Dr. Faustus discovers, after a long course of thumbing one's nose at God such grace is not forthcoming. Claudius knows that he is destined for hell, and by implication, he must have known that he was putting his soul in grave danger when he killed his older brother. Even knowing this, however, did not stop him. From a spiritual perspective, Claudius has not only sinned, but his logic has failed. He has deliberately chosen to worsen his life and his soul, with all the attendant consequences. Human judges can be bought off—often with a percentage of the ill-gotten gains— but there is no bribing God, and therefore no ultimate escape from one's crimes. Before the battle of Agincourt, Henry V tells the soldier Williams much the same thing about any criminals that might be in his army: "If these men have defeated the law and out run native punishment, though they can outstrip men, they have no wings to fly God." When Falstaff cries out on his deathbed, "God, God," perhaps he has in mind the judgment to which he will soon come.

Shakespeare examines the same situation in *Richard III*, where he contrasts the choices made by two men whom Richard has sent to kill his brother Clarence. In the second "murderer," Shakespeare portrays a failure to harden the heart: a belief in God—and the possibility of damnation—prevents the would-be killer from carrying out his orders. Having committed themselves to obey Richard, and having his warrant to kill Clarence, the murderers go to Clarence's cell, where he lies asleep:

Second Murderer: What, shall I stab him as he sleeps?

First Murderer: No: He'll say 'twas done cowardly, when he
                    wakes.

Second:	Why, he shall never wake until the great Judgement Day.
First:	Why, then he'll say we stabbed him sleeping.
Second:	The urging of that word, "Judgement," hath bred a kind of remorse in me.
First:	What, art thou afraid?
Second:	Not to kill him—having a warrant—but to be damned for killing him, from the which no warrant can defend me.
First:	I thought thou hadst been resolute.
Second:	So I am—to let him live.
First:	I'll back to the Duke of Gloucester [Richard], and tell him so.
Second:	Nay, I prithee stay a little: I hope this passionate humour of mine will change. It was wont to hold me but while one tells twenty.

(1.4.99–115)[19]

But counting to twenty only helps for a moment. Ultimately, the second murderer's fear of his accomplice, and of Richard, is outweighed by the more distant fear of judgment. Clarence wakes, and says: "I charge you, as you hope to have redemption, / By Christ's dear blood shed for our grievous sins, / That you depart and lay no hands on me: / The deed you undertake is damnable" (1.4.178–81). This additional reminder dissuades the second man, who even tries to save Clarence, but he is too late to stop the first murderer from stabbing Clarence in the back. Yet, the second man's action affirms that the right moral decision can be made, even under pressure.

The drama of choosing between heaven and hell displays a mindset that in sixteenth- and seventeenth-century England was virtually inescapable. Spiritually, people confronted judgment every day of their lives. Earthly trial and judgment externalized and dramatized the most fundamental facts of their relationship with God: that they were "destined unto judgment after all." No wonder that Shakespeare, the most capacious mind in English literature, was so concerned with it.

Shakespeare's scenes of judgment cannot be fully understood without reference to the theological status of law and adjudication in Elizabethan and Jacobean England. Even when we examine judgment in Shakespeare's plays most broadly, as the exercise of a human faculty, we need to be mindful of the theological subtext his audience brought to the theater: that man is a fallen creature whose ability to observe and reason has been severely occluded by original sin. Shakespeare examines judgment in a variety of ways, but this religious framework is always present.

Shakespeare and Moral Wisdom

Today it is typical in the humanities and social sciences to shun any claim that values or truths transcend time and place. Postmodernists, Marxists (the few that remain generally hang out in English departments, along with the last remnants of Freudians and Jungians), anti-foundationalists, and assorted new-leftists hold the view that human nature is so malleable that we are utterly the creatures of circumstance, our minds locked into the ideologies of our own times and places, out of communication with the past or with each other. They leave us with a picture of ourselves as completely isolated and alienated—quarantined in the present and utterly determined by culture: we cannot understand the past, or at best, we can only see it through the dark, ideological glass of our own time. Even if we could understand the past, it would not help us. This way of seeing the world, taught to a generation of undergraduates, is profoundly nihilistic, depressing, and illogical: nihilistic because it erases the past, and in so doing, forecloses any possibility of thinking critically about the present; depressing, because it isolates us from the accumulated store of human experience and wisdom, estranging us from our heritage; illogical, because at the same time theorists assert we cannot understand the past, that heritage is criticized as if it could be understood—and usually charged with being imperialistic, racist, patriarchal, deadeningly dualistic and rational, and generally un-PC. Undergraduates and graduate students who swallow these theories receive a double dispensation of resentment: they get to feel self-righteous and indignant about the history of the West while at the same time maintaining that they are cut off from it. One can feel quite superior from such a perch, and the desire to feel superior to everything is a virulent and Faustian academic disease.

Thus, although before 1970 most scholars recognized Christianity as one of the most influential forces in Renaissance culture, a religion that had to be understood if the Renaissance was to be understood, Shakespeare scholars of the past thirty years have largely ignored it in favor of examining "the margins" of Renaissance culture. As a result, students are far more likely to study cross-dressing in England, the gender quandaries posed by boys playing female roles, and how Shakespeare's plays served as propaganda for the despotic regimes of Elizabeth and James, than they are the religious beliefs that united and divided English society, and through which the most profound critiques of that society were expressed. To remove the most important aspect of the context for Renaissance literature is also to remove the core of that literature from the reach of a student's understanding.

Dr. Samuel Johnson faulted Shakespeare for not taking an explicit moral position in his plays. But Johnson wrote in the eighteenth century, when authors displayed morals in their novels like neon lights. If you missed the point in the story, you were likely to get it again, in essay form, in another chapter. Drama does not lend itself to moralizing by an authorial voice, and Shakespeare has too much finesse to browbeat his audience with an explicit moral. But his plays always raise moral issues and contain a moral dialogue. Characters judge other characters, often by an explicitly Christian code of ethics, and often by an ethics that would have been attributable to natural law—written in the hearts of men, as St. Paul says, and hence as available to antique Romans as sixteenth-century English theater audiences. The ethical tools for making judgments are contained in characters' speeches and actions, often those of the secondary characters, such as Kent in *King Lear,* Horatio in *Hamlet,* or Paulina in the *Winter's Tale,* who remain true to their friends and loyal to the truth. Though Shakespeare's major characters are more complex, and so more riddled with faults, they too have their epiphanies: Hamlet finally understands the value of faith as opposed to calculation; Isabel, in *Measure for Measure,* learns to forgive; Lear discovers compassion and finds that he is not "everything." Shakespeare's work is a lot less "multi-vocal" and ambiguous than modernists or postmodernists would like to believe, and more committed to Christian ethics than Dr. Johnson thought.

I am optimistic about our ability to understand the past, and I believe that studying it is one way to liberate ourselves from the cultural prisonhouses we have concocted during the last quarter century. One does not have to be religious to believe that morality and wisdom can transcend time and culture—an honest empirical look at the world will achieve the same result. In every culture, people function primarily in groups, and for groups to promote their own survival, cohesion needs to be maintained. It should come as no surprise, then, that basic moral rules promoting group cohesion *are* universal. Societies do not tolerate murder, theft, slander, fraud, the flouting of parental authority and responsibility, or adultery because they cannot survive long if they do. This list covers six of the Ten Commandments. (I am certainly not arguing that these rules are not broken. But to the extent that they are, and to the extent that a society tolerates or implicitly endorses their being broken, social cohesion is lost, and various social ills, with which we are all too familiar, follow.) In virtually all societies this list could be lengthened: promises must be kept, the injured should be compensated, agents should act in good faith to their masters, and, as Gilbert's Lord High Executioner says, the punishment should fit the crime. An enormous portion of the world's great literature, and virtually all of Shakespeare, examines what happens to individuals and societies when these moral rules are transgressed. To ignore the past, including its moral teachings, or to hold it in contempt, amounts to junking the moral treasure of Western culture. It is unfortunate, to say the least, that in English departments today students are so often cheated of the wisdom they hoped to find in literature, and instead are encouraged to feel morally superior for embracing radically skeptical and deterministic theories of what and how we can know.

Whether we accept or reject the religious views of Shakespeare's contemporaries, Shakespeare still presents the basic legal and moral problems that all societies must confront and at least partially solve in order to exist. This aspect of Shakespeare makes him well worth our consideration, not as an oddity, cast up from a time we can barely touch (and would not want to), but as a fellow human being, gifted with uncanny poetic skill, and who has much to teach us about ourselves, our problems, and our oft erring judgments.

In this book we will examine Shakespeare's presentation of judgment and trial as illuminated by the law, politics, and Christian beliefs of his day, all of which were so intermingled as to be inseparable. The first chapter, on *Henry VI, Part 2,* will deal with judgment in a kingdom where the rule of law is disintegrating. The second chapter, on *Hamlet,* will deal with human judgment as a faculty, its tendency to go wrong, and the ways in which it can be subverted. The third and fourth chapters are concerned with comedies in which long trial scenes function as religious allegories: *The Merchant of Venice* and *Measure for Measure.* The last two chapters examine three of Shakespeare's late plays. Chapter five looks at women on trial in *The Winter's Tale* and *Henry VIII.* Chapter six examines Prospero, in *The Tempest,* as a Christian judge who is preparing for his own final judgment. All quotations from the Bible are from the one Shakespeare knew, the Geneva Bible of 1560.[20] To give the reader some help, I have modernized some of the spellings.

During the course of the book, I will at times have some harsh things to say about current historical and feminist criticism. I have no objection to criticism that helps us to more adequately contextualize and thereby understand Shakespeare's work, whether it bears on Shakespeare studies or an understanding of Tudor and Jacobean politics or the relations between men and women during the Renaissance. Certainly some historical and feminist criticism does this, in whole or in part. What I object to is the use of Shakespeare as a soapbox, for the conspicuous display of trendy political positions, or more commonly, the distortion of Shakespeare's work, to accommodate arguments criticizing present social arrangements. Certainly there is much to criticize, but such criticism can be more directly and astutely accomplished by political thinkers whose education and background have given them the wherewithal to do it.

I suggest a job change for people who hold teaching positions in departments of literature but who are more interested in the advancement of certain political causes than in the books they teach. Let them enter politics, become lawyers, journalists, social workers, soldiers, even political scientists—or let them simply argue as well-informed citizens, outside the auspices of literary education. They could free themselves from the confines of literary criticism and more directly address the social injustices they recognize and seek to remedy. Rather than being limited to the confines of a classroom or a seminar at the MLA convention, they could loose their cloistered virtue to the world, and the world could respond. The rest of us could get on with enjoying Shakespeare.

I the Lord thy God am a jealous God, visiting the iniquity of the fathers upon the children unto the third and fourth generation of them that hate me.

Exodus 20:5

From Death and darke Oblivion (neere the same)
The Mistresse of Mans life, grave Historie,
Raising the World to good, or Evill fame,
Doth vindicate it to Eternitie.

High Providence would so: that nor the good
Might be defrauded, nor the Great secur'd
But both might know their wayes are understood,
And the reward, and punishment assur'd . . .

Ben Jonson's poem for the preface
to Sir Walter Raleigh's
History of the World

1

Henry VI, Part 2:
Judgment in a
Disintegrating Kingdom

God's Judgment on England

Ben Jonson's prefatory poem to Raleigh's *History* sets forth
the Renaissance belief that the writing of history is a moral
enterprise. Oblivion threatens to swallow the story of individuals and the entire human race from start to finish. It is the
work of "grave history," mankind's mistress, to keep this from
happening, so that people can understand how the world works
over the long course of time. What history teaches, according
to Jonson, Raleigh, and, as we shall see, Shakespeare, is that
a moral order governs the universe. Bad acts have bad consequences, and good acts good ones, both here and in eternity,
though in the fallen world, the bad often seems to overwhelm
the good. By displaying the moral pattern of cause and effect
throughout time, history displays the way God's natural law

works, vindicating its operation in the world. Thus history directs our conduct by providing us with examples to emulate and avoid.

Shakespeare wrote two tetralogies of history plays. The first series includes three plays about *Henry VI*, which are designated as *Parts 1, 2, and 3*, and *Richard III*. These plays were written between 1589 and 1591, at the beginning of Shakespeare's career, and capitalized on the patriotic fervor that followed in England after the Spanish Armada's destruction in 1588. The second tetralogy includes *Richard II, Henry IV, Parts 1 and 2*, and *Henry V*. These plays, though dealing with the portion of medieval history directly preceding the reign of Henry VI, were written after the first tetralogy, between 1595 and 1599.

Taken together, the eight plays deal with the consequences of Henry Bolingbroke's deposition of the rightful but tyrannous king, Richard II. Richard's deposition, which puts Bolingbroke on the throne as Henry IV, begins a series of civil wars and contentions that ripple through time and end in Shakespeare's histories only with the defeat of Richard III on Bosworth Field by Elizabeth I's grandfather, the Earl of Richmond, later Henry VII. Whether the chain reaction set in motion by Richard's deposition had in fact abated was a matter of some concern to the people of Shakespeare's day.

The whole dramatized history, extending from *Richard II* to *Richard III* (covering the period from 1388 to 1485) is a great cautionary tale of what happens to a realm when even a bad king is toppled. With the exception of *Henry V*, these histories focus on the sins and failings of the English, and are anything but celebratory. Yet, they were tremendously popular, which suggests a mindset in Shakespeare's pre-Romantic audience that is very different from ours, a keen sense that the world was one in which human failings were the rule rather than the exception: dangers had to be struggled against constantly and were to a great extent unavoidable. Shakespeare's history plays are about English politics, and the political and divine repercussions of political action. Shakespeare seeks to find and portray universal patterns of cause and effect in the history of nations, particularly England, and to present them through the medium of drama. In this sense, Shakespeare hunts the same game as the other historians of his day. Sir Walter Raleigh can be taken as a prominent example.

Raleigh, in the preface to his *History of the World* (1614), examined the judgments of God on people and nations throughout history, arguing that God's judgments were unchangeable and worked their way out over the "long processe of time." History, for Raleigh, was a record of God's action in the world. His succinct analysis of the history covered by Shakespeare's tetralogies is, according to Lily Bess Campbell, "the most explicit working out of history as presenting the judgments of God, that the English Renaissance produced."[1] Raleigh believed that after seizing the throne, any usurper's family line invariably ended, either in the third generation or with the third heir. Raleigh's theory represents the view most generally held by his contemporaries, and it so obviously informs Shakespeare's history plays that it could be taken as a summary of their plot and theme.

The Tudors took the line that deposing a king was always a sinful act, no matter how badly he ruled. God had given people certain rulers for his own reasons and it was not the prerogative of the people to contradict God by opposing his "deputies on earth." Sir William Baldwin, in the popular *A Mirror for Magistrates*, stated the idea as follows:

> For in dede officers be gods deputies, and it is gods
> office which they beare, and it is he which ordeyneth

> thereto suche as himselfe lysteth, good when he
> favoreth the people, and evyll whan he wyll punish
> them. And therefore whosover rebelleth against any
> ruler either good or bad, rebelleth against God, and
> shalbe sure of a wretched ende: For God can not but
> maintein his deputie.[2]

The inconsistency in this position, of course, was that the Tudors themselves had overthrown Richard III to get the throne; the Tudor response was that, nevertheless, they were *on* the throne. God had decided for them in battle, and if Henry VII had sinned in deposing Richard III, this furnished no moral justification for anyone to commit the sin of deposing them! Many people challenged this view, as perhaps does Shakespeare in *Macbeth* and *Richard III*. Some kings, these plays tell us, are just too horrible to maintain. However, we can take it as a starting point that in Shakespeare's mind, and in most of his contemporaries', deposing a king was almost always a mistake, fraught with evil consequences and prone to awaken God's wrath.

Raleigh sees in English history the perfect consistency of God's judgment on evil kings, most of whom he shows to be usurpers and lawbreakers. According to Raleigh, Richard II paid for the cruelty of his grandfather, Edward III, as well as for his own crimes:

> Richard the second . . . always tooke him-selfe for
> over-wise to bee taught by examples. . . . (who in
> regard of many deedes, unworthy of his Greatnesse,
> cannot bee excused, as the disavowing of him-selfe
> by breach of Faith, Charters, Pardons, and Patents),
> He was in the prime of his youth deposed; and
> murdered by his Cosen-germane and vassal, Henry
> of Lancaster, afterwards Henry IV.[3]

Here, Raleigh could be providing a thumbnail sketch of Shakespeare's *Richard II,* in which Richard makes the fatal mistake of banishing Henry Bolingbroke (Henry of Lancaster) for "twice five summers" and eventually seizing Bolingbroke's property for his own, without due process of law. Henry returns from banishment, and with the help of a powerful noble family, the Percys, regains his land, imprisons Richard, takes the throne, and instigates the deposed king's murder.

God's vengeance, however, falls on Henry IV, and again, the following could be the summary of Shakespeare's plot for seven of his histories, in historical order, from *Henry IV Part 1* through *Richard III,* but excluding *Henry V*:

> This King [Henry IV], whose Title was weake, and his obtaining the Crowne traitorous: who brake Faith with the Lordes at his landing, protesting to intend only the recoverie of his proper Inheritance; brake faith with *Richard* himselfe; and brake Faith with all the Kingdome in Parliament, to whom he swore that the deposed King should live. After that he had enjoyed the Realme some few yeares, and in that time had beene set upon all sides by his Subjects, and never free from Conspiracies and rebellions; he saw (if Soules immortall see . . .) his Grandchilde *Henrie* the sixt, and his Sonne the Prince, suddenly, and without mercy, murdered; the possession of the Crowne (for which he had caused so much blood to bee powred out) transferred from his race; and by the Issues of his Enemies worne and enjoyed. . . .
>
> Now *Henrie* the sixt, upon whom the great storme of his Grandfathers grievous faults fell, as it formerly had done upon *Richard* the Grand-childe of *Edward*: . . . Hee drew on himselfe and this Kingdome the greatest joynt-losse and dishonor that ever it sustained since the *Norman* Conquest.[4]

Henry VI lost the territories his father, Henry V, had gained in France, and through incompetence, as the Chorus in *Henry V* says, "made his England bleed." The house of York in deposing Henry VI committed its own sins, for which it's children would also pay: Edward IV, the Yorkist king, allowed his younger brother Richard to slaughter Henry VI's son, Edward, and to execute his own brother, Clarence. When Edward IV died, Richard imprisoned his nephews, Edward's two sons, in the Tower of London. Both were successors to the throne, and one, for a brief period, was King Edward V. Richard had the two boys murdered since their claim to the throne was superior to his.[5] Raleigh describes him as "the greatest Maister in mischiefe of all that forewent him," and he was destroyed in turn:

> And what successe had *Richard* himselfe after all these mischefes and Murders, policies, and counter-policies to Christian religion: and after such time, as with a most mercilesse hand hee had pressed out the breath of his Nephews and Naturrall Lords; other than the prosperity of so short a life, as it tooke end, ere himselfe could well looke over and discerne it? The great outcrie of innocent bloud, obtaining at Gods hands the effusion of his; who became a spectacle of shame and dishonor, both to his friends and enemies.[6]

Though the deposers of kings in these examples are taken by Raleigh as instruments of God's justice, they are not free from the crimes they themselves commit in the process of carrying out the divine doom, and it is important to see that Raleigh does not relate the deposition of the third-generation king or third heir only to his ancestor's usurpation, but also to the sins committed in excess of what was necessary to take the throne, sins attributable to the sheer lust for power and the willingness to kill people who got in the way. Henry IV doesn't merely take the throne from Richard—he instigates his murder and commits other crimes. Edward IV gratuitously slaughters Henry VI's son. Richard III paves his way to the throne with the dead bodies of his relatives, including the child King, Edward V.

Writing during the reign of James I, Raleigh takes his analysis a step further than anyone would have dared during the reign of Elizabeth, and applies this historical pattern to the Tudors. In stopping Richard III, Raleigh writes, Henry VII was no doubt the immediate instrument of God's justice, yet in the aftermath Henry executed people who had helped him to the throne and produced Henry VIII, one of the most merciless princes who had ever reigned anywhere. Thus, God cut off Henry VII's line with Elizabeth I, who died without issue. For two hundred years, the lines of all who had seized the English throne ended with either the third generation or the third heir. Campbell summarizes Raleigh's argument: "The throne that Edward III gained, his grandson Richard II lost; the throne that Henry IV gained, his grandson Henry VI lost; the throne that Edward IV gained, the third heir [Richard III] lost; the throne that Henry VII gained passed from the Tudors with the death of his grandchild Elizabeth. Such was the pattern of God's vengeance worked out in detail."[7] It was a pattern that the English had recognized and contemplated since the publication of John Hardyng's *Chronicle* in 1543.

Shakespeare's history plays reflect the pattern described by Raleigh. Thus, the scenes of judgment in Shakespeare's history plays, from *Richard II* to *Richard III*, take place in the larger context of divine judgment on the kings of England. What follows from this is that the king, "the fountain of justice," as Bacon put it, laboring under judgment himself, has great difficulty dispensing justice to the realm. The functioning of the judicial system thus serves as a prime indicator of the kingdom's health. Dysfunctional courts point to big political problems further up the line, and for Shakespeare, a political problem is also a religious one. Like a heart pumping tainted blood to the body politic, the King's spiritual infection is passed eventually through the courts to the whole realm. This is particularly true in the case of Shakespeare's hapless king, Henry VI.

The Case of *Thump v. Horner*

Henry VI, Parts 1 and *2* dramatize the state of England leading to the Wars of the Roses. The first part focuses on the English loss of France, which had been partially conquered by Henry V; the second concentrates on the court machinations of several factions contending for power under the weak and incompetent reign of Henry VI. *Henry VI, Part 3* puts the audience squarely into the English civil war and the defeat of Henry VI by Edward, Duke of York, later Edward IV; thus, the red rose of Lancaster, represented by Henry, goes down to the white rose of York.

   2 Henry VI covers fourteen years of English history, from 1441 to 1455. In the first scenes, Shakespeare orients his audience to the power struggle going on in Henry's court. The plot is crowded with incidents and characters and, unfortunately, is not easy to summarize. The reader need not swallow the following smorgasbord of characters all at once; we will be returning to them in more manageable bites. Humphrey, the Duke of Gloucester, and also Henry's uncle, is ruling England as Henry's "protector." The protector's job is to rule the kingdom until a child-king attains his majority. Since Henry VI was crowned in infancy, Gloucester has done the job for a long time, and in Shakespeare's play (though not historically) Henry allows Gloucester's protectorship to extend even into his adult years. Shakespeare does this to emphasize Henry's reluctance to be king. Unlike his father and grandfather, Henry has little will or talent to rule. God's judgment, apparently, is that Henry Bolingbroke's vaulting ambition to become king and establish a dynasty will be thwarted by his grandson's corresponding lack of ambition.

In the play Gloucester is referred to as "the good Duke Humphrey," and given the incompetence of his nephew-king, Humphrey is the last person who stands between England and civil disaster. The Duke of Suffolk, and Henry's new queen, Margaret, want to get rid of Humphrey to increase their power in the kingdom. Henry, who goes through the play uttering religious platitudes, is more suited to a monastery than a throne, and Margaret and Suffolk intend to rule with Henry as figurehead.

The Dukes of Somerset and Buckingham form another group that would like to eliminate Gloucester. Cardinal Beaufort, who hates Gloucester, and with whom he has been feuding for years, would simply like to kill the man, partly out of revenge and partly to gain power. Richard Plantagenet, the Duke of York, has a better hereditary claim to the throne than Henry and intends to take the crown by force; he wants to eliminate first Gloucester, then Henry, and then anyone else from the house of Lancaster who gets in his way. Power abhors a vacuum. The question in *2 Henry VI* is, who will occupy the vacuum?

Though ending with the battle of St. Albans, *2 Henry VI* is mainly about court intrigue, in which competing nobles use the judicial system to commit robbery or to undermine each other and thus corrupt the administration of justice. The play reaches most of its dramatic crescendos through trial scenes, of which there are, in whole or in part, eleven, far more than in any other play by Shakespeare. Five complete adjudications occur in the Folio version of the play and a sixth in

Quarto,[8] and both Quarto and Folio include parts of four other adjudications. In addition, both Quarto and Folio versions contain Cardinal Beaufort's deathbed scene, in which he imagines himself on trial before God for his part in Duke Humphrey's death. Both versions present the abuse by the nobles of the judicial process, the frantic reactions of the commons to the evident corruption in King Henry's court, and the chaos that results when different power groups rush to fill the vacuum left by Henry's *de facto* abdication.

The first scene dealing with the legal woes of England occurs in act 1, scene 3, and involves three petitions, two brought by "three or four petitioners" representing the township of Long Melford, and one by Peter Thump, an apprentice armorer. By chance, these petitioners are intercepted by Suffolk and Queen Margaret, who demand to see their petitions. Since the complaint of the people of Melford relates to some of the legal abuses that brought about the Cade Rebellion, depicted in act 4 of the play, I will defer discussing it until later in this chapter and begin with the first trial, which we might title *Thump v. Horner.*

Peter Thump's petition accuses his master, Thomas Horner, of treason, "for saying that the Duke of York was rightful heir to the crown" (1.2.25–6). Horner happens to be the Duke of York's armorer. Peter's accusations provide the occasion for a political coup of far more importance than the prosecution of Horner, because York, named in the petition, is competing with the Duke of Somerset for the Regency of France. Suffolk, who backs Somerset, sees this accusation of treason as a way to discredit York and thus to throw the regency to Somerset. Suffolk and the queen destroy the petitions of the men from Melford, partly because they want Peter Thump's suit to receive the privy council's full attention, so that suspicion will be focused on York.

These actions of Suffolk and Margaret combine total disrespect for the rule of law with political astuteness about how a seemingly minor detail, such as "management" of a court's calendar, can be used to manipulate politics. Since the value of a dramatic presentation is not lost on Suffolk, he opens the case before the King:

Suffolk: Please it your Majesty, this is the man [Peter Thump]
            That doth accuse his master of high treason.
            His words were these: that Richard Duke of York
            Was rightful heir unto the English crown,
            And that your Majesty was an usurper.

King: Say, man, were these thy words?

Horner: And't shall please your Majesty, I never said nor
            thought any such matter: God is my witness, I am
            falsely accused by the villain.

Peter: By these ten bones, my lords, he did speak them to
            me in the garret one night, as we were scouring my
            Lord of York's armour.

York: Base dunghill villain, and mechanical,
            I'll have thy head for this thy traitor's speech.
            I do beseech your royal Majesty
            Let him have all the rigour of the law.

Horner: Alas! my lord, hang me if ever I spake the words.
            My accuser is my prentice; and when I did correct
            him for his fault the other day, he did vow upon his
            knees he would be even with me: I have good witness
            of this: therefore, I beseech you Majesty, do not cast
            away an honest man for a villain's accusation.

                                        (1.3.181–202)

Suffolk attains his political ends since Gloucester appoints Somerset "Regent o're the French," given the suspicion cast on York. As to Thump and Horner, Gloucester issues this judgment: "And let these have a day appointed them / For single

combat, in convenient place." The *Thump v. Horner* trial then
stands adjourned until act 2, scene 3, in which the promised
trial by battle is staged. This serious conflict between a master and his apprentice, one which will be decided in trial by
combat, indicates that foundational rot has already entered
Henry's kingdom. To understand why, we need to examine the
Tudor family and its relation to the state.

Tudor doctrines of order and obedience established the
family as the fundamental political building-block of the ideal
commonwealth. With the father at the head, followed by the
eldest son, younger sons, wife, daughters, apprentices, and
servants, the extended family, in theory, reproduced in minia-
ture the social structure of the Tudor body politic. Challenges
to the family from within were the microcosmic counterpart of
political insurrection, and obedience to the family patriarch
prepared one for obedience to the king or queen.

Each year thousands of boys came to London to be apprentices, thus becoming members of new micro-political units:
the families of their masters. As Steven R. Smith writes, "Relying on his master for instruction as well as food, clothing
and shelter, the apprentice became a part of his master's household, and ideally lived under him as he would have under his
own father."[9] The nature of the master-apprentice relationship was set forth in guidebooks that recognized "the master's
responsibility for disciplining his apprentices, and the
apprentice's obligation to render complete obedience and faithful service."[10] In addition, the articles of indenture spelled
out the same covenant, stating that the apprentice would serve
seven years, "during which term the said apprentice his said
master well and truly shall serve, his secrets keep close, his
commandments lawful and honest everywhere he shall willingly do: hurt nor damage to his said master he shall none
do."[11] Thus, at the beginning of his indentures, the apprentice

swore a loyalty oath to this master, the leader of the body politic to which the apprentice would be most intimately connected.

In addition to his duties to his master, an Elizabethan apprentice also had duties to the state, the most relevant of which, in this case, was the statutory command to report treasonous utterances. Nothing illustrates the unease with which the Tudors occupied the throne, and their own sense of English instability, better than the proliferation of treason legislation and trials from the ascendancy of Henry VIII to the end of Elizabeth's reign. John Bellamy notes:

> Between 1485 and 1603, according to one calculation, there were no fewer than sixty-eight treason statutes enacted, though there had been less than ten in the period 1352–1485. This proliferation is explained by the fact that many Tudor acts were the by-product of royal concern over the succession to the crown and the king's ecclesiastical supremacy, problems previous kings did not face in the same form, and also by the reluctance of the Tudor monarchs to put their trust in judicial construction based on existing statutes.[12]

The psychological and social effect of this mass of treason legislation and the crown's willingness to use it as a means of destroying its enemies has yet to be fully examined by historians. But it certainly must have contributed to the lack of trust that historian Lacey Baldwin Smith describes as one of the period's most characteristic features.[13] Failure to report treason was itself treason, and against the Tudor craving for order and stability must be set the Tudor fear of betrayal— and the failure to betray.[14] The theme of "see much, say lytill, and lerne to suffer in tyme" was repeated throughout the poetry of the fifteenth century, when *Henry VI* takes place, and carried over into *Tottel's Miscellany*, a poetry anthology of the sixteenth century. The advice of fathers such as Sir William Wentworth, Sir Walter Raleigh, and Henry Percy, the ninth earl of Northumberland, to their sons, and of Thomas Elyot to his readers, was to guard one's speech, for indiscretion could be construed as treason, and ears were everywhere. Peter Thump is a fictional version of such a listener and Thomas Horner of such an indiscreet tongue-wagger.

The scene of an apprentice accusing his master must have been problematic for a Tudor audience. Rather than providing adequate reconciliation of the demands of family and state, the scene shows that these demands are potentially competitive and that the Tudor model of an organically whole kingdom in which all loyalty must flow to the crown is shaky at the core. For there is no doubt that Peter has taken the course required by Tudor law and propaganda. In the official statement of church doctrine known as "the bishops Book," the Fifth Commandment, "Honor thy father and thy mother," was interpreted to mean that a "subject must love the King, as the father of all his subjects, and . . . that a Christian must love the King more than he loved his natural father."[15] (Thus is religion distorted to fit political expediency, rather than serving as a foundation to which politics must conform—a problem confronted by Christ during his ministry and Christianity ever since.) But though Anglican doctrine emphasized that loyalty to the king took primacy over loyalty even to one's father, one might well question the zeal with which Peter has informed on his master, whose alleged treasonous utterances only stated the truth. York, the nearest descendant of Edward III's third son, Lionel, certainly has a better hereditary claim than Henry VI, who claims through John of Gaunt, Edward III's fourth son.

The scene sets forth the disquieting reality that people were not safe to speak their minds even in their own homes, that loyalty to the family and loyalty to the state could be at odds, and that, while a state cannot exist without stability in the family, the state's very efforts to purge itself of treason could undermine the harmony of family life and, in the long run, the state itself, since the family was the building block of the state. The episode demonstrates how easily one could prosecute a family grudge under the color of a treason accusation; Horner asserts that this is exactly what Peter is doing: "my accuser is my Prentice, and when I did correct him for his fault the other day, he did vow upon his knees he would be even with me." Secrets must be kept because anyone could be an informer, and Peter does reveal his master's secrets (in conformity to the treason laws, but against the articles of the typical indenture).

The contention within the kingdom about who should be on the throne has opened this breach in Horner's family. National tension, at the macrocosmic level, creates family tension at the microcosmic level, which in turn affects the state, in this case causing York to lose the regency of France to Somerset. Shakespeare is dramatically demonstrating that the state *is* an organic entity in which every part influences every other, and here the contending nobles are primarily at fault, since it is their dissension that produces civil war, even within the family. "He who troubleth his own household shall inherit the wind," and in this instance, the wind is the War of the Roses. The house of Horner, the master armorer, has its own civil war, shown in the scene of trial by combat in act 2, scene 3.

Trial by battle was born of the same medieval theory of divine intervention in judicial affairs that provided the basis for trial by ordeal.[16] Where proof of guilt was impossible to obtain, or when the only proof available was the word of accuser against accused, the judge, in evidentiary despair, abdicated as fact-finder and turned the proceedings over to God. Judicially decreed duels and ordeals are often said to form the beginnings of the law of evidence, if only as an acknowl-edgment of how inadequate human investigation can be. Trial by battle was decreed by Parliament in cases of alleged trea-son where there was no evidence to support the allegation except the accuser's word against that of the accused. Thus, in the confrontation between Thump and Horner, Shakespeare presents the usual case for trial by battle.

Though the theory of judicial duel was that "a weak, just man would defeat a strong, unjust man,"[17] several medieval authors argued that, judging by the results, God generally seemed to be on the side of the bigger, stronger, better-trained warrior. The story of David and Goliath was often cited as evidence of divine sanction, but Pope Nicholas I, as early as the mid-ninth century, attacked trial by battle, noting that "divine authority never sanctioned it as law . . . and those who practice it are only tempting God."[18] Though trial by ordeal, which had long been opposed by the church, was effectively destroyed by the Fourth Lateran Council in 1215, when clergy were forbidden to participate in the process, trial by battle, which had never been dependent on the participation of clergy, continued throughout the Middle Ages. (The last judicial duel to be fought in England occurred in 1492, although trial by battle was still technically available until 1819!)

Peter Thump may be cited as one of those participants who shared Nicholas I's doubts about divine intervention in judicially declared combat. "Alas! my Lord," Peter tells Gloucester, "I cannot fight; for God's sake, pity my case! The spite of man prevaileth against me. O Lord, have mercy upon me! I shall never be able to fight a blow. O Lord my heart!" (1.3.213–16)

Gloucester's reply is "Sirrah, or you must fight, or else be hang'd." The dilemma faced by Peter—whether to fight or be hanged—is historically accurate. Those who were doomed to participate in a judicial duel but refused to fight were sent to the noose, as were the defeated who clung to life long enough to be dragged to the gallows erected beside the field of combat. After the loser was killed—or finished off by hanging—he suffered the usual fate of traitors and was disemboweled, drawn, and quartered.

We can only speculate as to how this stage combat was produced for its original audience, but it is probable, from the tone of the scene, that it was milked for comedy. The action begins with the entourages of Peter and Horner entering at opposite doors, drinking heavily to the combatants. Horner is drunk, and though Peter wisely declines more drink, he might well have been played as somewhat inebriated. The weapons are not the swords of chivalrous combatants but staves with sandbags fastened at the ends, suggesting that the combat resembled a Punch and Judy show. The entertainment value is not lost on Henry's court, and Shakespeare provides a quick piece of characterization through queen Margaret's ghastly comment that she has purposely left court "to see this quarrel tried." Peter is described by York as "more afraid to fight" than any fellow he has ever seen. Peter, however, makes a better beginning than Horner. He prepares for death, giving away his few worldly possessions and invoking the name of God while Horner continues to drink and, in Quarto, invokes the name of a popular hero, Bevis of Southampton.

The broader social consequences of the family division between Thump and Horner manifest themselves in what becomes a vicarious struggle between masters and apprentices. Peter is urged by another apprentice to "fight for credit of the Prentises" (Quarto D1v). Horner, on the other hand, is repeatedly called "neighbor" by his companions, emphasizing that they are part of a distinct group in opposition to apprentices:

1. **Neighbor:** Here neighbor Horner, I drink to you in a cup of
                 sack. And fear not neighbor, you shall do well
                 enough.
2. **Neighbor:** And here neighbor, here's a cup of Charneco.
3. **Neighbor:** Here's a pot of good double beer, neighbor, drink
                 and be merry, and fear not your man.

(Quarto D1v)

Masters and neighbors form one cheering section and apprentices another. The scene—especially in the Quarto—portrays
a major rift in the Tudor ideal of organic family and political
harmony, while also demonstrating that microcosmic family
quarrels can have macrocosmic political consequences, by
spreading from two men to two categories of people.

Peter strikes the drunken Horner down, and Horner confesses treason before he dies. Peter cries, "Oh God! have I
overcome mine enemies in this presence? O Peter! Thou hast
prevail'd in right." Thus, the scene seems to end with the
weaker but just man winning, always a popular formula, and
the apprentices, who formed a large part of Shakespeare's audience, probably loved it. Their masters may have felt otherwise.

The historical account on which Shakespeare based his
battle between Horner and Thump appears in the histories of
Raphael Holinshed, John Stow, and Edward Hall, the principal chroniclers of Shakespeare's day. In all three histories the
apprentice indeed vanquishes his master, but that is where
the similarity between the sources and the play ends: in all of
the histories, the apprentice is a lying scoundrel. Stow gives
the most detailed account:

> John David [the basis for Thump] appeached his
> master William Catur [the basis for Horner], an
> armorer dwelling in S. Dunstons parish in Fleetstreet,
> of treason, and a day being assigned them to fight in

> Smithfield, the master being well beloved, was so
> cherished by his friends and plied so with wine, that
> being therewith overcome was also unluckily slain
> by his servant: but that false servant (for he falsely
> accused his master) lived not long unpunished, for
> he was after hanged at Tyborne for felony.[19]

Hall notes that the apprentice was hanged at "Tiborne" and
describes him as "a coward and a wretch," but does not indicate that the apprentice had falsely accused his master.
Holinshed's comment is that the master "was slain without
guilt. As for the false servant, he lived not long unpunished;
for being convicted of felony in court of assize, he was judged
to be hanged, and so was at Tiburne." The most vitriolic and
personal moral lesson to be derived from this incident is set
forth by Stow:

> Let such false accusers note this example, and look
> for no better end, without speedy repentance: my self
> have had the like servant that likewise accused me
> of many articles, he liveth yet, but hath hardly
> escaped hanging since, God make him penitent.[20]

The histories that Shakespeare drew on for his plot describe a
situation that is highly disturbing to their authors, who react
to the servant with unanimous indignation and disgust. This
reaction is matched by the dearth of facts indicating any guilt
on the servant's part. The authors merely assert that the servant was lying, as if there were no other possibility. They seem
outraged at the apprentice's disloyalty. Not only does the servant in challenging his master also challenge the family, but
he makes a mockery of the trial process. In the historians'
chronicles, God does not give the innocent party victory: so
much for the theological basis of trial by combat. The servant,
especially for Stow, represents a form of inescapable and yet

unreliable and corruptible surveillance, ready to take advantage of a slip of his master's tongue or to invent such a slip as a means of revenge.

One can always argue, as do Stow and Holinshed, that God will not be denied. They record, in support of that contention, that the apprentice was punished later at Tyburn, but this still leaves the problem of a dead William Catur, the master. Where was justice there? What happens to the master's now fatherless family? And how does the servant's eventual execution redress the abuse of judicial process, in which the master, though innocent, is legally killed and then, in all probability, drawn and quartered with his head set upon London Bridge as an example? The gloating of Stow and Holinshed over the apprentice's execution seems a rather ragged attempt to extract some kind of order out of an incident in which the Tudor ideology of obedience shows its fragility.

A good way to approach the question of Shakespeare's intentions in a play is to note the deviations between his script and the story as told by his sources. A large deviation, such as we have in the *Thump v. Horner* case, sometimes indicates where Shakespeare's meaning lies.[21] Shakespeare's point, which is continually developed through the play, is that dissension at the top of the social hierarchy spreads, and ongoing dissension leads to internecine combat and anarchy.

York's ambition to become king expresses itself in a conflict that he could never have foreseen: a trial by combat between two members of the lower orders, which escalates into a general breach between masters and apprentices, all of which plays itself out in a judicial system whose function is to dispense justice, thereby promoting God's will on earth. But corrupt leadership leads to the corruption of the courts, which are being used not for the purpose of promoting justice, but as political weapons. This shows contempt for God, and such blasphemy inevitably results in broader social evils: master is pitted against servant, class against class, and nobles against each other. The ripe fruit of such contempt for the judicial system will be the Cade Rebellion of act 4, which in turn displays dire consequences for religion. However, before we come to that episode, and the several trial scenes that it contains, we need to examine the fall of Duke Humphrey of Gloucester and his wife Eleanor.

The Judicial Destruction of Duke Humphrey and Eleanor

Suffolk's expertise at using the courts to further his political ambition continues with the entrapment of Duke Humphrey's wife, Eleanor Cobham, the Duchess of Gloucester. As Suffolk used Peter Thump to throw suspicion on the Duke of York, he now uses the trial of Eleanor for witchcraft and treason to destroy Gloucester, removing him as protector and setting him up for a treason trial of his own.

Eleanor is introduced early in the play as coveting her position as the protector's wife, which has made her *de facto* queen of England. Her animus to the new queen Margaret is energized when Margaret "accidentally" gives her a box on the ear. (Margaret adds insult to injury, saying she has mistaken Eleanor for a serving woman!) Eleanor responds, "Could I come near your beauty with my nails / I'd set my ten commandments in your face," and proclaims that she will be revenged.

Eleanor is an early shadow of Lady Macbeth. She and Humphrey recite their dreams to each other early in act I; Humphrey's is prophetic:

> Methough this staff, mine office-badge in court,
> Was broke in twain; by whom I have forgot,
> But, as I think, it was by th'Cardinal;

And on the pieces of the broken wand
Were plac'd the heads of Edmund Duke of Somerset,
And William de la Pole, first Duke of Suffolk.

(1.2.25–30)

On the other hand, Eleanor's dream is a treasonous wish-fulfillment:

Methought I sat in seat of majesty
In the cathedral church of Westminster,
And in that chair where kings and queens are
          crown'd;
Where Henry and Dame Margaret kneel'd to me,
And on my head did set the diadem.

(1.2.36–40)

Humphrey chides her for this dream and lets the audience know that this has been a constant theme of Eleanor: "And wilt thou still be hammering treachery, / To tumble down thy husband and thyself / From top of Honour to Disgrace's feet?" (47–49). But though Humphrey is angry with his wife, he loves her, and when she pouts because of his response he says, "Nay, be not angry; I am pleased again" (line 55). Thus, in a few lines, Shakespeare clearly establishes Eleanor as Humphrey's Achilles' heel and foreshadows what is to come.

Meanwhile, Suffolk and Cardinal Beaufort buy the help of a priest named Hume to lure Eleanor into a trap. Hume sets up a meeting between Eleanor and three people engaged in witchcraft, Margery Jourdain, John Southwell (also a priest), and Roger Bolingbroke, a "conjuror." The use of witchcraft, of course, is a crime in violation of laws based on Deuteronomy 18: 10–12:

Let none be found among you that maketh his son or
his daughter to go through fire, or that useth

> witchcraft, or a regarder of times, or a marker of the
> flying of souls, or a sorcerer, / Or a charmer, or that
> conselleth with spirits, or a soothsayer, or that asketh
> counsel at the dead / For all that do such things are
> abomination unto the Lord. . . .

Eleanor seeks to know her husband's future, the future of the King, and the Dukes of Suffolk and Somerset. A spirit is raised from hell, and he makes veiled prophesies of the fates of Henry, Suffolk, Somerset, and the Duke of Gloucester. As the spirit descends, York, Buckingham, and their men break in and arrest Eleanor.

Eleanor is convicted in act 2, scene 3, and sentenced to banishment on the Isle of Man, but first she must do three days of penance and walk the streets barefoot in a white sheet, holding a burning taper, a typical punishment of the ecclestiastical courts. To understand the humiliation in-volved—and its symbolic value—one has to remember that in those days, the streets functioned as open sewers. Gloucester, heart-broken, watches his wife's humiliation and makes a statement aligning himself with the rule of law:

> Eleanor, the law, thou seest, hath judged thee:
> I cannot justify whom the law condemns.
>
> **Exeunt Duchess and other Prisoners, guarded**
>
> Mine eyes are full of tears, my heart of grief.
> Ah! Humphrey, this dishonour in thine age
> Will bring thy head with sorrow to the grave.
> I beseech your Majesty, give me leave to go;
> Sorrow would solace and mine age would ease.
>
> (2.3.15–21)

The king, who is a spectator with other members of the court, gives Humphrey leave to go, but not until Humphrey gives up his staff, thus resigning his protectorship. Humphrey gives it up willingly, and Henry, in accepting it, ironically throws away the only prop sustaining him and England.

The last step for Gloucester's enemies is get rid of him completely, and Eleanor, when she takes leave of her husband to go into banishment, warns him at length that this is coming. He gives an uncharacteristically naïve reply, but one which the young Shakespeare evidently includes to underscore his main theme, the perversion of justice in England:

> Ah! Nell, forbear: thou aimest all awry;
> I must offend before I be attainted;
> And had I twenty times so many foes,
> And each of them had twenty times their power,
> All these could not procure me any scathe,
> So long as I am loyal, true, and crimeless.

> (2.4.58–63)

Shakespeare will show Humphrey's confidence to be utterly misplaced. After Gloucester's exit, Eleanor says she longs for death, "at whose name I oft have been afeard, / Because I wished'd this world's eternity." Like Claudius in *Hamlet* and the second murderer in *Richard III*, Eleanor realizes that she has willed all the wrong things, taking the false "eternity" of this world for the true eternity she will meet after death. This is the earliest occurrence of an Augustinian theme that recurs in Shakespeare's work from beginning to end: What constitutes readiness for death, and how does one become ready? What do people have to go through before they can say, as Hamlet does to Horatio, "The readiness is all. Let be"? Bishop Beaufort of Carlisle will shortly furnish an example of what readiness is not.

In act 3, scene 1, Gloucester is finally accused by Suffolk and Bishop Beaufort of treason. Rather than repeating the as-

sertion he made to Eleanor, that he cannot be convicted unless he is guilty, Humphrey now acknowledges that he *will* be
convicted, even though innocent:

> I shall not want false witness to condemn me,
> Nor store of treasons to augment my guilt;
> The ancient proverb will be well effected:
> A staff is quickly found to beat a dog!

(3.1.168–71)

The staff to which Humphrey refers recalls to the audience Humphrey's protectorship (symbolized by his staff of office), his dream, and his recent loss of power. Humphrey will
finally be beaten by the staff he had to give up when his protectorship came to an end. His enemies will wield the staff of
justice, now *only* a symbol, to secure his death.

King Henry is so vociferous in defense of Gloucester that
Margaret, Suffolk, and Beaufort decide they cannot afford to
bring Gloucester to trial. Unable to assassinate Humphrey judicially, they have him murdered in prison. In the subsequent
inquest, it is determined that Humphrey, whose eyes bulge
and hair stands straight, was strangled. Henry suspects Suffolk, but he does nothing. Though capable of grief, Henry is
incapable of action. He only watches passively and mourns as
his kingdom falls apart, expecting God to somehow protect
him because he is pure, though he makes no effort of his own.
Raleigh's judgment of Henry makes explicit what Shakespeare
demonstrates on stage: "Although he was generally esteemed
for a gentle and innocent prince, yet . . . as in condescending
to the unworthy death of his uncle of Gloucester, the main and
strong pillar of the house of Lancaster, he drew on himself and
this kingdom the greatest joint-loss and dishonour that ever it
sustained since the Norman Conquest."[22]

None of the people who plot to kill Duke Humphrey escape punishment. Beaufort is the first to feel God's wrath, and his death is a dramatic analog of Richard Hooker's funeral sermon about the inescapability of judgment. A messenger tells Henry that Beaufort is dying, and describes his state:

> Cardinal Beaufort is at point of death;
> For suddenly a grievous sickness took him,
> That makes him gasp, and stare, and catch the air,
> Blaspheming God, and cursing men on earth.
> Sometimes he talks as if Duke Humphrey's ghost
> Were by his side; sometime he calls the King,
> And whispers to his pillow, as to him,
> The secret of his overcharged soul . . .

> (3.2.368–75)

Beaufort has had no time to repent, and the suddenness of his illness makes it seem that he has been struck directly by God. His blasphemy and curses guarantee that his end will not be a happy one. Repentance and faith is possible for sinners at the last minute, but in Shakespeare's work there are no deathbed conversions. Habits of viciousness developed over a lifetime persist until the end. Beaufort has long exercised the fundamental option of turning his back on God and is dying in a state of mortal sin; in delirium he attempts a fevered defence, as if God could be tricked at the last moment:

> Bring me unto my trial when you will.
> Died he [Gloucester] not in his bed? Where should he
>   die?
> Can I make men live whe'r they will or no?
> O, torture me no more! I will confess.
> Alive again? Then show me where he is:
> I'll give a thousand pound to look upon him.
> He hath no eyes, the dust hath blinded them.
> Comb down his hair; look! look! it stands upright,

> Like lime-twigs set to catch my winged soul.
> Give me some drink; and bid the apothecary
> Bring the strong poison that I bought of him.
>
> (3.3.8–18)

Beaufort, apparently responding to messages that Humphrey is not dead, as in the eternal sense he is not, demands to look at him. But he can only see Humphrey as he was in death, with his hair like a sticky trap reaching up to catch Beaufort's soul. We get a sense of the torture Beaufort has gone through, for we can infer that his sudden illness is really suicide, the result of strong poison bought from an apothecary. But for Beaufort, who though a bishop harbors no noticeable trace of religious belief, suicide will not be the end of suffering, but only the beginning. "So bad a death," one of the witnesses says, "argues a monstrous life."

Richard Hooker noted in the funeral sermon, quoted in the introduction, that God's judgments sometimes do not fall until years or generations after the wrongdoing, but in this early play by Shakespeare, which lacks the subtlety of the plays shortly to follow, judgment follows hard upon the evil deed. Because of this, Shakespeare's theological ideas, which were those of his culture, stand in bold relief: God will judge wrongdoers and mete out punishment sooner or later; he works through the medium of history, and just as the history of Israel shows his personal involvement, so does that of England.

With Gloucester gone, and no one to control the infighting at court or to beware York's ambition, England is ripe for anarchy or civil war, and it gets both. So far I have concentrated on what has been going on around Henry, but Shakespeare takes pains to show how this king's inability to govern has resulted in the destruction of justice *throughout* the kingdom. To track the decay of the judicial system, we must return to those petitioners from Long Melford who entered the stage with Peter Thump; their discontent lies at the roots of the Cade rebellion, which takes up most of act 4.

Jack Cade and the Destruction of the Rule of Law

Shakespeare sets up the trial scenes of the Cade rebellion by introducing the corruption of justice in local courts when "three or four petitioners" of Melford are intercepted by the Duke of Suffolk and the Queen. Suffolk reads the petitions and finds that the first is against the servant of his ally, Cardinal Beaufort, as the petitioner says, "for keeping my house, and lands, and wife, and all from me" (1.3.17–18). The second petition is against Suffolk himself by another petitioner on behalf of his entire township "for enclosing the commons of Long Melford" (1.3.21–22). Enclosure was a kind of theft, the seizure, by local magnates such as Suffolk, of lands traditionally held in common and managed by the people. This complaint would particularly raise the hackles of Shakespeare's audience, since enclosure was extremely unpopular, condemned by the clergy and legislated against by parliament throughout the sixteenth century.

By showing the presentation of these petitions, Shakespeare provides background about the political condition of the realm and the people's perceptions of who can be trusted. The petitioners are seeking Duke Humphrey of Gloucester, the Lord Protector; in other words, they are seeking to present their petitions to the King's Privy Council, the strongest member of which is Humphrey, rather than to several other courts which could also provide a hearing, such as local manorial courts, courts of assize, or Common Pleas, which was the central civil court in London.[23]

The implication is that Suffolk controls the administration of justice in his own dukedom and that the petitioner for

Long Melford has been forced to bring his suit to Westminster, where, as a last resort, he hopes to get an impartial hearing from Gloucester. The petition against the cardinal's man illustrates that parts of England are in the grip of a few men who exercise power with no regard to law; in the case of Melford, those men are the Cardinal and Suffolk. Their pursuit of power at court mirrors how nobles govern throughout the countryside. In *The End of the House of Lancaster*, R. L. Story describes the situation in the years just preceding the Cade Rebellion and Wars of the Roses:

> The Yorkist manifesto of 1451 was not exaggerating when it said that riot, murder, robbery and the like had flourished in the time of Henry VI. . . . The feuds of the nobility in the more outlying parts of the kingdom attained the proportions of private wars. . . .
>
> Known offenders were sooner or later subjected to the formal procedures of the judicial system, but there was apparently little danger of conviction and punishment. Juries of country gentry would not convict their own kind. Instead of keeping order and protecting the weak, the law was more commonly misapplied to the advantage of those able to control it. The corruption and oppression of local government was the main burden of the Kentish rebels.[24]

Those Kentish rebels are Cade's men, historically a far more intelligent and responsible crew than Shakespeare's portrayal of them in act 4 suggests. Shakespeare's Cade is an energetic and rather comic thug. The real Cade had a good education, was probably a member of the "squirearchy" of Kent, and was therefore at least a gentleman. He and his followers presented a long complaint to the crown that included a catalog of judicial misconduct: the selling of the goods and property of those accused of treason before they were convicted (thus ensuring they would be); the lease ("farme") of judicial offices to people who used them to gain money through extortion and false accusations; the taking of default judgments against defendants who had been neither summoned nor notified of suits pending against them; and the illegal eviction of people from their property,[25] which is precisely the complaint of the first petitioner. "The complaint of the commons of Kent" does not reflect a rebellion aimed at anarchy; rather, it reflects genuinely the legal abuses of the time and a desire to see fair enforcement of the laws in place. Stowe comments that there was nothing in the articles "but seemed reasonable."[26]

The rebellion Cade led was several steps forward in sophistication from the John Ball Rebellion of 1381, in which killing all the lawyers, burning all the law books and legal records, and starting from scratch were the principle goals of the rebels. Dick the Butcher's cry, "The first thing we do, let's kill all the lawyers" (4.2.73) owes far more to Holinshed's portrayal of the Ball Rebellion than it does to Jack Cade's. Shakespeare takes both rebellions as his sources and conflates them to tell the story he wants.

In Shakespeare's adaptation of Holinshed's history, an additional piece of political machination helps to explain the Cade rebellion. Cade is commissioned by the Duke of York to start the rebellion so that York, who is in Ireland putting down another rebellion, can return to save England from anarchy. York sets up Cade as the problem that he, riding in on his "white horse," will come home to solve. To attract followers, Cade claims to be the last descendant of John Mortimer, who would have an even better hereditary claim to the crown than York or Henry. (Historically, Cade seems to have really believed this claim.)

Dick the Butcher's cry would have resonated with

Shakespeare's audience just as lawyer jokes do with us today. ("What do you call fifty lawyers chained together at the bottom of the sea?" "A good start.") Although humor at the expense of lawyers has its origins far back in Western culture, there is evidence that during the half-century leading to the English Revolution, the public's animus against lawyers reached unprecedented levels. As Wilfrid R. Prest explains in his book *The Rise of the Barristers*, the number of lawsuits filed during this period grew steadily, and the legal profession grew in proportion. Lawyers were commonly regarded as avaricious, covetous, dishonest, ambitious, and proud.[27] The perceived rarity of the "good" lawyer is evidenced by an epitaph that survives in three versions, one attributed to Ben Jonson: "See how God works his wonders now and then? Here lies a lawyer and an honest man."[28] Prest notes that "hostility towards common lawyers seems to have burgeoned precisely as the profession grew in size and social prominence during the sixteenth century."[29]

Shakespeare presents the rebels' preoccupation with judicial corruption through the mouth of Holland, a rebel who, just prior to Cade's entrance as the leader of the rebellion, says, "Let the magistrates be laboring men," preparing the way for Cade, putatively a laborer, to set up shop as magistrate for the masses. Cade himself does not advocate the destruction of the legal system as part of his platform, but he does make some utopian promises, not different in kind from many we hear today: "[that] seven half-penny loaves [shall be] sold for a penny; the three hoop'd-pot shall have ten hoops, and I will make it felony to drink small beer" (4.2.62–65).

Cade's trial scenes are darkly comic and turn the English court system on its head in much the same way that, during the carnival season, the King of Mardi Gras, or in England's case, The Lord of Misrule, turns topsey-turvey the established hierarchy and modes of conduct. One hardly knows whether to laugh or shudder at Cade's inverted trial scenes, which address legitimate grievances but attempt to solve them in horrific ways. Expand Cade's range of operation, send him across the channel, and you would get something like the Terror of the French Revolution. The following sections focus on Cade's trials.

The Trial of the Clerk, "Emmanuel"

The first judicial victim of Cade's court is Emmanuel, a clerk. His crime is that he can read and write. The grievances that Cade's men bring against Emmanuel are all connected with the misuse of writing for legal chicanery. Emmanuel's trial, however, amounts to a wholesale condemnation of literacy by the rebels, who always take their remedies to the violent extreme. Emmanuel, not the brightest of men, does not realize that his literacy is what dooms him until he is hung with his pen and inkhorn about his neck. The trial proceeds as follows:

Cade:	How now! Who's there?
Weaver:	The clerk of Chartham; he can write and read and cast accompt.
Cade:	O monstrous!
Weaver:	We took him setting of boys' copies.
Cade:	Here's a villain!
Weaver:	H'as a book in his pocket with red letters in't.
Cade:	Nay, then he is a conjurer.
Butcher:	Nay, he can make obligations, and write courthand.
Cade:	I am sorry for't. The man is a proper man, of mine honour; unless I find him guilty, he shall not die.

(4.2.80–90)

With Cade's "The man is a proper man, of mine / honour unless I find him guilty, he shall not die," Shakespeare gives us a parody of judicial pomposity and crocodile tears. The arbitrary use of power is rhetorically inflated to sound as if it were due process, and the exercise of deadly power, cloaked in sympathy. Cade continues his unintentional parody of judicial arrogance by using the condescending second person familiar ("thou") toward Emmanuel and calling him "Sirrah." Emmanuel, who quickly proclaims that he can read and write, does not realize that he has entered a jurisdiction in which that will get him killed.

One way to avoid hanging for a capital offense during Shakespeare's day was by claiming "benefit of clergy," otherwise referred to as knowing your "neck verse." Benefit of clergy was first instituted by medievals attempting to save priests, who were virtually the only literate members of society, from the hangman's noose. If one could read his neck verse in Latin, he was essentially given one free capital offense (excepting treason), though he carried a record of the decree for the rest of his life in the form of a branded thumb. For a second offense, no benefit was extended. Benefit of clergy was alive and well in Shakespeare's day, and Ben Jonson, another great dramatist of the period, claimed and received it after killing an actor in a duel. The court duly recorded its leniency on his thumb and Jonson refrained from killing actors thereafter. The neck verse, appropriately, was Psalm 51:1: "Have mercy upon me, O God, according to thy loving kindness: according to the multitude of thy tender mercies blot out my transgressions." Emmanuel's vociferous proclamations of his literacy are not going to get him off with a neck verse, but rather, in the court of Cade, provide the confession of his crime:

Cade: Come hither, sirrah, I must examine thee. What is

	thy name?
Clerk:	Emmanuel.
Butcher:	They use to write it on the top of letters. 'Twill go hard with you.
Cade:	Let me alone. Dost thou use to write thy name? Or hast thou a mark to thy self, like a honest plain dealing man?
Clerk:	Sir, I thank God I have been so well brought up, that I can write my name.
All:	He hath confess'd: away with him! he's a villain and a traitor.

(4.2.91–102)

The rebels' anger at the "benefit of clergy" claim is well founded. The practice allowed guilty first offenders to escape, while putting the innocent illiterate to execution. It was invoked with a regularity that continually displayed the system's unfairness: "Stone has suggested that 47% of the criminal classes of Jacobean London could read, since they successfully pleaded benefit of clergy. The Middlesex records in fact show 32% of the capital felons in the reign of Elizabeth and 39% in the reign of James successfully claiming clergy, a somewhat lower percentage than cited by Stone," reports historian David Cressy.[30]

Emmanuel bears little resemblance to Christ, but given the suggestiveness of his name, Shakespeare must certainly be making a point. "Emmanuel," meaning "God be with us," is especially significant in a time when the printed English Bible was becoming the presence and authority of God in the homes of England.[31] The word "Emmanuel" also has meaning in connection with education. One of the words which grammar school boys used to practice writing was "Emmanuel," and "Emmanuel" was often written at the top of letters, deeds, and other documents as a sign of piety. Emmanuel himself is associated with the teaching of grammar, since he has a school book with red letters, probably a copy of the *Primer*, which had capitals in red, and because he was taken "setting" or checking boy's copies of writing, which probably included the word "Emmanuel."[32]

If the clerk Emmanuel stands for anything, it is literacy, and if his death is a metaphoric crucifixion, it is "the Word," in all its associations, that is being executed. Like Cinna the poet in *Julius Caesar*, and for that matter Jesus, Emmanuel is a victim of the mob. His fate represents Christian humanism's worst nightmare: that something like the fall of Rome could happen again, that literacy and learning could be directly attacked, civilization plunged into another dark age, and the people denied the word of God. From a populist point of view, the scene demonstrates the frustration of the John Ball rebellion of 1381: "An attack on the records and recorders whose presence permitted and promoted the oppressive collection of revenues . . . the recording of arrears, and the registration of property so that it could be controlled and alienated by the state and its often corrupt agents."[33] But for Shakespeare and his audience, the execution of Emmanuel is an attack on literacy, and therefore religion. The scene demonstrates that England is caught in a vicious cycle. The flouting of religious principles through the corruption of the judicial system leads to the emplacement of unprincipled and unreasonable mob adjudications—lynchings in fact—which become another indirect attack on religion, the loss of which will only plunge the commonwealth further into anarchy.

One Court as Good as Another: The Sergeant-at-law's Trial

The next trial scene, which occurs only in Quarto, is even more savage. The trial of the Sergeant-at-law (a barrister) is a comic reversal of Suffolk's and Margaret's treatment of the first petitioner in 1.3, who complained that Cardinal Beaufort's servant had taken his house and wife and all. Here, the situation is turned upside down when the Sergeant-at-law complains to Cade that he has been dispossessed of his wife by Cade's men:

Sergeant: Justice, justice I pray you sir, let me have justice of
            this fellow here.

Cade: Why, what hast he done?

Sergeant: Alas, sir, he has ravished my wife.

Dick: Why my Lord, he would have prevented me. And I
            went and entered my
            action in his wife's paper house.

Cade: Dick, follow thy suit in her common place.
            You whoreson villain, you are a Sergeant, you'll
            Take any man by the throat for twelve pence,
            And arrest a man when he's at dinner.
            And have him to prison ere the meat be out of his
                mouth.
            Go Dick, take him hence, cut out his tongue for
                cogging
            Hough him for running and to conclude
            Brave him with his own mace.

                                    (Quarto, G2v)

This brief scene emblematizes the law as rape. The courts under the control of Suffolk have failed to provide a remedy for the "taking" of the first Melford petitioner's wife. Under these circumstances, it is metaphorically appropriate that Cade's man "Dick" likens rape to the serving of legal papers, entering his "action" in the Sergeant's wife's "paper house" (a paper house being the place where complaints—legal actions—are served). The law has become what it has been used to legitimize, and this being widely recognized, there is no longer any need to cloak rape with a veneer of legality—one simply proceeds directly to the rape, rape having become law. So Cade tells Dick to follow his suit in "the common place" of the Sergeant's wife, implying that she's a whore anyway.

The Sergeant is sentenced to be emasculated in two ways. First, he is to be deprived of that piece of anatomical equipment that he most relies upon to commit legal rapes—his tongue. He is to be "houghed" to keep from running, which has a double sense. "Houghing" is the clearing of one's throat as a lawyer might be expected to do before making a long speech, "running on." It is also the cutting of the hough sinew, the tendons behind the knee, an operation performed on cattle to keep them from running off. Here, the tongue fills in for the hough sinew: the Sergeant will never run off in court again. Cade's final order, that the Sergeant be braved with his own mace, implies that the Sergeant is to be literally emasculated. The joys of metaphoricity are connected to the joys of mutilation in a manner than must have been hilarious to the audience and quite gratifying for any unfortunate litigants in attendance. The Sergeant is hardly a sympathetic victim, not simply because he is a lawyer, but because he is stupid enough to seek relief from Cade and sycophantic enough to call him "sir" and treat him as a legitimate judge, a popular comment on lawyers' willingness to grovel to anyone or argue to any court to get what they want.

The Trial of Lord Say

The final trial in the Cade Rebellion is that of Lord Say, one of the king's councilors and a judge, who is accused of losing Maine and Normandy to France, speaking French, promulgating literacy, hanging those who cannot read, enforcing the criminal and tax laws, and putting an elegant footcloth on his horse. Again, the rebels' charges mix anger at legitimate grievances with large doses of comic—but dangerous—ignorance.

The rebels are particularly concerned with the loss of France, and they have legitimate reason to be angry, since many of them appear to be veterans of French campaigns. Dick the Butcher says, "We'll have the Lord Say's head for selling the dukedom of Maine" (4.2.153–54), and when the messenger arrives shouting that Lord Say has been captured, he says, "here's the Lord Say, which sold the towns in France" (4.7.18–19).

In Cade's extemporaneous indictment of Say, the first charge involves France: "What canst thou answer to my Majesty for giving up of Normandy unto Mounsieur Basimecu, the Dauphin of France" (4.7.25–27)? ("Basimecu" puns on *baise mon cul*: "kiss my backside.") Yet it is evident from the very beginning of the play that if anyone is to be credited with the loss of Maine, it is Suffolk, who has traded Maine and Anjou to bring Margaret to England. Somerset's ineffective government has cost the English Normandy. There is no indication in the play or in history of any involvement by Say. The rebels simply assume, with no proof at all, that Say is responsible, and their ignorance of the true political situation subverts their claims to rule.

The displacement of learning by ignorance is augmented by rebel errors in logic. The accusation against Say for speaking French forms the major premise of an erroneous syllogism which is set forth in this exchange between Cade and Sir Humphrey Stafford, who has been sent to stop the rebels:

Cade: . . . he [Say] can speak French;
            and therefore he is a traitor.

Stafford: O gross and miserable ignorance!

Cade: Nay, answer if you can: the Frenchmen are our
            enemies; go to then, I ask but this: can he that speaks
            with the tongue of an enemy be a good counsellor,
                or no?

                                            (4.2.159–65)

Playing with logic was a source of humor among many Renaissance writers, and here we see Shakespeare doing it in the same manner in which he gives malapropisms to other characters, like Bottom in *A Midsummer Night's Dream* or Dogberry in *Much Ado About Nothing*. Cade uses speaking "with the tongue of an enemy" in a double sense, providing an example of "the four terms fallacy." Syllogistically, Cade's speech also exemplifies the formal error of the "excluded middle": Say speaks French; our enemies speak French; therefore, Say is our enemy. (Try to imagine a popular audience today with the ability to pick up this kind of humor as the play or movie zips along.) There is comedy here, but also a trenchant comment on the mob's ability to reason. Stafford's comment, "O gross and miserable ignorance," accurately describes the foolishness of Cade's argument. Cade's ignorance and illogic provide a straightforward demonstration of the Elizabethan contention that the great herd of people is incapable of political thought—that democracy is virtually synonymous with anarchy, the rule of appetite rather than reason, and is indeed the worst form of government, if it can be called government at all.

Cade's second charge against Say, another piece of satire, is for promulgating literacy, and therefore repeats the charge against Emmanuel, doubly emphasizing the rebels' attack on learning:

> . . . Thou hast most traitorously corrupted the youth of the realme in erecting a grammar-school; and whereas, before, our forefathers had no other books but the score and the tally, thou hast caus'd printing to be us'd; and contrary to the King his crown, and dignity, thou has built a paper-mill. It will be prov'd to thy face that thou hast men about thee that usually

talk of a noun, and a verb, and such abominable words
as no Christian ear can endure to hear.

(4.7.30–39)

This parodies the opening statement of a prosecutor mar-
shalling evidence, both circumstantial and direct, in a treason trial. Say's associations are bad: he keeps company with
men who speak treasonously of nouns and verbs. Say builds
paper mills, putting him in the same category as basement
bomb manufacturers. He corrupts youth by erecting grammar
schools. Like a good prosecutor, Cade makes an appeal to the
jury's heritage: their forefathers didn't need any writing except for the score and tally.[34]

Cade goes on to set forth benefit of clergy as a grievance:
"Thou hast put them [poor men] in prison; and because they
could not read, thou hast hang'd them; when, indeed, only for
that cause they have been most worthy to live" (4.7.41–44).
Say defends himself ably, citing his record as a counselor and
judge:

Justice with favour have I always done;
Prayers and tears have mov'd me, gifts could never.
When have I aught exacted at your hands,
But to maintain the King, the realm, and you?
Large gifts have I bestow'd on learned clerks,
Because my book preferr'd me to the King,
And seeing ignorance is the curse of God
Knowledge the wing wherewith we fly to heaven,
Unless you be possess'd with devilish spirits,
You cannot forbear to murder me.

(4.7.64–73)

Here, Say speaks with the voice of Christian humanism,
defending his career as that of the good judge, an example of

which has already been provided by Duke Humphrey. The humanists believed that learning and the pursuit of truth would naturally lead men to God, because God was the ultimate truth to which all others led. Sidney sets out the humanist program in his *Defense of Poesy*, in which he argues that the purpose of literature is to instruct and delight, to furnish examples of goodness and virtue that inspire emulation: "Who readeth Aeneas carrying old Anchises on his back, that wisheth not it were his fortune to perform so excellent an act?" In this speech, Shakespeare dilates what was suggested by the hanging of Emmanuel, that the destruction of literacy is a satanic act— "devilish"—that prohibits Christians from obtaining what they need, which is knowledge, "the wing wherewith we fly to heaven."

The knowledge Say speaks of is most fundamentally that of the Bible, the word of God through which men acquire faith and salvation, but it also includes classical learning, science, law, the entire field of human investigation, which rightly understood reveals God's glory. Say argues that the destruction of "the Word," or even the word in general, is an attack on God. Thus, political dereliction and the craving for power work to the spiritual detriment of the country, and the Cade Rebellion is only one in a line of dominoes that has fallen because of the infighting at Henry's court. The undermining of government based on religious principle leads to attacks on religion which further undermine the government, and so on, possibly until total governmental collapse. Shakespeare's point is that getting off this merry-go-round, as it gains speed, is not easy. Each cause triggers a larger effect, and each effect, a more powerful cause, until the whirlwind of political and spiritual energy becomes a cyclone.

Death can be treated comically so long as the playwright presents a "biter gets bit" situation, or when the stage victim is so "unreal" in dramatic presentation that he evokes little or no pity. Say, a palsy-stricken old man, beaten up by a mob, has dramatic reality, as opposed to Emmanuel or the Sergeant-at-law, who go to death and dismemberment like cartoon cats. The execution of Say and his son-in-law, James Cromer, and the bringing on stage of one of their heads, marks the turning of Shakespeare's comic treatment of the Cade Rebellion toward a serious conclusion. The Rebellion is shortly put down; all the participants except Cade are forgiven by Henry, when they come to him with halters about their necks. Appropriately, Cade himself is killed by a Kentishman, Alexander Iden, who finds Cade hiding in his garden. Discovered in the garden of "Iden," one of England's snakes is crushed, thus completing Shakespeare's identification of Cade with Satan. Perhaps there are worse people than Cade in *2 Henry VI*, but there are none more dangerous, because Cade represents an attack on the very idea of government, and therefore, justice.

"Sacramental" Justice

Were we to read this play in a postmodern vein, which typically dismisses any idea of transcendent order, we might interpret Shakespeare's portrayal of the Cade Rebellion as an unmasking of the Tudor (and all other) judicial systems: a demonstration that judicial decision making is really just the exercise of raw power cloaked in the rhetoric of equitable language. Cade is not that much different than any other judge. He merely shows the judicial emperor to have no clothes by mimicking the language of the law whenever he renders a decision governed only by his lust to exercise power. However, the Cade Rebellion furnishes only three trial scenes in a play which is virtually constructed of them, and the play as a whole presents a much more complicated picture of judicial decision-making.

Earlier in the play, when Duke Humphrey decrees a trial

by combat between Thump and Horner, Shakespeare portrays the limits of judicial reasoning. Humphrey must decide a charge of treason by one man against another, but there is no way to determine whether the accuser or denier is telling the truth. Since the task is impossible for reason, Humphrey, in medieval fashion, decrees trial by battle, leaving God as the ultimate arbiter of justice. In this case, judicial reasoning abdicates in the face of utter uncertainty. There is no evidence on which to base a reasoned judgment, and so Humphrey is left with a judicial coin-flip. But there is another trial, in 2.1, unnecessary to plot development, but very important as a foil to all of *2 Henry VI*'s scenes of bad judgment. This scene shows what a smart judge operating fairly can accomplish. Here Gloucester plays the part of a good epistemologist, working his way to the truth through evidence and reason.

Saunder Simpcox is a beggar who claims to have just received his eyesight as the result of a miracle at St. Albans, a miracle he intends to cash in on. When Gloucester questions him, Simpcox is able to identify colors by name, a feat which, Gloucester points out, the formerly "blind man" could not manage, having had no opportunity to form links between the words for colors and the colors themselves. Gloucester's discovery of Simpcox's fraud is sound. Shakespeare does not show in *2 Henry VI* that forensic proof is impossible. He shows that it is difficult to come by, that the system is subject to serious corruption, and that corruption can dress itself in language suffused with legitimacy. The whole truth and nothing but the truth is, perhaps, an unreachable prize. Nevertheless, truth is the ideal toward which all good judges (and historians) work.

No one during Shakespeare's time ever claimed that an act of judgment was a sacrament. Yet Fortescue and the English common lawyers of the sixteenth century agreed that "the laws promulgated by man are decreed by God," and "guided and directed to us through divine grace." The application of law, it would seem, is God's grace made visible. The *Book of Common Prayer* gave a functional definition of "sacrament" as follows: "Sacraments ordained of Christ be not only badges or tokens of Christian men's profession, but rather they be certain sure witnesses, and effectual signs of grace, and God's good will towards us, by which he doth work invisibly in us, and doth not only quicken, but also strengthen and confirm our Faith in him."[35]

Fortescue's idea of the law thus comes close to being sacramental, for when rightly applied, law is a visible means of God's grace *to the body politic*, and it creates a corporate faith in the body politic in that godliness and justice are affirmed in every fair judgment. *2 Henry VI* is about a time in the history of England which was sacrilegious; the law, as an instrument of grace, was dragged through the mud, blasphemy starting from the top and working it's way down. Henry, a pious but totally incompetent king, leaves a power vacuum and his nobles woefully abuse the courts as they try to fill it. Biased and rapacious judgments arouse the wrath of the people, making them more manipulable to a demagogue like Cade, who is actually the puppet of one of the most powerful men in the kingdom, York, who will twist or destroy the law if that's what it takes to become king. The notion of duty to God and country is lost in all this, as Shakespeare's audience, Sir Walter Raleigh, and the historians of their day well knew. In the early 1590s, it being obvious that Elizabeth would die without an heir, Englishmen wondered if they were still caught in a cycle of punishment initiated two hundred years before. *2 Henry VI*, therefore, is not just history, but a tale of where Englishmen might find themselves yet. Each court proceeding was indeed a measure of the spiritual health of the realm.

James I on the kind of people who are haunted by spirits or demons:
[Such persons are of two kinds]: "Either such as being guiltie of greevous offenses, God punishes by that horrible kind of scourdge, or else being persons of the best nature peradventure, that yee shall finde in all the Countrie about them, God permittes them to be troubled in that sort for the trial of their patience, and wakening up of their zeal, for admonishing of the beholders, not to truste over much in themselves . . ."

Daemonologie, Edinburgh, 1597

Vanity of vanities saith the Preacher: vanity of vanities: all is vanity. / What remaineth unto man in all his travails, which he suffreth under the sun? / One generation passeth, and another generation succeedeth. . . . / I have considered all the works that are done under the sun, and behold, all is vanity, and vexation of the spirit. / That which is crooked, can none make straight: and that which faileth cannot be numbered.

Ecclesiastes, 1:2–4; 14–15

Whosoever shall seek to save his life shall lose it; and whosoever shall lose his life shall preserve it.

Luke 17:33

2

Hamlet
and the Limits
of Human Judgment

Hamlet and *King Lear* are regarded, rightfully, as Shakespeare's two most profound tragedies. Hamlet, who loses faith in humanism's rosy assessment of mankind's capabilities, and Lear, who finds himself in a universe without justice, abandoned by the gods, sum up between them a disenchantment with the world that spoke strongly to the pessimistic turn of the European mind, of which both the medieval world and the dawn of nihilistic modernity partake.[1] However, the Renaissance is also characterized by its classically inspired view of human potential and its hopes for exploration and progress. Hamlet, straddling the chasm between the modern and the medieval, is a fractured human being in search of some unifying and sustainable sense of who he is, indeed, of what "man" is; if only he could fit the pieces of himself together, he would have a fulcrum from which to act on the world. This fulcrum is what he searches for, with all his intellectual might, throughout the play. No character in Shakespeare reasons with more diligence to judge the right course of action, and thus no one comes up harder against the limitations of human judgment than Hamlet.

Would You Trust this Ghost?

Hamlet begins with men cold and sick at heart on the battlements of Elsinore. Their leader, King Hamlet, has recently died; Norway threatens invasion, and two of the watchmen, Marcellus and Barnardo, have twice seen what appears to be the ghost of their recently dead king stalking the walls. Horatio, a scholar from Wittenberg who is visiting Denmark, has been recruited by the watchmen to observe the apparition and to speak to it, so he also waits, though with hearty disbelief that the ghost will appear.

Horatio is one of Shakespeare's most fascinating secondary characters. A student from a Protestant university known for its radical views, he is a skeptic who seems to share the belief of both Catholics and Protestants that "ghosts" were not the souls of the departed but more likely demons. Horatio is steady, calm, and observant, and his talents as a dispassionate intellectual and an acute advisor are commissioned many times in the play. We get a sense of Horatio's intellectual carefulness in his first short speech. As Horatio joins the watchmen, Barnardo greets him: "Say, what, is Horatio there?" Horatio laconically replies, "A piece of him," meaning that only a bit of him thinks this cold outing is worthwhile. Of course, the ghost does appear, and Horatio, skeptical no longer, says: "Before my God, I might not this believe / Without the sensible and true avouch / Of mine own eyes" (1.1.59–61). God's name and heaven are invoked many times in speeches that take place on the walls of Elsinore, and at first they may seem to be mild oaths, but psychologically, they impress an audience as attempts to establish closeness with God in the face of supernatural terror.

Horatio hypothesizes that the apparition's appearance forebodes some cataclysm in the state, as did the ghosts that "did squeak and gibber in the Roman streets" the night before Caesar was murdered. When the ghost appears a second time, in an attempt to make it stay, the watchmen go so far as to strike at it with their "partisans," or spears, but this has no effect, and the ghost leaves upon the crowing of the cock, in Horatio's description, "like a guilty thing upon a fearful summons."

Marcellus, for one, wishes that spirits would stay out of the human world, and out of his fear he recalls a story about the rooster that is almost a prayer for God to purify his creation:

> Some say that ever 'gainst that season comes
> Wherein our Saviour's birth is celebrated,
> This bird of dawning singeth all night long;
> And then, they say, no spirit dare stir abroad,
> The nights are wholesome, then no planets strike,
> No fairy takes, nor witch hath power to charm,
> So hallow'd and so gracious is that time.

(1.1.163–70)

Marcellus's story suggests that during the season of Advent, Christ's victory is commemorated by a demonstration of divine power. In his ministry, Jesus demonstrated his power over sin, death, and the devil (in part, by casting out demons); the story implies that a remainder of that power exists in a partially restored creation during the season preceding Christmas, when spirits are forbidden to walk abroad. Marcellus clearly wants to believe the story, and even the cautious Horatio, who might have dismissed it out of hand hours before, must at least acknowledge the possibility it might be true: "So have I heard, and do *in part* believe it" (italics added).

At this point, no one has made a judgment about the nature of what they have seen. They have not even used the word "ghost," and Horatio certainly does not jump to the conclusion that the apparition is the ghost of Hamlet's father—quite the opposite. In Horatio's first speech to the spirit, he asks its identity and in fact assumes that it has not only "usurped" the time of night in which it appears, but also *the form* of King Hamlet. Appearances are not to be trusted: "What are thou that usurp'st this time of night / Together with that fair and warlike form / In which the majesty of buried Denmark / Did sometimes march?" (1.1.49–52). As morning breaks, the men decide to tell Hamlet what they have seen.

Mourning for the death of his father, frustrated by his mother's marriage to his uncle Claudius, angry that Claudius is on the throne instead of him, Hamlet is primed to hear what Horatio and the guard have to say. But Hamlet is a student of Wittenberg too, and he does not just swallow a story. Horatio describes what he has seen, and Hamlet cross-examines Horatio, Marcellus, and Barnardo point by point, not just to satisfy his curiosity, but to *verify* their story. This is the first we see of a Horatio-like trait in Hamlet. He too tries to make his judgments on the basis of evidence and reason rather than passion, though given the stress he is under, this takes a tremendous act of the will:

Hamlet:	Arm'd, say you?
All:	Arm'd, my lord.
Hamlet:	From top to toe?
All:	My lord, from head to foot.

Hamlet:	Then saw you not his face?
Horatio:	O yes, my lord, he wore his beaver up.
Hamlet:	What look'd he, frowningly?
Horatio:	A countenance more in sorrow than in anger.
Hamlet:	Pale, or red?
Horatio:	Nay, very pale
Hamlet:	And fix'd his eyes upon you?
Horatio:	Most constantly
Hamlet:	I would I had been there.
Horatio:	It would have much amaz'd you.
Hamlet:	Very like. Stayed it long?
Horatio:	While one with moderate haste might tell a hundred.
Marcellus and Barnardo:	
	Longer, longer.
Horatio:	Not when I saw't . . .
Hamlet:	I will watch tonight. Perchance 'twill walk again.
Horatio:	I war'nt it will
Hamlet:	If it assume my noble father's person,
	I'll speak to it though hell itself should gape
	And bid me hold my peace.

(1.2.226–46)

In this exchange, Shakespeare conveys important clues about Hamlet's intellect and state of mind. First, Hamlet is canny. He sets a little trap for these witnesses who have told him they have seen an apparition that looks like his father. Was he wearing armor? From head to toe. Then his face could not have been seen; your identification is questionable. Ah, but he wore his helmet visor up. There is a discrepancy between the watch and Horatio about how long the specter stayed, though Horatio, with characteristic precision, notes the possibility that his two companions are referring to other sightings.

Hamlet will also watch, but he too is reluctant to characterize what has been seen as his father's ghost, even if it bore his father's form: "If it *assume* my noble father's person, I'll speak to it," he says (emphasis added).

Well, if the apparition is not the ghost of Hamlet's father, what could it be? Certainly many Elizabethans did believe in ghosts. But they also believed in demons and attributed to them the ability to take on any shape or to impersonate any-thing—even the ghost of a dead father. This possibility never leaves the consciousness of Hamlet or Horatio, and later in the play Hamlet acknowledges that melancholy people such as himself are especially susceptible to demonic temptation. James I wrote his book *Daemonolgie* because it was evident to him that witches and demons were active in the land, and that their activity had increased: "The fearefull abuondinge at this time in this countrie of these detestable slaves of the Devill, the Witches or enchaunters, hath moved me (beloved reader) to dispatch in post, this following treatise. . . ." The possibil-ity that the apparition is a demon angling for Hamlet's soul is made explicit in act 1, scene 4, where Hamlet meets "the ghost." When Hamlet sees him, he says:

> Angels and ministers of grace defend us!
> Be thou a spirit of health or goblin damn'd,
> Bring with thee airs from heaven or blasts from hell,
> Be thy intents wicked or charitable,
> Thou com'st in such a questionable shape
> That I will speak with thee. I'll call thee Hamlet,
> King, father, royal Dane.

> (1.4.39–45)

The first line, of course, is a plea for divine assistance, since Hamlet knows he and the men with him are possibly confronting the demonic. Hamlet specifically acknowledges that the specter could be a "goblin damn'd," who brings with it "blasts from hell." However, it comes in such "questionable shape," i.e., a shape that invites questions, that Hamlet must speak to it, and Hamlet makes a decision to call it by the name of what he wants it to be—the spirit of his father. Hamlet knows, in a sense, that he is just assigning the thing a name, but that he does name it suggests the passions boiling inside him and the danger of his desire to believe.

The apparition beckons for Hamlet to follow it, and Horatio, in a speech that echoes Hamlet's line about hell itself gaping, pleads with Hamlet not to go:

> What if it tempt you toward the flood, my lord,
> Or to the dreadful summit of the cliff
> That beetles o'er his base into the sea,
> And there assume some other horrible form
> Which might deprive your sovereignty of reason
> And draw you into madness?

> (1.4.69–74)

James I says in *Daemonologie* that demons tempt men "to obtaine one of two thinges . . . The one is the tinesell of their life, by inducing them to such perrilous places at such time as he either followes or possesses them which may procure the same [and this seems to be what worries Horatio about the "dreadful summit,"—the possibility that the demon will deprive Hamlet of his sovereign reason and lead him over the edge]. The other thing that he prizes to obteine by troubling of them is the tinsell of their soule, to mistrust and blaspheme God."[2]

The conversation between Hamlet and the apparition he has chosen to call his father can be viewed, without interpretive squirming, as one of temptation, and to see how this works, it is necessary to backtrack a bit to Hamlet's first soliloquy, so that we can get a fix on his state of mind. It is the content of Hamlet's troubled mind that would furnish a satanic tempter the material with which to work.

Hamlet's mother has married a man he does not like, and so soon after his father's death that "the funeral baked meats did coldly furnish forth the marriage tables," which makes Hamlet suspect his mother's loyalty to his father. The kings of Denmark are elected by a group of powerful nobles, and Hamlet, probably in Wittenberg at the time of his father's death, was gone when his uncle Claudius "popped between [him] and his election." Human life seems to have lost its meaning for Hamlet, the entire country having put away his father so quickly, and later in the play he says ironically, "There's hope a good man's memory may outlive his life half a year." But Hamlet senses something behind all the hurry, as if he'd gotten a whiff of something "rotten in Denmark," some abomination at the core, just beyond his perception. In this context, Shakespeare gives us Hamlet's first soliloquy:

> O that this too too sullied flesh would melt,
> Thaw and resolve itself into a dew,
> Or that the Everlasting had not fix'd
> His canon 'gainst self-slaughter. O God! God!
> How weary, stale, flat and unprofitable
> Seem to me all the uses of this world!
> Fie on't, ah fie, 'tis an unweeded garden
> Grows to seed; things rank and gross in nature
> Possess it merely.
>
> (1.2.129–37)

In several of his many soliloquies, Hamlet will ask the question of whether life is worth living, and here he shows himself to be of a very modern temper. For a person of the Middle Ages would not have posed this question. The answer was too obvious: of course life was not worth living! Man's existence was a trial to be gotten through, like a life sentence on Alcatraz, and for believers death was a blessed release to heavenly freedom. But because Hamlet—the Renaissance man—has one foot in the modern world and one in the medieval, he believes that man's life should amount to something important. He has imbibed the spirit of the Renaissance, which revived the conviction of the Greeks that this earthly life has potential meaning, and therefore we must use it to accomplish great things. As Hamlet later expresses it, "What a piece of work is a man, how noble in reason, how infinite in faculties, in form and moving how express and admirable, in action how like an angel, in apprehension how like a god: the beauty of the world, the paragon of animals. . . ." (2.2.303–07). Man is a creature *designed* to explore the universe and accomplish wonders. He is almost a partner with God. His reason makes him so; without it man is no more than a beast, an automaton. Late in act 4 Hamlet poses the same question about man's purpose with the same sense of wonder:

> What is a man
> If his chief good and market of his time
> Be but to sleep and feed? A beast, no more.
> Sure he that made us with such large discourse,
> Looking before and after, gave us not
> That capability and godlike reason
> To fust in us unus'd.

(4.4.33–39)

Why did God give us reason, part of which consists in the ability to consider both the past and the consequences of our actions for the future—in other words, why were humans given free will and the ability to make prudent decisions—if they were not supposed to use them? But Hamlet's understanding of what makes life valuable has been challenged by everything that has happened since his father's death. Particularly his mother's "o'er hasty" marriage to a man Hamlet cannot respect. The implied slight to his father's stature has started Hamlet thinking about whether human accomplishment, in the face of death, is anything but trivial. The medieval side of Hamlet begins to chafe the modern; the mystery of our ultimate end throws human ambition into question. Hamlet's morbid disgust at his mother's unfaithfulness is what especially opens him to demonic temptation, since this is where his reason is least engaged. The following statement in Hamlet's first soliloquy, expressing anguish at his mother's remarriage, will be repeated by the apparition to Hamlet almost verbatim, as if it were flinging Hamlet's own thoughts back to him, telling Hamlet exactly what will push him most quickly to revenge:

> That it should come to this!
> But two months dead—nay, not so much, not two—
> So excellent a king, that was to this [Claudius]
> Hyperion to a satyr, so loving to my mother
> That he might not beteem the winds of heaven
> Visit her face too roughly. Heaven and earth,
> Must I remember? Why, she would hang on him
> As if increase of appetite had grown
> By what it fed on; and yet within a month—
> Let me not think on't—Frailty, thy name is woman—
> A little month, or ere those shoes were old
> With which she follow'd my poor father's body,
> Like Niobe, all tears—why, she—
> O God, a beast that wants discourse of reason
> Would have mourn'd longer—married with my uncle,
> My father's brother—but no more like my father
> Than I to Hercules. Within a month,
> Ere yet the salt of most unrighteous tears
> Had left the flushing in her galled eyes,

> She married—O most wicked speed! To post
> With such dexterity to incestuous sheets!

(1.2.137–57)

Hamlet's father is the sun god Hyperion, associated with reason and masculine vigor, while Claudius is a mere satyr, half goat, and with a goat's lustful disposition. Hamlet's mother here is described almost in parasitical terms: she would hang on King Hamlet, like a leech perhaps, hanging on more tightly as it sucks blood, except that now Gertrude's appetite is feeding as happily on Claudius's love as it did on her first husband's, and she gets more hungry for Claudius the more of him she gets. Gertrude, Hamlet implies, is a creature of appetite, and when her host dies, she finds another. The imagery of feeding parasites and worms occurs throughout the play, and most forcefully, as an echo of this soliloquy, in the ghost's speech to Hamlet.

The apparition first tells Hamlet that it is not residing in heaven: "My hour is almost come / When I to sulph'rous and tormenting flamers / Must render up myself" (1.5.2–4). Rather, it seems to be in purgatory:

> I am thy father's spirit
> Doom'd for a certain term to walk the night,
> And for the day confin'd to fast in fires,
> Till the foul crimes done in my days of nature
> Are burnt and purg'd away.

(1.5.9–14)

The ghost names Claudius as his murderer, which is just what Hamlet suspected at some level, or perhaps wanted to believe: "O my prophetic soul!" Hamlet says. But then the ghost repeats back to Hamlet the very thoughts that Hamlet has voiced in his first soliloquy, with the same kinds of com-

parisons: Claudius a beast, Gertrude a parasite, and King
Hamlet a creature of light and heaven:

Ghost: Ay, that incestuous, that adulterate beast,
             With witchcraft of his wit, with traitorous gifts—
             O wicked wit, and gifts that have the power
             So to seduce!—won to his shameful lust
             The will of my most seeming-virtuous queen.
             O Hamlet, what a falling off was there,
             From me, whose love was of that dignity
             That it went hand in hand even with the vow
             I made to her in marriage, and to decline
             Upon a wretch whose natural gifts were poor
             To those of mine.
             But virtue, as it never will be mov'd,
             Though lewdness court it in a shape of heaven,
             So lust, though to a radiant angel link'd,
             Will sate itself in a celestial bed
             And prey on garbage.

                                              (1.5.42–57)

The ghost accuses Gertrude of committing adultery with
Claudius. Echoing Hamlet's line in the soliloquy describing
Gertrude as hanging on King Hamlet, the ghost says, "what a
falling off was there," implying that she is like a leech that
falls off its host once sated with blood. The imagery of parasitical feeding continues. The ghost likens Gertrude to the
very opposite of virtue, for virtue, though it is courted by lewd-
ness disguised as "a shape of heaven," will still be faithful;
but "lust," which Gertrude now personifies, even if married to
a radiant angel, will be unfaithful and leave to "prey on garbage." Claudius, of course, is the garbage, and Gertrude the
maggot. But who is the radiant angel? It can only be King
Hamlet, since Gertrude is the one who has fallen off him, pre-
ferring Claudius.

The irony in the ghost's statement is that he, confined to "fast in fires" to purge his sins, likens himself to an angel or saint. The irony deepens as the ghost, already in purgatory, convinces Hamlet to commit the sin of taking revenge: "If thou didst ever thy dear father love . . . Revenge his foul and most unnatural murder" (1.5.23, 25). How much more hellish will King Hamlet's time in purgatory be for encouraging a sin of the most serious kind? And what kind of father would want to put his son's soul in danger by persuading him to commit such a sin?

At first, Hamlet is quick to agree to take revenge: "Haste me . . . that I with wings as swift / As meditation or the thoughts of love / May sweep to my revenge," but when the ghost leaves, Hamlet acknowledges that his pledge to take revenge may embrace evil: "Shall I couple hell?" he says; that is, shall I join myself, possibly with the demonic, to take revenge for my father's death? Hamlet, his knees giving way, fights to collect his wits, and pursues the task of bringing his wits to bear for the next two acts.

Shakespeare's audience, both Catholic and Protestant, would almost certainly have seen the "ghost" as a demon in disguise. The contemporary Protestant view of ghosts, expressed by Lewes Lavater in 1572 was that God did not let the dead return:

> For if dead persons had returned backe again into this life, the wicked spirit the divell would easily have devised many sleights & wiles, & brought in much deceit into the life of man. And therfore god hath clean shut up this dore of deceit, & not permitted any dead man to returne hither & shewe what things be done in the other life, least the divell might gredely catch this occasion to plant his fraudulent policies.[3]

James I says the same in *Daemonologie*,[4] and as Eleanor Prosser notes in her fine book, *Hamlet and Revenge,* "the average Elizabethan was bombarded with these arguments."[5] Since departed souls did not return, ghosts were either demons or angels, but the latter possibility was considered extremely slight. If the apparition appeared to the credulous, to children, and above all to melancholics;[6] if it appeared at night, especially midnight; if it appeared in deserted places, like the battlements of a castle, and wanted to isolate one person from the rest of his fellows, it was virtually certain to be demonic. If it urged the commission of sin there was no question that the apparition was a tempter from hell, and this the ghost does by urging Hamlet to take revenge. Aside from taking the appearance of a snake and squirting venom from its fangs, there is little more the ghost can do to identify itself as a demon.

Hamlet is traditionally known as "the vacillating prince," the man whose character flaw is that he cannot make up his mind. Lawrence Olivier's portrayal of Hamlet was inspired by this view, together with the idea of Ernst Jones, one of Freud's disciples, that Hamlet is Oedipally motivated in seeking revenge. But because of the nature of the ghost, we see that Hamlet has an overwhelming reason to be cautious. The deed that the ghost is tempting Hamlet to commit settles the ghost's identity. Revenge was strongly condemned by the Anglican church of Shakespeare's day. Prosser explains:

> Revenge was a reprehensible blasphemy, as the most frequently cited Scriptural text made clear: "Dearly beloved, avenge not yourselves, but rather give place unto wrath: for it is written, Vengeance is mine; I will repay, saith the Lord." Echoes of this divine command and promise reverberate throughout Elizabethan literature, and not merely in didactic works. . . .

> The primary argument against revenge . . . was
> that the revenger endangered his own soul. No matter
> how righteous a man might think his motives, the act
> of revenge would inevitably make him as evil as his
> injurer in the eyes of God.[7]

Though Hamlet, after his initial meeting with the ghost, tells Horatio "it is an honest ghost, that let me tell you," he also tells Horatio that he is going to pray, and once Hamlet has recovered himself he sees that he cannot simply take the ghost's word, for all the reasons previously mentioned. But Hamlet, as we shall see later in the play, is not so much interested in establishing the truth of the apparition's identity as he is in finding out whether the "ghost" has told him the truth about Claudius. To verify what the ghost is saying becomes Hamlet's major concern in the first half of the play, and he brings his best judgment to bear in constructing a situation that will elicit proof of Claudius's guilt, the famous "Mousetrap," in which a play becomes the thing to plumb the conscience of Claudius. Hamlet has ample reason to wait until he has further evidence of Claudius's guilt, but even if that evidence is obtained, taking revenge is something at which a Christian prince would balk. Contrary to the view most modern critics have taken,[8] Hamlet's caution, and his waiting, is justified, even though Hamlet berates himself for taking such a path.

Mousetraps Galore

The second and third acts deal with verifying the ghost's story and Hamlet's anger at himself for not taking revenge. Shakespeare poses a question that greatly concerns him in many of his plays: How do we distinguish who people are from who they pretend to be? This issue is raised very early in the play when Hamlet's mother suggests that his mourning is excessive. After all, she tells him, the death of fathers is common; "Why seems it so particular with thee?" she asks. Hamlet responds:

> Seems, madam? Nay, it is. I know not 'seems.'
> 'Tis not alone my inky cloak, good mother,
> Nor the customary suits of solemn black,
> Nor the windy suspiration of forc'd breath,
> No, nor the fruitful river in the eye,
> Nor the dejected haviour of the visage,
> Together with all forms, moods, shapes of grief,
> That can denote me truly. These indeed seem,
> For they are actions that a man might play,
> But *I have that within which passes show,*
> These but the trappings and the suits of woe.
>
> (1.2.76–86; italics added)

How can *seeming* be distinguished from *being*? This question takes on heavy thematic weight in the tragedies of *King Lear* and *Othello,* and is of central importance in many of Shakespeare's plays, such as *Much Ado about Nothing, Measure for Measure, The Winter's Tale,* and *Richard III.* As an actor and playwright, Shakespeare participated in a medium where the putting on and doffing of roles, in the quick succession of repertory theater, would have daily raised the issue of whether men have stable characters. Shakespeare is perhaps a bit obsessed with whether sincerity is possible. Don't we continually take on roles, and even when we are alone, don't we play to ourselves, becoming both actors and audiences? Can any of us look inside and find a genuine, innermost soul, or do we just see one role layered on top of another? How do we tell a sincere act from acting? As Hamlet notes in his commonplace book, immediately after his first meeting with the ghost, "One may smile and smile and be a villain—at least I am sure it may be so in Denmark." With respect to each other,

Hamlet and Claudius will both confront the problem of seeming versus being, and they will also face it as they peer into themselves.

Thus, the problem of finding out "who our seemers be" occurs in Hamlet at two levels. Superficially, various characters want to know what others are really up to. Claudius wants to know whether Hamlet is really mad, or just feigning. Polonius wants to confirm his pet theory that Hamlet has gone mad because Ophelia has rejected him. Hamlet has many such questions: Did Claudius really murder his father? Or to put it another way, is the "ghost" telling the truth? Does Ophelia love him, or is she duplicitous, as Hamlet's mother apparently was to his father? At a deeper level, Hamlet's introspective soliloquies show that he is searching for his proper role as a prince, a son, and finally, as a Christian. But *Hamlet,* like *Oedipus,* poses the question on a more profound and general level. "What is a man . . . ?" (4.4.33) Hamlet asks in his last soliloquy, and it is the question he has been asking by implication throughout the play.

Hamlet, of course, takes a role himself. He "seems" throughout the play, feigning madness; however, his "lunacy" seems to draw more attention to him than such a plotter would desire, and the cause of Hamlet's lunacy, and what it might be covering up, is what principally concerns Claudius until Hamlet's killing of Polonius. We may well ask what Hamlet is trying to achieve by feigning this affliction. I think the answer is that Hamlet cannot reveal what he is really struggling with, and so he takes the only role that might camouflage the genuine turbulence of his soul. Hamlet is distraught; he can't hide it, but by attaching the name of "madness" to his state of mind, he hides his knowledge of his father's murder and his desire to avenge it. Being "mad" is the most natural part for Hamlet because he is constantly struggling to keep his emotions under control and his reason engaged, to keep from becoming "passion's slave." But Hamlet is not passion's slave—at least not most of the time—and even before the scene in which Claudius and Polonius spy on Hamlet and Ophelia, Claudius senses Hamlet's madness is artificial. He asks Guildenstern and Rosencrantz: "[C]an you by no drift of conference / Get from him why he *puts on* this confusion?" (3.1.1–2; italics added). Though "puts on" does not necessarily mean "feigns," it does imply that Hamlet's condition is "not altogether involuntary."[9] Claudius clearly feels threatened by Hamlet.

Claudius and Polonius at first try to find answers to their questions by a combination of spying and ingratiation. This behind-the-curtains business is endemic to the court of Denmark; Polonius even spies on his own son, Laertes. First Polonius attempts to "board" Hamlet through conversation, but Hamlet has not the least trust in Polonius, so the old man gets nothing but thinly veiled insults. Then Claudius procures spies that Hamlet would be comfortable with, and might talk freely to, his old school chums, Rosencrantz and Guildenstern. But Rosencrantz and Guildenstern's initial fumbling does nothing but put Hamlet on his guard. Finally Polonius, believing that Hamlet has gone mad because of unrequited love for Ophelia, attempts to prove his theory by getting the two together, while he and Claudius watch.

When Hamlet walks in the lobby, Polonius says, speaking of Ophelia as if she were a bitch in heat, that he will "loose" his daughter to him, in the hope that Hamlet will reveal his love for Ophelia, especially if she rejects him. However, Hamlet realizes that Ophelia is allowing herself to be made a spy. He probably detects Polonius in his hiding place, and the trap elicits an emotional explosion from him, as Ophelia, the last woman in whom he had a shred of trust, confirms his worst thoughts about female "frailty." Hamlet asks her "Where is your father?" and she lies to him: "At home, my Lord." Hamlet loses control of his rage at this point, and is often portrayed as getting very rough with Ophelia; he ends his "get thee to a nunnery" tirade with a barely masked threat to Claudius: "Those who are married already—all but one—shall live; the rest shall keep as they are" (3.1.149–51). Polonius clings to the idea that love has brought about Hamlet's insanity, but Claudius dismisses the notion. He has seen enough to know that Hamlet is a danger to him. Whatever the cause of Hamlet's madness, Claudius's best judgment tells him that Hamlet must be gotten rid of.

The employment of Rosencrantz and Guildenstern, and even more so of Ophelia, is a step up, in sophistication, from mere spying. Claudius and Polonius construct situations very much as a psychologist would construct an experiment to encourage the person being observed to reveal himself. These proto-experiments in the field of forensic psychology, which offer the observed some cheese, will provide evidence of the observed's state of mind or motivation, provided the cheese is taken. Thus, the characters gather evidence to make more informed judgments about each other, which in turn will influence their decisions and courses of action. By staging "The Mousetrap," Hamlet simply turns the tables, using against Claudius the same structure of experiment and observation that Claudius used against him, but in a far more sophisticated and effective way.

Hamlet's "Mousetrap" comes out of his love for drama. To confirm the ghost's story, he will show Claudius a scene that depicts the ghost's description of his father's murder. If Claudius shows any signs of guilt, Hamlet will know what to do:

I have heard

> That guilty creatures sitting at a play
> Have, by the very cunning of the scene,
> Been struck so to the soul that presently
> They have proclaim'd their malefactions.
> For murder, though it have no tongue, will speak
> With most miraculous organ. I'll have these players
> Play something like the murder of my father
> Before mine uncle. I'll observe his looks;
> I'll tent him to the quick. If a do blench,
> I know my course.

> (2.2.584–94)

Hamlet needs to know beyond a doubt that the apparition is telling the truth, and he is careful to take precautions against his own prejudice. Rather than just watching Claudius himself during the performance of "The Mousetrap," he will bring in another, more dispassionate observer. This person is, of course, the observer of all observers, Horatio, and Hamlet calls on him for the same reasons that Marcellus and Barnardo did. Hamlet and Horatio will form a pair of observers, as did Claudius and Polonius, and they too will watch for a disclosure. Horatio represents a way of being in the world that Hamlet would like to emulate, and his compliment to Horatio stresses the equipoise that the sound master of judgment must maintain:

> Since my dear soul was mistress of her choice,
> And could of men distinguish her election,
> Sh'ath seal'd thee for herself; for thou hast been
> As one, in suff'ring all, that suffers nothing,
> A man that Fortune's buffets and rewards
> Hast ta'en with equal thanks; and blest are those
> Whose blood and judgment are so well commeddled
> That they are not a pipe for Fortune's finger
> To sound what stop she please. Give me that man

That is not passion's slave, and I will wear him
In my heart's core, ay, in my heart of heart,
As I do thee.

(3.2.63–74)

When the murder is played before Claudius and he rises stricken from his seat, stopping the play, Hamlet celebrates wildly, telling Horatio that he will "take the ghost's word for a thousand pound." Horatio responds less enthusiastically. Hamlet claims that his theatrical-forensic triumph ought to get him "a fellowship in a cry of players," i.e., a job, perhaps a full share, in a theatrical company. Horatio's laconic reply, "Half a share," is typical of him, and it comments, I believe, on some of the flaws in the execution of Hamlet's "Mousetrap."

Why shouldn't Hamlet get a full share? What might Horatio think has cast some doubt on the Mousetrap's trustworthiness as a conscience catcher? The easiest answer is that Hamlet's obstreperous behavior during the play has scared Claudius. In many productions of *Hamlet*, such as Kenneth Branagh's, or even Nichol Williamson's more restrained one, Hamlet is so over the top in his behavior during "The Mousetrap" that he himself seems threatening. But assuming that we have a more urbane and controlled Hamlet (which would make more sense, since he does want his trap to reveal the truth) there is still another problem with the construction of Hamlet's experiment. Claudius murdered his brother to get his kingdom and his queen. In Hamlet's play it is a *nephew*, Lucianus, who murders his uncle, Gonzago. Claudius, even if he were innocent, would have every right, given Hamlet's erratic behavior, to take this as a barely veiled threat. Since Claudius's reaction to "The Mousetrap" could verify either of two hypotheses, it ultimately fails to reveal the truth. This may be why Horatio only votes Hamlet "half a share" in a company of players. Has Hamlet's desire to find Claudius guilty made him construct a trap that is biased?

When we read or watch *Hamlet,* it is sometimes difficult to keep in mind that Hamlet has much less information about Claudius than we do. For instance we overhear Claudius in act 3, scene 1, when he virtually confesses. Before Hamlet meets Ophelia in the lobby, Polonius gives her a prayer book to make Hamlet less suspicious. Polonius notes: "'Tis too much prov'd, that with devotion's visage / And pious action we do sugar o'er / The devil himself" (3.1.47–49). This cuts Claudius deeply; he says in an aside:

> How smart a lash that speech doth give my
>   conscience
> The harlot's cheek, beautied with plast'ring art,
> Is not more ugly to the thing that helps it
> Than is my deed to my most painted word.
> O heavy burden!
>
>   (3.1.49–54)

The audience will decide Claudius's guilt at that point, and if there is a shadow of a doubt left, his attempt to remove that "heavy burden" through confession (3.3.36–72; a soliloquy as brilliant as any of Hamlet's) will dissolve it. But Hamlet sees neither speech. What if the audience had only the information that Hamlet has? Then the difficulty of Hamlet's judgment of Claudius's guilt would be apparent, as would Hamlet's difficulty in deciding on a course of action. In this play, Hamlet never knows for *certain* about his father and Claudius, and he is never able to come up with a plan to avenge his father; at best, in act 5, he finds that Claudius has killed his mother accidentally in an attempt to kill him. No matter how he may berate himself for not acting, Hamlet has come up against the wall that stands between human judgment and the exact truth, a wall familiar to lawyers, clients, juries, and judges. This is the wall at which evidence fails and where, in some matters, judgment must yield to faith. The transformation of Hamlet, after he has hit this wall, is the subject of the last two acts.

"When our deep plots do pall . . ."

In the first four acts Hamlet wants to control his own destiny and that of Denmark. He even arrogates to himself the God-like power of determining whether a soul will go to heaven or hell when he refrains from killing Claudius, who is on his knees trying to confess. Hamlet wants to take Claudius in the full flower of his sins, sending him to hell, and not when his repentance has cleared the slate with God, when killing Claudius might send him to heaven. (The irony is twofold; Claudius has not been able to repent and Hamlet's temporary megalomania prevents him from committing the sin of murder while at the same time leading him into the sin of presumption.) Thus, in trying to avenge his father, Hamlet commits the blasphemy of trying to outwit God, of making his will prevail over the divine will, not only in taking vengeance in this world, but also beyond the grave. Hamlet's melancholy has indeed become a spiritual corrosive.

Hamlet's soliloquies, breakthroughs both in that dramatic form and the art of characterization, show a man at war with himself. In the soliloquy of 2.2.544–601, Hamlet first berates himself for not feeling enough grief about his father to avenge his murder, then he falls into ranting, imagining that Claudius is humiliating him, tweaking his nose and pulling his beard; in the midst of all this spilt rage, Hamlet startlingly sees himself from an independent perspective and realizes he has been playing the part of an outraged son, which makes him feel ashamed of himself: "Why, what an ass am I," he says. Why is he unpacking his heart with words? Why is he "acting" when he should be taking action?

The same problem gnaws at Hamlet in the soliloquy of 4.4.32–66. As he sees Fortinbras's army tramping through Denmark on its way to fight over a piece of land in Poland, so small that it will not hold the contending armies nor provide room enough to bury the dead, Hamlet is envious. This, Hamlet says, is what honor is all about: fighting over nothing when honor is at stake. Hamlet believes that all occasions inform against him, indicting him for not having taken revenge, and the sight of the Norwegian army accuses him most of all. He admires Fortinbras, if for no other reason than the man can make a decision and act on it. Again, we do not have to accept Hamlet's self-evaluation, and we can question whether he ought to admire such a military expedition, but it is certain that Hamlet's ability to contain himself is exhausted, and his Errol Flynn-like adventures on the way to England bear this out.

In Hamlet's internal rage, one extreme—his desire to act— is balanced by another, his repeated questioning of whether life is worth living and whether human actions matter at all. This concern is addressed by the soliloquies of acts 1 and 4, which we have already considered, and by the famous "To be or not to be" soliloquy, which, located at the center of the play in act 3, also forms the heart of its plot and theme. When Hamlet says the question is "to be or not to be," he is referring not to suicide but to the act of revenge. Should he kill Claudius or not? That is the question. But his musings quickly morph into a more general evaluation of human life and whether it is worth living:

> To die—to sleep,
> No more; and by a sleep to say we end

> The heart-ache and the thousand natural shocks
> That flesh is heir to: 'tis a consummation
> Devoutly to be wish'd. To die, to sleep;
> To sleep, perchance to dream—ay, there's the rub:
> For in that sleep of death what dreams may come,
> When we have shuffled off this mortal coil,
> Must give us pause—there's the respect
> That makes calamity of so long life.
> For who would bear the whips and scorns of time,
> Th' oppressor's wrong, the proud man's contumely,
> The pangs of dispriz'd love, the law's delay,
> The insolence of office, and the spurns
> That patient merit of th' unworthy takes,
> When he himself might his quietus make
> With a bare bodkin?

> (3.1.60–76)

This is perhaps the most poetic rendering in English of the basic human question: "What's the point?" which is closely related to another, "Why me?" a question Hamlet asks by implication after meeting the ghost: "The time is out of joint. O cursed spite, / That ever I was born to set it right" (1.5.196–97).

Both of these questions are tightly bound up with the problem of death. Death relativizes and shrinks the importance of everything. Facing it squarely poses a perennial human difficulty, expressed by Omar Khayyam in the *Rubaiyat,* by the Preacher in *Ecclesiastes,* and by Boethius in *The Consolation of Philosophy,* a very popular book in the Renaissance and one Shakespeare would have known. Is everything we do under the sun merely vanity? Hamlet asks himself that question throughout the play whenever he thinks of mankind's great potential and of the small, insignificant space in which it must be used. Hamlet, like all of us, must work his way through the problem of death in order to know who he is and what he is to

do during the vanishing and unstable strand of his life. Hamlet's
questions, of course, are religious ones, questions that even
the most die-hard postmodernist, wary of all ultimate expla-
nations and "meta-narratives," will finally have to confront.
As David Lodge's academic postmodernman, Morris Zapp, discovers in *Small World*, death is the one thing that cannot be
deconstructed.[10]

In the "To be or not to be" soliloquy, Hamlet recognizes
that his fear of death is at least partly connected to his fear of
the consequences of sin, specifically, the sin of revenge:

> Who would fardels bear,
> To grunt and sweat under a weary life,
> But that the dread of something after death,
> The undiscover'd country, from whose bourn
> No traveler returns, puzzles the will,
> And makes us rather bear those ills we have
> Than fly to others that we know not of?
> Thus conscience does make cowards of us all.
>
> (3.1.76–83)

However we read this soliloquy, as the contemplation of
suicide, murder, or both, Hamlet is contemplating mortal sin,
which would send him to hell rather than purgatory. Hamlet's
religious faith is a hash of contradictions. He takes the Christian cosmos for granted, but God's law frustrates him, and he
pushes against it. He does not obey God because to do so is
right. Rather, he hesitates to kill Claudius, or himself, for fear
of the consequences—"conscience doth make cowards of us
all." Hamlet's fear is understandable. After all, he has just
met a spirit who claims to be doing time in purgatory, and the
picture the "ghost" has painted of his lodgings is not pretty:

> But that I am forbid

> To tell the secrets of my prison-house,
> I could a tale unfold whose lightest word
> Would harrow up thy soul, freeze thy young blood,
> Make thy two eyes like stars start from their spheres,
> Thy knotted and combined locks to part,
> And each particular hair to stand an end
> Like the quills upon the fretful porpentine.
>
> (1.5.13–20)

If this is purgatory, what could hell be like? Hamlet is so convinced of the existence of heaven and hell that he actually
refrains from taking revenge on Claudius for fear of sending
him to heaven! He wants Claudius to experience just what his
father may be experiencing, or worse. Yet Hamlet's presumption in thinking that he can decide the fate of a soul is perhaps the worst sin he commits in the play, and a stunning
piece of self-deception.

Yet, Hamlet finally transcends his problems and achieves
an acceptance of fate and death that allows him to act. How
does this happen? Two important scenes occur before Hamlet
goes to his fatal duel with Laertes. One is the graveyard scene;
the other is Hamlet's recounting of his sea adventures to
Horatio. The graveyard scene, act 4, scene 1, recalls the journey of Odysseus to Hades and what he learns there about how
death shrinks accomplishment. Better to be a live slave than
a dead hero, a mere shadow in hell, Achilles tells Odysseus—
and this from a man more zealous in promoting his own fame
than any Greek at Troy.[11] As Hamlet looks at the collection of
skulls the gravedigger throws up, he asks Horatio, already
knowing the answer: "Dost thou think Alexander looked o'
this fashion i' th' earth?" As the gravedigger applies his shovel
and more skulls fly up from the grave, destined for the char-
nel house, Hamlet imagines the lives of lawyers and land

speculators (of which Shakespeare was one). They are the most
uselessly ambitious of all, and yet they represent all humanity, all of whose efforts are vain in the shadow of death:

> Why may not that be the skull of
> a lawyer? Where be his quiddities now, his quillities,
> his cases, his tenures, and his tricks? Why does he
> suffer this mad knave now to knock him about the
> sconce with a dirty shovel, and will not tell him of his
> action of battery? Hum, this fellow might be in 's
> time a great buyer of land, with his statutes, his
> recognizances, his fines, his double vouchers, his
> recoveries. Is this the fine of his fines and the
> recovery of his recoveries, to have his fine pate full of
> fine dirt?

(5.1.96–106)

Hamlet jokes about death as it interrupts the habits of
men in general, making a mockery of their greed and short-
sightedness, and his death (and ours) is linked to theirs simply by virtue of his having been born. The gravedigger gives
the audience the startling bit of news that he became a
gravedigger on the day Hamlet was born, thirty years before,
on the very day that King Hamlet slew King Fortinbras of
Norway. The gravedigger, it seems, has been waiting for Hamlet since the day of his birth. "Who builds stronger than a
mason, a carpenter, or a shipwright?" the gravedigger riddles
Hamlet. It is the grave-digger, for his houses last till doomsday.

Hamlet is forced to meet death not just as a universal
fact, but as a personal one. The gravedigger has put Hamlet in
mind of his own death. Hamlet remembers Yorick, the court
jester of his youth, with sadness. Then Ophelia's funeral procession enters, and all he can do is grieve. Hamlet never

reaches an airy, philosophical superiority to death, and we never get the impression that any of his questions about the significance of human life have answers that can be articulated. Rather, Hamlet comes to an accommodation of death that cannot be intellectualized. His questions about life and its purposes have worn themselves out and are replaced by submission to Providence. This comes about for Hamlet not through thinking, but through the cessation of thinking, and it happens in that part of the world emblematic of change, the sea. Later, in Elsinore, Hamlet explains to Horatio that while on the ship bound for England with Rosencrantz and Guildenstern, something happened to him:

> Sir, in my heart there was a kind of fighting
> That would not let me sleep. Methought I lay
> Worse that the mutines in the bilboes. Rashly—
> And praised be rashness for it: let us know
> Our indiscretion sometime serves us well
> When our deep plots do pall; and that should learn us
> There's a divinity that shapes our ends,
> Rough-hew them how we will—
>
> (5.2.4–11)

The "mutines in the bilboes" are mutineers clamped in the hold, representing the mutiny that has been going on in Hamlet's heart since the beginning of the play. But the mutiny within Hamlet has been quelled, and part of the reason is that Hamlet knows now that he cannot control his own destiny. His deep plots have palled. His judgment has exercised itself to exhaustion. He is left with the understanding that divinity shapes our ends; divinity decides finally what our ends are to be and how they will be achieved. Horatio responds, "That is most certain."

What rescues Hamlet from going to England and his death

seems pure luck. While Rosencrantz and Guildenstern are asleep, Hamlet opens the packet they have with them and unseals their commission to England, wherein he finds orders that upon their arrival, his head is to be struck off. He just happens to have his father's signet in his purse, so he is able to write a new commission to England ordering the death of Rosencrantz and Guildenstern, and he seals the letter with the official stamp of Denmark. His luck continues. His ship is attacked by pirates, and he does an Errol Flynn-like swing from one ship to the other; the ships are parted, and Hamlet, now the pirates' prisoner, convinces them to return him to Denmark. As Hamlet says, his return is "most strange," coming about without thinking, plotting, or exercise of judgment, but through a course of events so improbable that they could only have been shaped by Providence.

When he is invited to the fencing contest with Laertes, Hamlet is virtually certain that it is a trap, and Horatio tries to convince him not to go. Hamlet replies with the definitive insight of the play, the anagnorisis of the tragic hero:

> We defy augury. There is special providence in the
> fall of a sparrow. If it be now, 'tis not to come; if it be
> not to come, it will be now; if it be not now, yet it will
> come. The readiness is all. Since no man, of aught
> he leaves, knows aught, what is 't to leave betimes?
> Let be.

> (5.2.215–20)

Prediction, plots—none of these matter to Hamlet anymore. He has, essentially, received the gift of faith, a spiritual condition ultimately attributable to God and unexplainable by reference to any series of events or experiences. He does not try to postpone the time of his own death, and he does not go into the duel with thoughts of killing Claudius. Death will come when it will come—for human beings as well as for sparrows—and the final arbiter is Providence, what God has decided, not man. Hamlet's speech alludes to Matthew 10:28–31, Jesus' commission to his disciples when he sent them out to preach and heal, knowing that they would encounter danger and threats to their lives:

> And fear ye not them that kill the body, but are not able to kill the soul: but rather fear him, which is able to destroy both body and soul in hell. / Are not two sparrows sold for a farthing, and one of them shall not fall on the ground without your Father? / Yea, and all the hairs of your head are numbered.

This was a popular verse for English ministers preaching on Providence, which the Elizabethans understood to operate in two ways. There was God's general providence, by which nature was ordered according to law, and there was special providence, which worked its way out in the lives of individuals and nations. The seventeenth-century preacher Ralph Walker states that "[t]he Providence of God is a worke of God by which hee doth most wisely, freelie, and mightily, and excellently well governe all things for the manifestation of his great goodness and glorie."[12] Walker's contemporary, Peter Baro, gives a similar definition: "We call Gods Providence, a perpetuall and unchangeable disposition and administration of all things that be."[13] Writers disagreed on whether Providence impinged on free will. Those of Calvinist leanings believed it did; adherents to Roman Catholic theology did not. But neither group disputed that ultimate outcomes were in God's control, no matter what decisions humans made.[14]

Providence includes the full range of natural law, spiritual and physical; disobedience of the spiritual laws governing life carries with it consequences that are as unavoidable as the laws of gravity for those who step off tall buildings. As Presbyterian minister James Montgomery Boice puts it, "If anger and tension go unchecked, they produce ulcers or high blood pressure. Profligacy is a path to broken lives and venereal disease. Pride will be self-destructive. These spiritual laws are the equivalent of the laws of science in the physical creation."[15] The consequence of Providence is not to relieve us of the need to be prudent or to make informed and reasoned judgments, but to "relieve us from anxiety in God's service."[16] This is what Hamlet's final reliance on Providence does for him. He has tried to be responsible, though he failed by killing Polonius; he has berated himself for not taking revenge, yet he has not taken it. His judgment has extended itself as far as it can, and now that thought has run out, Providence is what is left. Hamlet will enter the duel without anxiety, not only because he is ready to meet death, but also because he knows he is only an actor in a divine plan that will work its way out no matter what he does.

"The readiness is all," he says, a line Shakespeare liked so much he virtually repeats it in *King Lear*. It alludes to Luke 12:40 and Matthew 24:10, "Therefore be ye also ready: for in such an hour as ye think not the Son of man cometh." Resignation to death was a popular sermon topic in Renaissance England, and Bishop Latimer, in a sermon before Edward IV, sets forth a fuller explanation of what readiness for death would have meant to Shakespeare's audience:

> *Unusquisque enim certum tempus habet praedefinitum a Domino:* "For every man hath a certain time appointed him of God, and God hideth that same time from us." For some die in young age, some in old age, according as it pleaseth him. He hath not manifested to us the time because he would have us

at all times ready; else if I knew the time, I would presume upon it, and so should be worse. But he would have us ready at all times, and therefore he hideth the time of our death from us. . . . But of that we may be sure, there shall not fall one hair from our head without his will; and we shall not die before the time that God hath appointed unto us: which is a comfortable thing, specially in time of sickness or wars. . . . There be some which say, when their friends are slain in battle, "Oh, if he had tarried at home, he should not have lost his life." These sayings are naught: for God hath appointed every man his time. To go to war in presumptuousness, without an ordinary calling, such going to war I allow not: but when thou art called, go in the name of the Lord; and be well assured in thy heart that thou canst not shorten thy life with well-doing."[17]

Being truly ready for death transforms Hamlet. In accepting death, he finds life. In submitting to Providence, Hamlet preserves his soul. His anxiety vanishes, along with the need to exert control over events; death, which has been Hamlet's real nemesis all along, will come when God wills it and with the consequences He desires, and for the first time, this is good enough for Hamlet.

The call to the fencing "contest" is Hamlet's call to war and he goes cheerfully. Hamlet's mind is not on revenge when he goes to fence with Laertes; rather, he goes with an alert and open mind, not knowing what will happen, not rehearsing the possibilities, yet ready to respond to whatever happens.

Hamlet's transformation is powerfully demonstrated in his duel with Laertes. A "three touch" underdog, Hamlet still feels he will "win at the odds," acknowledging Laertes to be the better swordsman. Yet, Hamlet scores the first two hits and outplays Laertes throughout the match. The script provides plenty of opportunity for a director to present a Hamlet who is "playing over his head," and many actors have enacted this scene *as* play (consider Lawrence Olivier's jump from the balcony or Nicol Williamson's behind-the-back swats at Laertes). When Gertrude dies from drinking the poison meant for Hamlet, and when Hamlet discovers that his wound from Laertes's envenomed sword is fatal, he finally kills Claudius, not in revenge, but in the heat of action, carrying the fight to someone who has fatally attacked him.

Has Hamlet died well? I think so. He exchanges forgiveness with Laertes, who believes that Claudius has been "justly served," killed by his own poison. Hamlet, trying to be a responsible prince to the end, thinks lastly of the state, endorsing Fortinbras as Claudius's successor, and getting Horatio's promise to tell his story, so that he will not leave a "gored name" behind. This is not just a matter of vanity with Hamlet. When Hamlet kills Claudius, the courtly audience shouts "Treason, treason." The bare events they have seen, without explanation, will tell a lie. As a political leader, Hamlet has a duty to set a good example, to endorse loyalty to the state, not treason. Clearing his name is a political as well as personal task. The few drops of poison that he drinks at the end will hurry his death, but not cause it. When Hamlet dies and Horatio says "Good night, sweet prince, / And flights of angels sing thee to thy rest," the audience can reasonably assume that Horatio's benediction will come true. If the ghost is a demon, it has been defeated.

When Horatio begins to tell Hamlet's story, he says that his audience will hear "Of carnal, bloody, and unnatural acts"—the marriage of Claudius and Gertrude, and Claudius's murder of King Hamlet—and "Of accidental judgments," which would include Hamlet's killing of Polonius and Claudius, and the unplanned deaths of Laertes and Gertrude. Hamlet's "accidental judgment" is the foil to his great efforts to judge well; it demonstrates that good judgment is important, but infallible judgment impossible. Deep plots must give way to the irresistible workings of Providence.

If one be in debt and danger of the Law, to have a Brother of the same bloud . . . will little avail him, except he will also come under the Law, that is, become his Surety, and undertake for him. And such was our estate. As debtors we were, by vertue of . . . the handwriting that was against us. Which was our Bond, and we had forfeited it. . . . Therefore Hee became bound for us also, entred bond anew, took on Him, not only our Nature, but our Debt. . . . The debt of a Capitall Law in Death.

Launcelot Andrewes,
1609 Christmas sermon on
Galatians 3:3–5

3

The Merchant of Venice: Judgment and the Essence of Love

The Merchant of Venice is a comedy that is also a near-tragedy, a Christian allegory, and a fairy tale. Shakespeare had no compunctions against mixing genres or even blending them. Here, he gives us a blend. In traditional allegory, characters were one-dimensional, merely signs standing for ideas. The medieval Vice displayed vice, Faith displayed faith, and Everyman displayed mankind in the act of choosing. But the people of *The Merchant of Venice,* in addition to their allegorical component, display complex personalities marked by inconsistency, flaws, and the capacity, at times, to transcend themselves through virtuous action. Such characters do not usually inhabit allegories or fairy tales. This combination of allegorical purity, fairy tale structure, and realistic treatment of character makes *The Merchant of Venice* a "problem play"

for critics who prefer consistency to imaginative richness. But
Shakespeare's story, because of its generic blend, is able to
use one genre, the allegorical, as a foil for another, the realistic.

Allegory and fairy tale are genres of the ideal, and thus
furnish a schematic of life's courses, which ways to take and
which not to. But realism is the genre of how life actually is;
opposing these genres allows the playgoer to judge the real by
reference to the ideal. In *The Merchant of Venice*, Shakespeare's
most intellectual comic heroine, Portia, specifically draws our
attention to the gulf between morality and performance in an
early speech that contrasts how easy it is to *know* what is good
with how hard it is to *do* good:

> If to do were as easy as to know what were good to do,
> chapels had been churches, and poor men's cottages
> princes' palaces,—it is a good divine that follows his
> own instructions,—I can easier teach twenty what
> were good to be done, than be one of the twenty to
>   follow
> mine own teaching: the brain may devise laws
> for the blood, but a hot temper leaps o'er a cold
> decree. . . .

> (1.2.12–19)

Portia's admission, though spoken playfully, must be taken
as a serious answer to critics who contend that *Merchant* is
repulsive because the Christian characters are anti-Semitic
or fall short of Christian spiritual ideals and are therefore hypocritical. Even Paul said, "For I do not the good thing, which I
would, but the evil, which I would not, that do I" (Romans
7:19). The question the play asks is not whether Jews or Christians are better at following a spiritual ideal; the question is
which spiritual ideal one should aspire to follow: that of Old

Covenant legalism (as derived from the Pharisees) or New Covenant sacrifice and forgiveness. Shakespeare's answer is given in the trial and judgment that take up all of act 4. On the literal level, the trial portrays a case to enforce a bizarre contract, but on the allegorical, it figures forth the judgment—and means of justification—of the individual soul before God. It is impossible to understand the moral or spiritual content of the play if the allegorical dimension goes unrecognized.

Recovery of the allegorical element in *Merchant* began with Sir Israel Gollancz in 1931, was elaborated by a distinguished line of critics, and achieved its fullest development by Barbara Kiefer Lewalski in 1962.[1] Since then, their interpretation, which presents Christian beliefs in a favorable—even inspirational—light, has largely been eclipsed by critics who attack the play and the allegorical interpretation as being anti-Semitic, sexist, heterosexist, or naïve.[2] Yet, this frequently produced play is often exciting and uplifting on stage, while also comic and intensely suspenseful. The experience of a good production of *Merchant* shatters the axe-grinding criticism of the play trotted out in "hermeneutically suspicious"[3] journal articles and graduate seminars. In this chapter I hope to add a little to what the line of allegorical critics have already said so well, but mainly I will recapitulate and defend their readings of *Merchant*, which I believe to be essentially correct.[4]

The Antagonists: Antonio and Shylock

The Merchant of Venice combines two fairy tales, one about a loan, which is secured by a pound of the debtor's flesh, and another about winning a princess and her kingdom by choosing correctly among three "caskets," the right casket being the one that contains the princess's picture. Shakespeare links these two tales by making the debtor, Antonio, secure the loan so that he can finance the effort of his friend, Bassanio, to win the "princess," Portia. The man to whom Antonio pledges his flesh is Shylock, the Jewish usurer.

The play begins in the middle of a conversation, with a response to a question that the audience must infer. In the first two lines, Antonio says to Solanio and Salario, the other two characters on stage: "In sooth I know not why I am so sad; / It wearies me, you say it wearies you." Solanio and Salario, referred to as "the Salads" by some Shakespearean actors, prefigure Rosencrantz and Guildenstern in that they are as distinguishable from each other as two pieces of lettuce in a bowl. Together, they form a Venetian chorus that helps to fill in background, elicit information, and represent community values and attitudes. Antonio's response to their concerns about his melancholy, "you *say* it wearies you," puts us on our guard about the sincerity of these two, although it may just express Antonio's exasperation at the Salads' prying.[5]

The opening conversation reveals much about the condition of Antonio's spirit and that of Venice. Antonio declares, "I have much ado to know myself," a phrase that would have recalled to an Elizabethan audience the Delphic Oracle's two pieces of advice: "Know thyself," and "Nothing too much." Antonio recognizes that he is struggling to understand himself, but the audience has yet to find what has put him in this state. Unfortunately for Antonio, Solanio and Salario are all too happy to assist in determining the cause of his malady, and they both credit it, automatically, to worry about commercial ventures. Antonio has invested in six voyages, and the Salads weigh Antonio as they would themselves: their minds would be tossing on the ocean until their ships returned home, laden with merchandise. For Salario, such worries would occlude all other thoughts, including those religious:

> I should not see the sandy hour-glass run
> But I should think of shallows and flats,
> And see my wealthy Andrew dock'd in sand
> Vailing her high top lower than her ribs
> To kiss her burial; should I go to church
> And see the holy edifice of stone
> And not bethink me straight of dangerous rocks,
> Which touching but my gentle vessel's side
> Would scatter all her spices on the stream,
> Enrobe the roaring waters with my silks,
> And in a word, but even now worth this,
> And now worth nothing?

(1.1.25–36)

The hourglass was often used as a *momento mori*, or remembrance of death, in order to stir religious understanding of the transitory nature of life, and thus to admonish Christians to take care of their souls. Yet, for Salario, such thoughts easily vanish in the face of worries about money; even on the way to church, and presumably at church too, "the holy edifice of stone" would make him think only of the dangerous rocks that might break his trading vessels into pieces. The easy assumptions of Salario and Solanio point to the conflict between commercial and Christian values in Venice, and the displacement of the latter by the former. Salario assumes that Antonio would be obsessing about the fate of his ventures because that is what Salario, as a typical Venetian, would do; thus Shakespeare's first move is to blur distinctions between Venetian Christians and stereotypical Jews.

Gratiano, who comes in later with Antonio's friend, Bassanio, makes much the same charge as Salario, though there is no evidence that Gratiano cares much for the things of this world. He simply tells Antonio, "You have too much respect upon the world: / They lose it that do buy it with much

care" (1.1.74–75). This Christian commonplace is derived from
Matthew 16:25–26: "For whosoever will save his life, shall
lose it: and whosoever shall lose his life for my sake, shall
find it. / For what shall it profit a man though he should win
the whole world if he lose his own soul?" But Antonio, knowing Gratiano's reference, asserts that on this point he is not
spiritually muddled: "I hold the world but as the world
Gratiano" (1.1.77).

All of these speeches, and many more, take as their center of gravity a passage from Matthew that constitutes the play's
thematic center:

> Lay not up treasures for your selves upon the earth,
> where moth & canker corrupt, & where thieves dig
> through, and steal. / But lay up treasures for your
> selves in heaven, where neither the moth nor canker
> corrupteth, and where thieves neither dig through,
> nor steal. / For where your treasure is, there will
> your heart be also. / . . . No man can serve two
> masters: for either he shall hate the one, and love the
> other, or else he shall lean to one, and despise the
> other. Ye can not serve God and riches. / . . . Therefore
> take no thought, saying, What shall we eat? or what
> shall we drink? or wherewith shall we be clothed? /
> ...But seek ye first the kingdom of God and his
> righteousness, & all these things shall be ministered
> unto you. (Matthew 6:19–33)

Shakespeare takes these precepts from the Sermon on the
Mount as one moral measure of his characters, and Antonio is
put to the test first. When Bassanio asks for financial help
from Antonio so he can outfit himself to woo Portia, it becomes clear that Antonio has a motive to say no. Antonio's
melancholy arises from Bassanio's desire to marry. With
Bassanio's marriage, the relationship between these close
friends will change. Of necessity, Portia will become the most

important person in Bassanio's life, making Bassanio's friendship to Antonio secondary. Antonio feels the forthcoming dimi-
nution of his bond to Bassanio as a great loss. Helping Bassanio
to succeed with Portia is directly contrary to what Antonio
might selfishly desire, which makes it all the more admirable
that Antonio helps Bassanio anyway.

Bassanio has been a spendthrift, a type of prodigal son,
disabling his estate "by showing a more swelling port" than
his "faint means would grant continuance." He has borrowed
a lot of money from Antonio, and owes him more than anyone.
When he promises to pay Antonio everything he owes if Antonio will only "invest" in his venture to marry the rich Portia,
Antonio becomes impatient. It hurts him that Bassanio is asking him to make the loan as one businessman to another, rather
than as a friend:

> You know me well, and herein spend but time
> To wind about my love with circumstance,
> And out of doubt you do me now more wrong...
> Than if you had made waste of all I have.

> (1.1.153–57)

Antonio is willing to press himself to the utmost to help
his friend. "My purse, my person, my extremest means," are
yours, he tells Bassanio, acting in accordance with biblical
injunctions that Shakespeare's audience knew well:

> Give to every man that asketh of thee: and of him
> that taketh away thy goods, ask them not again / And
> if ye lend to them of whom ye hope to receive, what
> thank shall ye have? For even the sinners lend to
> sinners, to receive the like. / Wherefore...doe good,
> & lend, looking for nothing again, and your reward
> shall be great. (Luke 6:30, 34–35)

Antonio's love expresses itself not just for Bassanio, but to others whose debts he has paid or to whom he has lent money gratis. Thus, Antonio is established at the beginning of the play as a figure of one aspect of Christian love, generosity. Later in the play, when he is prepared to lay down his life for Bassanio, Antonio will become the allegorical form of love in its most perfect form, sacrifice: "I am a tainted wether of the flock, / meetest for death," he will say, as Shylock prepares to collect the pound of flesh nearest Antonio's heart. Antonio will rise to Christianity's highest ideal of love: "Greater love than this hath no man, than any man bestoweth his life for his friend's life" (John 15:13).

W. H. Auden, in 1962, suggested that it made the most sense to play Antonio as being in love with Bassanio, and that fear of losing Bassanio is the cause of Antonio's sadness. Many directors and critics have taken Auden's suggestion and have portrayed Antonio as having an unrequited homosexual attraction to Bassanio. However, in Elizabethan culture, which was much less guarded about emotion than ours, heterosexual men stated very openly that they loved each other, with no erotic connotation necessarily attached. In addition, it is a familiar theme in Shakespeare's plays that friends of the same sex must adjust when one of them marries or falls in love. This theme is displayed by Hermia and Helena in *A Midsummer Night's Dream,* Claudio and Benedick in *Much Ado about Nothing,* and Mercutio and Romeo in *Romeo and Juliet.* However, there is no evidence that homosexual relationships are being threatened for any of these pairs or that Antonio feels sexual attraction to Bassanio.

It is a measure of the critical influence of gender politics that a homosexual crush rather than close male friendship has become for many critics the most convincing explanation of Antonio's behavior throughout the play. Yet nothing in the play suggests that the bond of friendship between them needs to be sexualized to make Antonio's devotion to Bassanio credible. Certainly an Elizabethan audience, accepting biblical strictures about sex between men,[6] would have avoided the play *en masse* had they thought Shakespeare was implying that Antonio was sexually attracted to Bassanio. *The Merchant of Venice*, however, was a very popular play, revived many times, and this is the best evidence for what Shakespeare had in mind and what his audience must have understood.

I do not mean to suggest that *Merchant* should not be staged today in accordance with Auden's suggestion, or that it should not be performed in Victorian costume, as was Olivier's version. But I think it is important to keep in mind that none of these options would have been intended by Shakespeare or apprehended by his audience. Though we interpret Shakespeare with minds shaped by our own time and place, remaking Shakespeare in our own image is different from interpreting him, for the latter requires us to make the effort to understand Shakespeare on his own terms.

Shylock, in opposition to Antonio, takes as his motto, "Fast find, fast bind— / A proverb never stale in thrifty mind" (2.5.53–54): Get your hands on money as fast as you can and keep it. Mammon is Shylock's god, and if he has ever read Ecclesiastes, he has not taken it seriously: "He that loveth silver, shall not be satisfied with silver, & he that loveth riches, shall be without the fruit thereof; this also is vanity" (Ecclesiastes 5:9). A few verses later, the Preacher states: "There is an evil sickeness that I have seen under the sun: to wit, riches reserved to the owners thereof for their evil" (Ecclesiastes 5:13).[7] Certainly, Shylock's miserliness works only to his injury. Shakespeare gives us a hint that Shylock's life was not always this way, when Shylock, a widower, refers to the love he had for his wife, Leah. But Shylock's spirit has withered as his obsession with money has grown. Now he lives with a daughter who cannot stand him, who is trapped in a house that shuts its windows against the world, and who will leave him as soon as she can. His most intimate relationship is with his worst enemy, Antonio, and he can only achieve intimacy through hate.

Shylock hates Antonio, as he says, because he is a Christian, but most of all, because Antonio has interfered with Shylock's profits as a moneylender:

> I hate him for he is a Christian:
> But more, for that in low simplicity
> He lends out money gratis, and brings down
> The rate of usance here with us in Venice.
> I will feed fat the ancient grudge I bear him.
> He hates our sacred nation, and he rails
> (Even there where merchants most do congregate)
> On me, my bargains, and my well-won thrift.

> (1.3.37–45)

Although it is an academic faux pas to discuss characters as if they were real, a dramatist who is a master at characterization almost always implies a fuller life behind his characters than is explicitly revealed, a region that the imaginations of actors and audiences are invited to explore. (Harold Bloom, in *Shakespeare: The Invention of the Human*, argues that Shakespeare virtually created this sense of the unplumbable interiority of character.[8]) In this instance I have to wonder whether Shylock is telling the complete truth, or whether he is rationalizing a hatred that he maintains as a last connection to another human being. Does a perverse desire for intimacy fuel Shylock's desire to take a pound of Antonio's flesh, nearest the heart, as Antonio writhes under the blade?

When Shylock's daughter Jessica elopes with the Christian Venetian Lorenzo, taking much of Shylock's treasure with her, the loss of his daughter stings Shylock, but the loss of his money stings him more: "I would my daughter were dead at my foot, and jewels in her ear: would she were hears'd at my foot, and the ducats in her coffin" (3.1.80–82). Shylock's inability to sympathize, even with the suffering of his own people, demonstrates his immense self-centeredness. Only when a loss occurs *to him* can he feel the calamity of the Diaspora:

> Why there, there, there, there! a diamond gone cost
> me two thousand ducats in Frankfort,—*the curse
> never fell upon our nation till now, I never felt it till
> now*—two thousand ducats in that, and other
> precious, precious jewels.

(3.1.76–80; italics added)

Even the revenge that Shylock wants to take against Antonio is finally motivated more by a love of money than his desire to lash out against Christian Venice: "I will / have the heart of him if he forfeit, for were he out of / Venice I can make what merchandise I will" (3.1.116–18). Yet if Shakespeare meant Shylock to be a mere caricature of the money-grasping Jew, the diabolical shedder of Christian blood, his imagination transcended his prejudice. For though Shylock is a vengeful killer, Shakespeare has also made him a human being, which is perhaps more than we can say of Shakespeare's gentiles Iago or Richard III. Shylock is clearly a victim of unchristian behavior and prejudice, and while his moral stature is low, that of Christian Venice is not high. When Antonio comes to borrow money, Shylock stands up for himself courageously, and we learn that Antonio's behavior toward him in the past has not conformed to Christian principles of kind-

ness and charity. One cannot help but admire Shylock for turning the tables on Antonio, as the truth comes out about how he
has been treated:

> Signior Antonio, many a time and oft
> In the Rialto you have rated me
> About my moneys and my usances:
> Still have I borne it with a patient shrug,
> (For suff'rance is the badge of all our tribe)
> You call me misbeliever, cut-throat dog,
> And spet upon my Jewish gaberdine,
> And all for use of that which is mine own.
> Well then, it now appears you need my help:
> Go to then, you come to me, and you say,
> "Shylock, we would have moneys," you say so:
> You that did void your rheum upon my beard,
> And foot me as you spurn a stranger cur
> Over your threshold, money is your suit.
> What should I say to you? Should I not say
> "Hath a dog money? is it possible
> A cur can lend three thousand ducats?" or
> Shall I bend low, and in a bondman's key
> With bated breath, and whisp'ring humbleness
> Say this:
> "Fair sir, you spet on me on Wednesday last,
> You spurn'd me such a day, another time
> You call'd me dog: and for these courtesies
> I'll lend you thus much moneys"?

> (1.3.101–24)

Antonio does not deny any of this; rather, he seems proud
of it, and he is no doubt humiliated by having to ask Shylock
for anything. It is a mark of his love toward Bassanio that he is
willing to deal with Shylock at all; and it is a mark of his
detestation of Shylock that he responds as follows:

> I am as like to call thee so again,
> To spet on thee again, to spurn thee too.
> If thou wilt lend this money, lend it not
> As to thy friends, for when did friendship take
> A breed for barren metal of his friend?
> But lend it rather to thine enemy,
> Who if he break, thou may'st with better face
> Exact the penalty.

$$(1.3.125\text{--}32)$$

Many in Shakespeare's audience probably agreed with Antonio's stand against taking interest, though lending at interest was alive and well in Shakespeare's England. At the same time, Shylock may well have asked, and Shakespeare's audience may well have had the question in their minds: How is it that a Christian can justify spitting on people? Shakespeare uses irony here at Antonio's expense. Antonio will go on to claim that Shylock, like the devil, can quote scripture to his own purposes, and yet Antonio, who bases his detestation of usury on Luke 6:27–35, fails to follow the general precepts set forth in that passage:

> But I say unto you which hear, Love your enemies: do well to them that hate you. / Bless them that curse you, and pray for them which hurt you. / And unto him that smiteth thee on the one cheek, offer also the other: & him that taketh away thy cloak, forbid not to take thy coat also. / *Give to every man that asketh of thee: and of him that taketh away thy goods, ask them not again.* / And as ye would that men should do to you, so do ye to them likewise / For if ye love them which love you, what thanks shall ye have? for even the sinners love those that love them. / And if ye lend to them of whom ye hope to receive, what thanks shall ye have? For even the sinners lend to sinners, to receive the like. / Wherefore love ye your

enemies, and do good, and *lend, looking for nothing
again,* and your reward shall be great, and ye shall
be the children of the most High: for he is kind unto
the unkind, & to the evil. (italics added)

Of course, Antonio is the kind lender of this passage, not only
giving to his friend Bassanio, but also paying the debts of others who owe Shylock money, and of course, Shylock is the
opposite, loving no one and wanting his money with interest.
Yet Antonio fails the other, more difficult requirement of this
passage, as do most of us: Shylock is his enemy, and Antonio
treats him as such. Antonio, like Isabella in *Measure for Measure* and Prospero in *The Tempest,* has much to learn about
forgiveness, and he does learn. Unfortunately, at the end of
the trial scene, most productions focus exclusively on Shylock's
agony, rather than on Antonio's decision to forgive Shylock,
which is the key turning point for both men.

For Bassanio's sake, Antonio agrees to a "merry bond"
with Shylock, in which a loan of three thousand ducats will be
secured by a pound of Antonio's "fair flesh." This bond is
proposed as a jest by Shylock, burlesquing Christian folklore
that would have Jews, in an unholy inversion of the Eucharist,
eating Christian flesh and drinking Christian blood. Shylock
uses the image of the bloodthirsty Jew against Antonio, saying
essentially: "This is what you think I am? All right. I'll play
the part." Antonio perceives Shylock's irony and readily ac-
cedes to the bond, which is interest free. He says "there is
much kindness in the Jew," and puns as Shylock exits: "Hie
thee gentle Jew / The Hebrew will turn Christian." But
Bassanio, who has tried to dissuade Antonio from signing, says
"I like not fair terms, and a villain's mind."

Bassanio, Portia, and the Caskets

As the play moves from the gritty naturalism of Venice to the sweeter atmosphere of Portia's Belmont ("beautiful mount"), the genre of the play shifts to fairy tale. Shakespeare's source for this portion of *Merchant* was the *Gesta Romanorum,* in which a shipwrecked maiden must demonstrate her worthiness to marry an emperor's son by choosing the correct "vessel" from three possibilities: one of gold, one silver, and one lead, each bearing a different inscription. The vessel of gold is inscribed, "Who so chooseth mee shall finde that he deserveth"; the silver, "Who so chooseth me shall finde that his nature desireth"; and the lead,"Who so chooseth me shall finde that God hath disposed." The maiden picks the lead vessel, demonstrating her faith in God, and this, of course, is the correct choice, for what better foundation is there for marriage than faith and the acceptance of God's will? She opens the vessel to find it filled with jewels, signifying, among other things, that God takes care of those who put their faith in him. Here Shakespeare's source is straightforwardly allegorical, and Shakespeare retains allegory as a foundational element in his recreation of the casket story.

Based on Bassanio's description of Portia to Antonio, many critics have argued that Bassanio's motive for marrying is solely mercenary, a reading that certainly undercuts the allegorical component of Bassanio's quest. Bassanio tells Antonio:

> In Belmont is a lady richly left,
> And she is fair, and (fairer than that word),
> Of wonderous virtues,—and sometimes from her eyes
> I did receive fair speechless messages:
> Her name is Portia, nothing undervalu'd
> To Cato's daughter, Brutus' Portia,
> Nor is the wide world ignorant of her worth,
> For the four winds blow in from every coast

Renowned suitors, and her sunny locks
Hang on her temples like a golden fleece,
Which makes her seat of Belmont Colcho's strond,
And many Jasons come in quest of her.
O my Antonio, had I but the means
To hold a rival place with one of them,
I have a mind presages me such thrift
That I should questionless be fortunate.

(1.1.161–76)

Bassanio does mention Portia's wealth first, but dowry was openly discussed in planning any Elizabethan marriage,[9] and Bassanio is hoping for a loan from Antonio that he will be able to repay. Bassanio emphasizes Portia's beauty and character— "nothing undervalued to Cato's Portia," which is high praise indeed—and that when they met before, Portia seemed genuinely inclined to him. The match between the two is what Jane Austen would call happy, wise, and reasonable; they are neither Romeo and Juliet nor Anthony and Cleopatra, but they are exhilarated with each other, alike in values and birth, and suited for the social role they will play in Italian society.

For her part, Portia waits in Belmont, bound to go through with the casket game devised by her late father and set forth in his will, which provides that any man may win Portia's hand in marriage by picking the casket that contains Portia's portrait. The game is governed by several rules. Those which must be observed by the suitors are noted by Aragon, the second man to try his luck in the game:

I am enjoined by oath to observe three things,—
First, never to unfold to any one
Which casket 'twas I chose; next, if I fail
Of the right casket, never in my life
To woo a maid in way of marriage:
Lastly,

> If I do fail in fortune of my choice,
> Immediately to leave you and be gone.

>   (2.9.9–16)

Portia may provide no clues, true or false, as to which casket holds the portrait. Moreover, Portia feels that as an obedient daughter, she has no choice but to play the game. "So is the will of a living daughter curb'd by the will of a dead father" (1.2.23–25), Portia says ruefully. But though Portia is unhappy with her situation, fearing that she will be chosen by the wrong man, her maid Nerrisa says,

> Your father was ever virtuous, and holy men at their
> death have good inspirations,—therefore the lott'ry
> that he hath devised in these three chests of gold,
> silver, and lead, whereof who chooses his meaning
> chooses you, will no doubt never be chosen by any
> rightly, but one who you shall rightly love.

>   (1.2.27–32)

Thus Portia, as the prize heiress, occupies the place held by the emperor's son in the *Gesta Romanorum*, but she must also exercise the faith of the shipwrecked maiden, relying on the scheme that her father—"virtuous and holy"—has set upon to exclude unworthy husbands. And the father's scheme has both folk wisdom and spiritual logic behind it. First, the rule that prevents losers from marrying will deter anyone who would settle for a wife other than Portia—mere fortune-hunters being less likely to risk their future sustenance on one chance. Second, a man truly worthy of Portia will understand the meaning of love and go directly to the lead casket. Indeed, though Portia is surrounded by a giddy Frenchman, a drunken German, a silly Englishman, and various other unsuitables, these suitors all finally leave Belmont because they will not risk the penalty for losing the casket game. And those who stay must confront the trap of exposing themselves and their values by choosing among the three caskets, each of which will mirror the spirit of the chooser.

The first suitor brave enough to play the game is Morocco, who in many ways is a sketch of Shakespeare's later creation, Othello. Morocco has Othello's openness, honesty, and courage—and also, some of his barbarity. He also has some of Othello's insecurity; fearing that Portia will judge him on the basis of his skin color, he proposes to open a vein, demonstrating that his blood is a richer red "than that of the fairest creature northward born." And like Othello, Morocco finally lacks sufficient faith for love; ironically, the suitor most concerned that he will be judged by appearance is himself taken in by appearances.

In Shakespeare's version of the casket game, the gold casket bears the inscription "Who chooseth me will gain what many men desire"; the silver, "Who chooseth me shall get as much as he deserves"; and the lead, "Who chooseth me must give and hazard all he hath." Morocco's reasoning is that many men desire Portia, and therefore the gold casket must be the right choice. Although logical, Morocco is incorrect from the Christian perspective because love is not about getting what we desire but about our willingness to give and hazard all for the beloved, with no thought of gain. This is the very essence of Christian love, demonstrated by Christ's willingness to suffer death by crucifixion for the sake of humanity. Morocco's boastfulness about his military exploits and being beloved by "the best virgins" of his clime, and his vaunting language, make him, as Barbara Lewalski says, a type of the man caught up in worldly values.

After Morocco loses and exits, Portia bids him "a gentle riddance," indicating some respect for Morocco. Her next line,

"Let all of his complexion choose me so," has been taken in recent scholarship as a sign of Portia's racism, but this is another example of how "the hermeneutics of suspicion," motivated by the perverse desire to find moral rot at the foundation of Western literature, results in crude reading. In Renaissance England the word "complexion" could mean either the quality of one's skin, including its color, or the quality of one's temperament. When put in context with Portia's preceding line, and earlier lines when Portia tells Morocco that she is not governed by naïveté as to appearances, the idea that Portia is a racist becomes hard, though not impossible, to maintain. From Portia's point of view, it could well be that Morocco's temperament, governed by bodily humors that are not well balanced, tends more to the "choleric" and impetuous end of the personality spectrum.[10] Given the differences in their backgrounds and temperaments, Portia's gentle riddance of Morocco is far more prudent than, say, Desdemona's taking of Othello against her father's wishes, and it is little indication of a racist disposition.

The second suitor to play the game is Aragon, who believes that love should go with merit, and that no man deserves Portia more than he. His pride has so disabled his ability to love that he does not even consider the lead casket—does not even read its inscription—but ignores it as "base lead," clearly not good enough for him. He rejects the gold casket because it is what "the fool multitude," led only by appearances, would choose. Aragon is so narcissistic that he would undoubtedly make a horrible husband. When he opens the silver casket he finds, essentially, a picture of himself, "the portrait of a blinking idiot" (2.9.54). As Morocco fails because of his worldliness, Aragon fails because of his arrogance. Lewalski explains:

Aragon, the Spaniard—the very embodiment of Pride
according to the Elizabethan caricature—is the type
of Pharisaical self-righteousness: his sonorously
complacent language about the barbarous multitudes
and the faults of others rather suggests the "sounding
brasse" and "tinckling cymbale" of Paul's image (I
Cor. xiii.1), and certainly recalls the Pharisee's prayer.
But through its first line, "The fire seven times tried
this," the scroll refers Aragon to the twelfth Psalm,
which denounces vanity and proud speaking. . . .
Also, the blinking idiot within the casket mutely
testifies that since all men are sinners, pharisaical
pride is folly."[11]

Bassanio, the fairy-tale third suitor, is, according to the
dictates of genre, bound to make the right choice. The allegorical nature of the casket story intensifies in the speeches
of Portia, leading up to Bassanio's "hazard." Waiting for
Bassanio's judgment, Portia declares her allegorical status.
Saying, "I stand for sacrifice," she compares herself on the
one hand to Hesione, who had to await rescue from the sea
monster by Hercules, and on the other to the essential element of Christian love. "Go Hercules," she tells Bassanio,
who chooses the lead casket, identifying himself with the ethic
of sacrifice for which Portia also stands. He recognizes that
the inscription on the lead casket shows it to be the true con-
tainer of Portia's portrait: "He who loves must give and hazard
all he hath."

Barbara Lewalski explains that "at the allegorical level,
the caskets signify everyman's choice of the paths to spiritual
life or death. This analogy is explicitly developed in the 'Moral'
appended to the casket story in the *Gesta Romanorum*,"[12] in
which the emperor represents God, the son of the emperor,
Christ, and the maiden, mankind. The moral declares: "The
Emperour sheweth this Mayden three vessels, that is to say,

God putteth before man life & death, good and evill, & which of these he chooseth hee shall obtain."[13] The gold and silver vessels both represent ways to spiritual death, but the lead represents the way to spiritual life:

> By the third vessel of lead full of golde and precious stones, we ought to understand a simple life and a poore, which the chosen men choose, that they may be wedded to our blessed Lorde Jesu Christ by humilitie and obeisance, and such men beare with them precious stones, that is to saye, faith and hir fruitfull workes, pleasinge to God: by the which at the judgement day they be espoused to our Lord Jesu Christ and obtaine the heritage of heaven.[14]

Thus, though the wedding of Portia and Bassanio is performed off stage, we see the essence of a wedding ceremony on stage. Portia and Bassanio make vows of love to each other, and religious declarations—Portia's "I stand for sacrifice," and Bassanio's choice of the lead casket—which link their marriage to spiritual marriage with Christ. In dramatic form, this is a repetition of words familiar to all of Shakespeare's audience, those said by the priest at the beginning of every wedding ceremony as set forth in the *Book of Common Prayer:* "we are gathered together, here in the sight of God . . . to join together this man and this woman in holy matrimony . . . signifying unto us the mystical union, that is betwixt Christ and his Church."[15] Thus, Portia and Bassanio symbolically identify with the ethic of self-sacrifice at the heart of Christianity. Antonio has hazarded everything he has, including his life, for Bassanio, and Portia does the same, giving herself and everything she has to Bassanio with the conveyance of her ring:

> Myself, and what is mine, to you and yours
> Is now converted. But now I was the lord

Of this fair mansion, master of my servants,
Queen o'er myself: and even now, but now.
This house, these servants, and this same myself
Are yours, my lord's!—I give them with this ring . . .

(3.2.166–71)

What is clearly a joyful, even a thankful giving by Portia
has become an occasion for feminist critics to unmask the
patriarchal hegemony of Shakespeare and his day, in which
women are not only deprived of their property but made to say
they enjoy its taking. While I certainly do not want to plump
for Renaissance England's property arrangements, those contemporary essays which focus on Portia as victim seem to me
among the most impoverished readings of Shakespeare's work
to date.[16] Because they ignore the Christian context of the play,
these critics also fail to understand the nature of love as understood by Shakespeare and his audience and the way that
love is demonstrated. The ethic of self-sacrifice, which in
marriage is mutual, can only be seen by such feminist authors
as masked selfishness, and thus the beauty of the play to the
people of its own time—a beauty we can still touch—is lost to
the well-stocked resentments of our own.

Portia's sacrifice is a serious one. Like Antonio, she bets
everything she has, herself and her property, on Bassanio's
faithfulness and love. Her sacrifice is not as great as Antonio's,
who hazards his very life for Bassanio—with much less chance
of recompense. It remains to be seen whether Bassanio has it
in *him* to really hazard everything he has for love. The end of
act 3 gives him his chance. Receiving a message that Shylock
intends to collect his pound of flesh from Antonio, Bassanio
hastens back to Venice to help his friend. Portia and Nerrisa
follow him, disguising themselves as the judge Balthasar and
his clerk, so that they may decide Antonio's case. Thus, the

ideal world of Belmont insinuates itself into the mercenary precincts of Venice.

Shylock's Suit to Enforce His Bond

Nevill Coghill traced the theme of the trial scene, which constitutes the fourth act of *The Merchant of Venice*, to the medieval works *Piers Plowman* and *The Castle of Perseverance*. In *Piers*, Christ's right to deprive Hell of sinners is debated by "The Four Daughters of God," Mercy, Truth, Righteousness, and Peace:

> Briefly, their argument is this: under the Old Law, God ordained punishment for sin in Hell, eye for eye and tooth for tooth. But under the New Law of His ransom paid on Calvary, He may with perfect justice redeem "those that he loved," and this justice is His mercy. The new Law does not contradict, but complements the Old, Mercy and Truth are met together, Righteousness and Peace have kissed each other.
>
> Almost exactly the same argument is conducted by the same four daughters of God at the end of *The Castle of Perseverance*, a morality play of the early fifteenth century. The protagonist, *Humanum Genus*, dies in sin and comes up for judgment. Righteousness and Truth demand his damnation, which the play would show to be just. Mercy and Peace plead the Incarnation, and *Humanum Genus* is saved.[17]

In the trial scene of act 4, Portia becomes the representative of the New Covenant, which emphasizes God's mercy, and Shylock the Old Covenant, which demands perfect adherence to the law.[18] Coghill is careful not to oversimplify this contrast:

> The two principles for which, in Shakespeare's play,
> [Jew and Gentile] stand, are both inherently right.
> They are only in conflict because, whereas God is
> held to be absolutely just as He is absolutely merciful,
> mortal and finite man can only be relatively so, and
> must arrive at a compromise. In human affairs either
> justice must yield a little to mercy, or mercy to justice;
> the former solution is the triumph of the New Law,
> and the conflict between Shylock and Portia is an
> exemplum of this triumph.[19]

Lewalski adds to this reading by noting that the phrases in the Lord's prayer, translated in the Geneva and Bishop's Bibles as "Forgeve us our dettes, as we forgive our deters," is alluded to twice in the trial scene, "making the debtor's trial in the court of Venice a precise analog of the sinner's trial in the court of Heaven."[20] Such analogies were commonly made by clergymen in Elizabethan England, Lewalski notes, furnishing the example of William Perkins in his *Exposition of the Lord's Prayer:* "For even as a debt doth binde a man, either to make satisfaction, or els to goe to prison: so our sinnes bindes us either to satisfie Gods justice, or else to suffer eternall damnation."[21]

Though the trial scene operates at an allegorical level, it is presented naturalistically; the characters are complex, sometimes selfish, and often torn between opposing loyalties. Though Portia's appearance as judge is fantastic—an importation of Belmont's fairy-tale style into the grittier precincts of Venice—the trial has elements of realism that make the threat to Antonio's life theatrically credible and serve as a foundation for suspense. To understand how the bond functions at both levels, we need to return to the scene in which it was created.

A lawsuit to enforce a contract is always a battle of words

over the meaning of words. In the case of Antonio's bond with Shylock, the fencing over what words will mean occurs at the very beginning of the bond's creation. When Bassanio asks Shylock for the loan of three thousand ducats, Antonio to be bound as surety, the following exchange occurs:

Shylock: Three thousand ducats for three months, and
           Antonio bound.

Bassanio: Your answer to that.

Shylock: Antonio is a *good* man.

Bassanio: Have you heard any imputation to the contrary?

Shylock: Ho, no, no, no: my meaning in saying he is a *good*
           man, is to have you understand me that he is
               sufficient.

                              (1.3.8–15; italics added)

This passage dramatizes a temporary breach in communication that Shylock corrects with great amusement. Shylock has attached a business meaning to the word "good" and Bassanio a moral one. The misunderstanding demonstrates Shylock's and Bassanio's habitual modes of operation. Shylock, the man of commerce, the usurer, immediately consults the balance book before making a decision on whether a man is "good"; Bassanio, the aristocrat, attaches to the word "good" a whole complex of ethical standards including generosity, hospitality, reputation, honesty, *noblesse oblige*—those virtues Englishmen associated with honor. Bassanio is not a complete babe in the woods regarding commercial ventures, and he probably offers Antonio's reputation for honor as assurance to Shylock that Antonio will consider himself morally bound to pay the bond. Shylock, however, empties the word "good" of its ethical content and, since he has the upper hand in this transaction, seizes control of the language in which the loan will be negotiated, displacing the language of honor with that of commerce.

Shylock sows the seeds of his own destruction when he attempts to wrest the legal-commercial system of Venice to the noncommercial purpose of revenge. In Venice, all ducats are created equal. So long as a person has money, does not break the law, and gears his actions to the making of more money, his conduct and motives will be accepted by the state as reasonable, though he be an outsider of questionable morality. However, Shylock's stated reason for taking the bond is to foster love and friendship between himself and Antonio, and thus Shylock ironically takes the first step away from commercial behavior:

Shylock: I would be friends with you, and have your love,
            Forget the shames that you have stain'd me with,
            Supply your present wants, and take no doit
            Of usance for my moneys, and you'll not hear me,—
            This is kind I offer.

Bassanio: This were kindness.

Shylock: This kindness will I show,
            Go with me to a notary, seal me there
            Your single bond, and (in a merry sport)
            If you repay me not on such a day
            In such a place, such sum or sums as are
            Express'd in the condition, let the forfeit
            Be nominated for an equal pound
            Of your fair flesh, to be cut off and taken
            In what part of your body pleaseth me.

Antonio: Content in faith, I'll seal to such a bond,
            And say there is much kindness in the Jew.

Bassanio: You shall not seal to such a bond for me,
            I'll rather dwell in necessity.

Antonio: Why fear not man, I will not forfeit it,—
            Within these two months, that's a month before

> This bond expires, I do expect return
> Of thrice three times the value of this bond.

Shylock:　O father Abram, what these Christians are,
> Whose own hard dealings teaches them suspect
> The thoughts of others! Pray you tell me this,
> If he should break his day what should I gain
> By the exaction of the forfeiture?
> A pound of man's flesh taken from a man,
> Is not so estimable, profitable neither
> As flesh of muttons, beefs, or goats,—I say
> To buy his favour, I extend this friendship,—
> If he will take it, so,—if not, adieu,
> And for my love I pray you wrong me not.

Antonio:　Yes Shylock, I will seal unto this bond.

Shylock:　Then meet me forthwith at the notary's,
> Give him direction for this merry bond—
> And I will go and purse the ducats straight,

> ···

Antonio:　Hie thee gentle Jew.
> The Hebrew will turn Christian, he grows kind.

(1.3.134–70; 173–74)

Shylock's stated intention is to take the forfeiture provision as a joke. Shylock twice calls the bond a "merry bond" and the whole transaction a "merry sport." Shylock pokes fun at Bassanio for even suggesting that Antonio is putting himself in danger, or that Shylock would collect a pound of flesh. Antonio understands that the bond is, in fact, a no-interest loan, the pound of flesh clause being a jest: "I'll seal to such a bond, / And say there is much kindness in the Jew."

The context of the bond's formation is not only one of jest but of love. Shylock says he wants to "buy" Antonio's love, demonstrating that he is as unfamiliar with love as Bassanio is with business terms. The entire transaction is framed by

two similar statements. Shylock begins by saying, "I would be
friends with you and have your love. . . . This is *kind* I offer,"
and Antonio ends, saying "The Hebrew will turn Christian,
he grows *kind*." In the first instance, the word "kind" has two
meanings. One, most obviously, is that Shylock is being kind,
in the most profoundly Christian way, by helping his enemies.
(Thus, he shames Antonio.) The second use of "kind," not lost
on Bassanio, is that Shylock intends to pay back Antonio *in
kind* for his previous insults. This use is also synonymous with
"like." Shylock is growing—becoming—more *like* a gentile
and a Christian, the meaning Antonio emphasizes with the
preceding pun, "Hie thee *gentle* [gentile] Jew."

The dialogue of love and game that forms the context of
the bond's creation is ephemeral and vanishes with the bond's
formation. However, the bond as text remains and floats free
from the context that would limit its meaning, allowing Shylock to demand an interpretation of the bond that is "literal"
in only the most superficial sense. The bond, essentially, will
pass from an interpretive environment governed by merry sport
and love to a more restrictive environment governed by the
letter of the law (without the spirit) and by the values of commerce, which require all debts to be paid. Portia, as judge,
will have the task of placing the bond back into its context,
hoisting Shylock on his own petard by carrying his interpretation to its logical extreme. At the same time, she will place the
bond in its allegorical context, urging forgiveness of "debt"
and demonstrating the spiritual consequences of demanding
justice unleavened with mercy.

Shylock's case, in act 4, lasts 410 lines. When played
well, this scene can hold an audience in such suspense that
its ending comes with a collective gasp of relief. Shylock's
case can be divided into three parts: the attempt by the duke
and Portia to get Shylock to settle according to Christian prin-

ciples of mercy; Portia's judgment of both Antonio and Shylock; and Antonio's forgiveness of Shylock. Portia's sly acqui-
sition of her husband's wedding ring when she is disguised as
the judge, Balthasar, forms the bridge to the last act.

Shylock, stung by his daughter's betrayal, is as Antonio
describes him: "obdurate" to collect his pound of flesh. When
the duke asks Shylock to not only forgo exacting the bond's
penalty, but also to "Forgive a moiety of the principal" of the
loan, Shylock reminds him that Venice can exist as a center of
trade and finance only if it enforces contracts: "If you deny it,
let the danger light / Upon your charter and your city's freedom!" When Bassanio tries to get Portia (as Balthasar) to over-
ride Venetian law, she essentially repeats what Shylock has
told the duke:

> It must not be, there is no power in Venice
> Can alter a decree established:
> 'Twill be recorded for a precedent,
> And many an error by the same example
> Will rush into the state,—it cannot be.

> (4.1.214–18)

Here Portia states the familiar principle of *stare decisis*—precedent is not to be lightly overturned. The law must be pre-
dictable for citizens to establish and maintain stable relationships with each other; law by judicial fiat, which is just another form of tyranny, leads to chaos.[22] Venice seems to have
no judicial course of action but to enforce Shylock's bond, and
so it is logical that both the duke and Portia start with extra-
judicial appeals, attempting to get Shylock to settle. This effort corresponds with the practice of Shakespeare's day and is
based on two Bible passages addressing how Christians ought
to deal with each other: "Agree with thine adversary quickly,
whilst thou art in the way with him, lest thine adversary de-

liver thee to the judge, and the judge deliver thee to the sergeant, and thou be tossed into prison" (Matthew 5:25); and
"Now therefore there is utterly a fault among you, because ye
go to law one with another: why rather suffer ye not wrong?
Why rather sustain ye not harm? Nay, ye yourselves do wrong,
and do harm, and that to your brethren" (I Corinthians 5:7–8).

These biblical injunctions to settle amicably, out of court,
were taken very seriously by the Anglican Church, especially
with regard to cases involving usury. During the sixteenth century, England enacted a series of conflicting laws, alternately
allowing usury and disallowing it, in whole or in part; but con-
servative writers argued that all usury was wrong. Men were
not only subjects of the state, but of the church as well, and
biblical injunctions against the taking of interest (Deuteronomy
23:19–23, Exodus 22:25, and Leviticus 25:35–37) had to be
followed no matter what laws were enacted. According to R.
H. Tawney, the general policy of the Privy Council with regard
to creditor and debtor was

> to try to secure the settlement of disputes out of court
> through the good offices of a friend, an influential
> neighbour, or when necessary, an arbitrator appointed
> by itself. The justices of Norfolk are instructed to
> put pressure on a money-lender who has taken "very
> unjust and immoderate advantage by way of usury."
> The Bishop of Exeter is advised to induce a usurer
> in his diocese to show "a more Christian and
> charytable consideration of these his neighbours."...
> It is evident that under Elizabeth the government kept
> sufficiently in touch with the state of business to know
> when the difficulties of borrowers threatened a crisis,
> and endeavoured to exercise a moderating influence
> by bringing the parties to accept a compromise.[23]

From a business perspective, the duke's suggestion that Shylock forgive a moiety (half) of the principal of Antonio's debt is absurd, but from the Christian perspective what the duke says makes sense. Yet, the duke is being hypocritical, demanding that Shylock be a better Christian than the Christians of Venice. This is not lost on Shylock:

> You have among you many a purchas'd slave,
> Which (like your asses, and your dogs and mules)
> You use in abject and in slavish parts,
> Because you bought them,—shall I say to you
> Let them be free, marry them to your heirs?
> Why sweat they under burthens? let their beds
> Be made as soft as yours, and let their palates
> Be season'd with such viands? you will answer
> "The slaves are ours,"—so do I answer you:
> The pound of flesh which I demand of him
> Is dearly bought, 'tis mine and I will have it:
> If you deny me, fie upon your law!
> There is no force in the decrees of Venice:
> *I stand for judgment,*—answer, shall I have it?

> (4.1.90–103; italics added)

Again, Shakespeare deliberately blurs the moral distinctions between Shylock and his Christian opponents. Shylock at least is not a slave-holder. He does not want a whole man—only a pound of a man. In this passage Shakespeare gives Shylock his allegorical status: "I stand for judgment." Later, Shylock will say, "I stand here for law." Shylock represents the Old Covenant, with its demand for strict adherence to the law, and the law of Venice does seem to resemble the law of the Old Covenant, since as both the duke and Portia maintain, it cannot be set aside. Every jot of it must be obeyed; and as Antonio is condemned under it, so is all mankind condemned under Old Testament law, because no one can keep it perfectly. Only the New Covenant of justice through faith can save mankind, all of whom are in Antonio's position:

> But now is the righteousness of God made manifest without the Law, having witness of the Law and of the Prophets, / *to wit,* the righteousness of God by the faith of Jesus Christ, unto all, and upon all that believe. / For there is no difference: for all have sinned, and are deprived of the glory of God, / And are justified freely by his grace, through the redemption that is in Christ Jesus, / Whom God hath set forth to be a reconciliation through faith in his blood to declare his righteousness, by the forgiveness of sins that are passed through the patience of God. (Romans 3:21–25)

God's mercy is freely given, and when Portia, disguised as Balthasar,[24] tells Shylock that he must be merciful to Antonio, Shylock replies, "Under what compulsion must I?" It is a similar answer to that which he gives the duke, who asks, "How shalt thou hope for mercy, rend'ring none?" echoing James 2:12: "For he shall have judgment without mercy, that hath shewed no mercy; and mercy rejoiceth against judgment." Shylock replies: "What judgment shall I dread, doing no wrong?" But the two verses preceding James 2:12, those just quoted from Romans, and many others state that no one can keep the law perfectly, and therefore all are justly condemned.

Shylock, who now becomes a representative of unalloyed adherence to the law and judgment by its strict application, simply does not understand mercy. He does not understand he also is a sinner and lawbreaker, especially in his attempt to commit the judicial murder of Antonio, his merciless behavior to other debtors, and his miserable treatment of his daughter Jessica. In all of this, Shylock also breaks the law of the Old Covenant. As David Ariel explains in *What Jews Believe,*

"Because people are created in the image of God, any offense against another person is an offense against God. The call to imitate the moral character of God is the challenge placed before every human being. According to the Torah, murder is not only a criminal act but an attack upon the very image of God inherent in each person."[25] By either Jewish or Christian standards, Shylock needs mercy as much as anyone, but he is blind to his own breaches of the law, and therefore his own guilt and condemnation. Shylock will have to be confronted with his own status as a lawbreaker before he can value mercy. He will have to go to school under the law before he can appreciate forgiveness.[26]

Nevertheless, Portia gives Shylock every chance to change his course. First, she urges him to settle with the most famous speech in the play, the thematic centerpiece of *The Merchant of Venice,* which incorporates the doctrine of Romans 3:21–25 and Galatians 3:3–5:

> The quality of mercy is not strain'd,
> It droppeth as the gentle rain from heaven
> Upon the place beneath: it is twice blest,
> It blesseth him that gives, and him that takes,
> 'Tis mightiest in the mightiest, it becomes
> The throned monarch better than his crown.
> His scepter shows the force of temporal power,
> The attribute to awe and majesty,
> Wherein doth sit the dread and fear of kings:
> But mercy is above this sceptred sway,
> It is enthroned in the hearts of kings,
> It is an attribute of God himself;
> And earthly power doth then show likest God's
> When mercy seasons justice: therefore Jew,
> Though justice be thy plea, consider this,
> That in the course of justice, none of us
> Should see salvation: we do pray for mercy,
> And that same prayer, doth teach us all to render

The deeds of mercy. I have spoke thus much
To mitigate the justice of thy plea,
Which if thou follow, this strict court of Venice
Must needs give sentence 'gainst the merchant there.

(4.1.180–201)

Portia does not argue that mercy should utterly displace justice in earthly courts, but that mercy should *season* justice,
that the two ideals should work together. But Shylock wants
justice unseasoned with any mercy, and by his reply, he puts
himself deliberately under a law that shows no mercy: "My
deeds upon my head! I crave the law," he says. Not until Shylock refuses from Bassanio settlement offers of twice and then
ten times the amount of what Antonio owes, Bassanio pledg-
ing "my hands, my head, my heart," does Portia proceed to
render the famous verdict that Shylock can have his pound of
flesh, provided that not one jot of Antonio's blood is spilt, thus
making the same kind of spiritual distinction between flesh
and blood that is made in the Eucharist. Shylock can only say
in astonishment, "Is this the law?" since the law is what he
has bound himself to. Portia takes her literalness further: Shylock must take a pound of flesh exactly, no more and no less.
Lastly, as Shylock tries to recover at least his principle, he
runs into a difficulty that threatens his very life, for it turns
out that Shylock has broken a law, and the breaking of law,
without Christ's redemption, is spiritual and eternal death.
Portia tells him:

It is enacted in the laws of Venice,
If it be proved against an alien,
That by direct, or indirect attempts
He seek the life of any citizen,
The party 'gainst the which he doth contrive,
Shall seize one half his goods, the other half
Comes to the privy coffer of the state,

> And the offender's life lies in the mercy
> Of the Duke only, 'gainst all other voice.

(4.1.344–52)

Thus do Portia and the duke, as judges, play the part of God, while Shylock plays the unregenerate sinner who has demanded judgment of others but cannot withstand judgment himself. Shylock runs into Matthew 7:1–2: "Judge not, that ye be not judged / For with what judgment ye judge, ye shall be judged, and with what measure ye shall mete, it shall be measured to you again." Now it is up to Antonio, who has spat upon Shylock, to become a better Christian by imitating Christ and extending mercy to a murderous enemy. Antonio becomes the intercessor for Shylock. The duke pardons Shylock his life before he asks, and Antonio convinces the duke to return to Shylock the half of his goods that would be confiscated by the state, and to put the half that would go to Antonio into trust for the benefit of Shylock's daughter, Jessica, and her husband, Lorenzo, all of Shylock's money going to this couple on his death, all of which mercy is contingent on Shylock becoming a Christian. In response to this, Shylock says, "I am content," but I have never seen a performance of the play in which that line did not manifest agony, though sometimes Shylock tries to mask his pain.

The forcible conversion of Shylock from Judaism to Christianity has been portrayed on stage and taken by critics as the most horrendous example of anti-Semitism in the play. In the 1980 BBC production,[27] starring Warren Mitchell as Shylock, an enormous cross is hung from Shylock's neck by Solanio and Salario, and it weighs on him like a millstone. Lawrence Olivier portrayed Shylock's agony with a long off-stage howl. Yet in Shakespeare's time, Antonio's provision, along with his division of Shylock's property, would certainly have been seen

as an act of redemptive kindness. Shylock, whose soul was in
danger of hell, now at least has a chance to save himself by
becoming a Christian, and the symbolic redemption of his fine
by Antonio is part of this logic. The court scene has demonstrated that reliance on the law to the exclusion of mercy only
kills. Shylock, who asked for such an application of the law—
even though he had sealed explicitly to a merry bond, a bond
made in sport—now is trapped by the same mechanism which
he would have used to murder Antonio. "For as thou urgest
justice, be assur'd / Thou shalt have justice more than thou
desir'st," Portia tells him after he has repeatedly rejected mercy
for Antonio. "The Jew shall have *all* justice" (italics added).
Like a lost soul, Shylock cannot even save his principal. He
gets nothing but the forfeiture. But with Antonio's extension
of mercy, the possibility that Shylock will accept God's mercy
becomes possible.

Many critics have made arguments about anti-Semitism
in *Merchant* that have to be taken seriously,[28] and an honest
reading needs to address these head-on. Shakespeare had little
understanding of Judaism. The same, of course, could be said
of Calvin, Luther, and the Roman Catholic Church of the day.
As an allegorical figure, Shylock is, by New Testament standards, a fair representation of Pharisaical legalism. However,
recent scholarship shows that the Pharisees had a far more
complex understanding of mercy and justice than the New
Testament indicates.[29] And at the time of the Renaissance,
Shylock is certainly not a fair representation of Jewish ethics,
which are based on respect for all people, since all are created in the image of God. Though Shakespeare is very careful
to distinguish Christian ideals from Christian conduct, he does
not do the same for Judaism, and this, at times, gives the play
an anti-Semitic tone. Shakespeare did not create a good Jew
to serve as Shylock's foil,[30] and the play contains no speeches

voicing the moral precepts of Judaism, which acknowledge the value of mercy.[31] Moreover, Shylock's request to Tubal to meet him at the synagogue, implying they will meet there to firm up the plot against Antonio (3.2.115–20), appeals to familiar anti-Semitic canards, as exemplified by some of Luther's worst writing: "Be on your guard against the Jews, knowing that wherever they have their synagogues, nothing is found but a den of devils in which sheer self-glory, conceit, lies, blasphemy, and defaming of God and men are practiced most maliciously...."[32] Shylock is many times referred to as a devil, a familiar label during Shakespeare's time for Jews. And there is Gratiano's gratuitous nastiness after Shylock agrees to convert to Christianity: "In christ'ning shalt thou have two godfathers— / Had I been judge, thou shouldst have had ten more, / To bring thee to the gallows, not to the font" (4.1.394–96).

Yet Shakespeare represents Shylock as a human being who still mourns for the wife he lost when he thinks of the ring he was given by Leah when he was a bachelor, the ring that his own daughter has stolen and sold for a monkey. His assertions that he too is a human being who can bleed, and his testimony about how he has been treated by Antonio, all force the audience to see him as more than the stock villainous Jew. Attaching to the play the anti-Semitic epithet is simplistic. If Shakespeare was anti-Semitic, his imaginative sympathy for his characters and his sense of human fallibility astonishingly transcended his sixteenth-century English prejudices.

The lines in *The Merchant of Venice* that trouble us most are those which seem to attribute Shylock's viciousness to the Jews as a people, such as these from Antonio to Bassanio, who has been trying to reason Shylock out of his hatred:

> I pray you think you question with the Jew,—
> You may as well go stand upon the beach
> And bid the main flood bate his usual height,

> You may as well use question with the wolf,
> Why he hath made the ewe bleak for the lamb:
> You may as well forbid the mountain pines
> To wag their high tops, and to make no noise
> When they are fretten with the gusts of heaven:
> You may as well do any thing most hard
> As seek to soften that—than which what's harder?—
> His Jewish heart!
>
> (4.1.70–80)

These lines, in their allegorical dimension, speak primarily to spiritual conditions. Shylock's hard-heartedness derives from the Jewish refusal to accept Jesus as the Messiah, despite his miracles and sermons. Thus, Jesus explains to his disciples that he teaches in parables to insinuate himself into the hearts of his people; because Israel's heart is "calloused" (Matthew 13:15) it must be penetrated subtly. From the viewpoint of Renaissance Christianity, Jesus' failure to penetrate the hearts of the Jewish nation was not for lack of effort:

> O Jerusalem, Jerusalem, which killest the prophets,
> and stonest them that are sent to thee, how often would
> I have gathered thy children together, as the hen
> gathered her brood under her wings, & ye would not!
> / Behold, your house is left unto you desolate; and
> certainly I tell you, ye shall not se me until the time
> come that ye shall say, Blessed is he that cometh in
> the name of the Lord. . . . (Luke 13:34–35)

The attitude displayed in the New Testament toward the Jews is not one of hatred, but of love, hope, and admittedly, frustration. Paul emphasizes God's care for Israel and prophesies that finally "all Israel will be saved" (Romans 12:26). This is not a matter of choice, Paul says, but of election, and Shylock's conversion could have been seen as the allegorical fulfillment of this promise. That many twentieth-century Jewish critics find this repulsive is understandable. But from Shakespeare's perspective, it is a measure of good fortune. In a society that rightly prides itself for religious tolerance and that would violently fracture without it, we are wise to reject the idea of forced conversion to anything. But as students of literature, we are obliged to develop a historical imagination, to connect with the past sufficiently to avoid mistaking a generous act for a contemptible one, even if our notion of generosity is different from that of the Elizabethans. Shakespeare's characterization of Shylock has to be read in the literary context in which he worked. Hard-heartedness was a spiritual condition that Christians not only applied to Jews, but to themselves,[33] and in Renaissance drama, Christians sometimes came off worse in comparison to Jews and infidels.[34]

The Ring Game

The "Ring Game," which has its culmination in act 5, begins in the trial scene of act 4. In stressing the friendship between Antonio and Bassanio, Shakespeare also emphasizes how far Antonio and Bassanio are from recognizing that Bassanio's marriage to Portia must be taken as the most important relationship in his life. While Antonio is used by Shakespeare as a figure of Christ during the trial scene, ready to give his body and blood for his friend, his allegorical function is interwoven with his selfish need to compete with Portia for Bassanio's love. This is revealed in Antonio's "last words" to Bassanio:

> Commend me to your honourable wife,
> Tell her the process of Antonio's end,
> Say how I lov'd you, speak me fair in death:
> And when the tale is told, bid her be judge
> Whether Bassanio had not once a love.

> (4.1.269–73)

Shylock is stropping his razor on the sole of his shoe, and
Bassanio, I think, can be forgiven for giving Antonio the declaration of love he so much wants to hear, one that values him
even over Portia:

> Antonio, I am married to a wife
> Which is as dear to me as life itself,
> But life itself, my wife, and all the world
> Are not with me esteem'd above thy life.
> I would lose all, ay sacrifice them all
> Here to this devil, to deliver you.

                                        (4.1.278–83)

Gratiano, who follows Bassanio's lead like a puppy, is always compelled to become part of what is happening, and he
gratuitously chimes in that he wishes his wife were in heaven
so she could entreat God to change "this currish Jew." At this
point, Shylock, perhaps thinking of Jessica, gets the funniest
and most satirical line in the play: "*These* be the Christian
husbands." Portia, who can certainly understand the pressure
on Bassanio to make such a declaration of love to Antonio,
cannot help but feel displaced. Her dry comment on Bassanio's
declaration is, "Your wife would give you little thanks for that."
She and Bassanio have been made "one flesh" through marriage, and his primary loyalty must be to her as hers is to him.
Antonio, for all his sacrifice for Bassanio, has not yet given
and hazarded all he has because he will not sacrifice the place
he wants to hold in Bassanio's heart. The ring game, which
Portia will initiate at the end of the trial scene, becomes the cata-
lyst by which the relationship of Antonio and Bassanio must
necessarily be adjusted in recognition of Bassanio's marriage.

After the trial, Bassanio wants to give Balthasar (Portia)
the three thousand ducats that were to have been paid in satisfaction of Shylock's bond. Such a gift, after the decision of

the case, would not necessarily have been taken as improper in sixteenth- century England, but Portia refuses it. However, when she sees the ring she has given Bassanio, which, if removed, would "presage" the end of his love to her, she begs that he give it to her, and Bassanio, though he does not want to give it up, is compelled to do so by Antonio, who has just put his life on the line for his friend: "My Lord Bassanio, let him have the ring, / Let his deservings and my love withal / Be valued 'gainst your wife's commandment" (4.1.445–47). Bassanio gives Portia the ring, sending it by Gratiano. Thus begins a comic parody of the trial scene, with Portia retaining the role of judge and taking the additional role of Shylock, demanding the law upon Bassanio's head. Bassanio becomes the sacrificial victim until Antonio once again interposes himself. Bassanio's giving of the ring is the comic counterpart of Antonio's pledge of a pound of flesh. The ring represents Portia and all of Belmont, as Portia says when she first gives it to Bassanio. If Bassanio has not hazarded everything he has by giving up the ring for his friend, in the realm of comedy he has come close. When Portia seems to threaten the very existence of her marriage by saying she will be as liberal as Bassanio, and deny nothing to the judge who got the ring—not even her body and her husband's bed—Antonio is finally compelled to give up his last and strongest desire:

> I am th' unhappy subject of these quarrels.
> ....
> I once did lend my body for his wealth,
> Which but for him that had your husband's ring
> Had quite miscarried. I dare be bound again,
> My soul upon the forfeit, that your lord
> Will never more break faith advisedly.
>
> (5.1.238, 249–53)

Having achieved what she wants and her marriage needs, Portia discloses herself as the judge who got the ring. All is well and more than well, since in Belmont, as in heaven, those who sacrifice are repaid many times. Barbara Lewalski, who took the allegorical interpretation to its finest and most thorough development deserves the last word:

> In Belmont all losses are restored and sorrows end: Bassanio wins again his lady and all Belmont; Antonio is given a letter signifying that three of his argosies are returned to port richly laden; and Lorenzo receives the deed naming him Shylock's future heir. Lorenzo's exclamation, "Fair ladies, you drop manna in the way of starving people" . . . sets up an implied metaphor of the heavenly communion. Here all who have cast their bread upon the waters in the "ventures" of Christian love receive the reward promised:
>
> > *Whoever shall forsake houses, or brethren, or sisters, or father, or mother or wife, or children, or landes, for my names sake, hee shal receive an hundreth folde more, and shal inherite everlasting life (Matt. xix: 29).*[35]

The rich reward for venturing to love is itself exemplified in Belmont, where the play ends. How, one might ask, would *The Merchant of Venice* have ended if Shakespeare had decided not to import the fairytale magic of Portia and her home? What if commercial Venice had had to resolve its own problems of law and morality? The answer, perhaps, is given in *Measure for Measure*, in which Shakespeare poses a challenge to romantic comedy that even he cannot surmount.

Judge not, that ye be not judged. / For with what judgement ye judge, ye shall be judged, and with what measure ye mete, it shall be measured to you again. / And why seest thou the mote that is in thy brother's eye, and perceivest not the beam that is in thine own eye? / Or how saist thou to thy brother, Suffer me to cast out the mote out of thine eye, and behold a beam is in thine owne eye? / Hypocrite, first cast out the beam out of thine own eye, and then shalt thou see clearly to cast out the mote out of thy brother's eye.

Matthew 7:1–5

Values may easily clash within the breast of a single individual; and it does not follow that, if they do, some must be true and others false. Justice, rigorous justice, is for some people an absolute value, but it is not compatible with what may be no less ultimate values for them— mercy, compassion—as arises in concrete cases. . . . We are doomed to choose, and every choice may entail irreparable loss.

Isaiah Berlin,
The Crooked Timber of Humanity

4

Measure for Measure: Trial as Political Theater

Like *The Merchant of Venice*, Shakespeare's *Measure for Measure* combines elements of folklore (a ruler going disguised among his people, a bed trick), realism, and allegory. It is even more steeped in Christian doctrine than *Merchant*, more problematic in structure, and more complicated in theme. Whereas in *The Merchant of Venice* allegory was fully integrated into the play, accessible to the audience but not to the characters, in *Measure for Measure* Duke Vincentio deliberately stages an allegorical trial—in effect, a morality play—for the benefit of his subjects. (This, as we shall see, gives him much in common with James I, who was crowned shortly before the play was produced.) Thus, the theater audience encounters allegory as a play within a play. Although *Measure for Measure* examines the competing claims of justice and mercy, it goes beyond *The Merchant of Venice* in posing an additional question to the audience: To what extent can a secular state, administering the criminal law to preserve its existence, integrate Christian ideals of mercy and forgiveness into its judicial system? From beginning to end, Duke Vincentio's problem is to find an adequate answer to this question.

The State of Vienna and Its "Duke of Dark Corners"

At the start of *Measure for Measure,* Shakespeare presents Duke Vincentio as a ruler of integrity and intelligence faced with several problems, most of his own making. Vincentio's major failure as a ruler has been excessive leniency—if not downright negligence—in the enforcement of criminal laws. In Vienna, according to the duke, a lack of restraint during the previous fourteen years has resulted in near anarchy:

> We have strict statutes and most biting laws,
> The needful bits and curbs to headstrong jades,
> Which for this fourteen years we have let slip;
> Even like an o'ergrown lion in a cave,
> That goes not out to prey. Now, as fond fathers,
> Having bound up the threatening twigs of birch,
> Only to stick it in their children's sight
> For terror, not to use, in time the rod
> Becomes more mock'd than feared; so our decrees,
> Dead to infliction, to themselves are dead,
> And Liberty plucks Justice by the nose,
> The baby beats the nurse, and quite athwart
> Goes all decorum.
>
> (1.3.19–31)

"Jades" are willful, headstrong horses, and Vincentio's polity, he believes, is full of them, doing whatever they want. Although Vincentio has allowed this situation to develop, he does not want to take responsibility for rectifying it. He tells

his confidant, Friar Thomas, that it would be for him tyranni-
cal to punish the people for what he has "bid them do," for, he
acknowledges, we bid evil deeds be done whenever we give
them "their permissive pass / And not the punishment" which
they deserve (1.3.37–39). Sexual offenses in particular have
had their permissive pass in Vienna, giving rise to an epi-
demic of venereal disease, a number of abandoned children,
and the weakening of marriage—problems not unknown to
our own time.

The duke's other failing, closely related to the first, is that
he does not like to engage in public display. He is a man who
prefers privacy to political ceremony. He knows that he needs
to be seen by his people to set a good example and to exhort
them to lead virtuous, law-abiding lives, but he is embarrassed
by the excessive praise his people pay him, repelled by the
obeisance and flattery he must endure in public. As Friar
Thomas later comments, the duke is a man who knows himself—a high compliment—and therefore can sense the gulf
between himself and the ceremonial role he plays as
duke. What bothers Vincentio is the dissonance between his
private self and the one he must craft for the public:

> I love the people
> But do not like to stage me to their eyes:
> *Though it do well,* I do not relish well
> Their loud applause and aves vehement;
> Nor do I think the man of safe discretion
> That does affect it.
>
> (1.1.67–72; italics added)

It *would* do well for the duke to put himself in the public
eye, to provide a good example, to create confidence in his
authority, and he recognizes his dereliction in this regard. The
duke's unfortunate solution, since he cannot seem to do his

duty, is to have someone else do it, and to this end he appoints Angelo to be his deputy, to "duke it in his place," while he, supposedly, goes to Poland on a diplomatic mission. Let Angelo restore the law; let him be the lightning rod for the people's ire. Here Vincentio is following Machiavelli's astute political advice: if there is hatchet work to do, get someone else to do it. Let someone else attract the people's hatred, someone who can be scapegoated if necessary.

Vincentio does want Angelo to do an honest job of governing, the main part of which consists in dispensing justice, but he does not completely trust Angelo, whose cold rectitude might be hiding corruption. The duke therefore decides to stay in Vienna, disguised as a friar, to see whether Angelo will be corrupted by power:

> Lord Angelo is precise;
> Stands at guard with Envy; scarce confesses
> That his blood flows; or that his appetite
> Is more to bread than stone. Hence shall we see,
> If power change purpose, what our seemers be.

(1.3.50–54)

Similarities between the duke and James I have been widely recognized for years,[1] and readings based on the connection are familiar.[2] The duke's problems are similar to those of James. "Anarchy" and prostitution in the suburbs were all contemporary issues in London. The marriage laws of England were in severe confusion and clandestine marriage was common. England's new king undoubtedly had severe doubts about the trustworthiness of some of his new courtiers, as Walter Raleigh soon discovered, and it has long been remarked how James and the duke share an aversion to public display and an introverted love of study (like Prospero, in *The Tempest*), particularly of religion and theology.

The first act, therefore, sets up the problem of a duke who understands the value of law enforcement, who understands the value of ceremony and theatricality in government—as does James I in *Basilikon Doron* and Machiavelli in *The Prince*—but still cannot make himself engage in the necessary public relations work.[3] He does not mind being prince, but he does not want to play the role of prince. As a result the people of Vienna have become unsure of who the duke is or what he stands for, just as the people of London may have been unsure of who their new Scottish king was, and what he stood for. Later, Lucio, a soldier of fortune, habitué of brothels, cynic, and libertine, will articulate public opinion when he speaks "but according to the trick" (i.e., according to fashion) in referring to Vincentio as "the old fantastical Duke of dark corners," not only implying that the duke is promiscuous (and already James's attraction to boys had been noticed[4]), but emphasizing his avoidance of public appearance. Though Lucio continually demonstrates his willingness to sacrifice truth to his own vanity (as proved beyond a doubt in Isabella's "trial" in act 5), his slander is dangerous, and the duke must realize that his own failure to achieve a public identity has prepared the soil in which such lies can take root.

The duke sets himself two tasks: he must find out whom he can trust and he must reestablish his authority. He needs to rediscover his dukedom, the image he conveys to his subjects, and the moral quality of his lieutenants in much the same way James, in the first year of his reign, had to discover his new kingdom and assess the loyalty of those courtiers left from Elizabeth's reign. A reading of the play that celebrates James's first year as king would have the duke triumphant on all fronts.

Thus, Vincentio needs to apply to himself the argument he uses to convince Angelo to take public office:

Heaven doth with us as we with torches do,
Not light them for themselves; for if our virtues
Did not go forth of us, 'twere all alike
As if we had them not. Spirits are not finely touch'd
But to fine issues; nor nature never lends
The smallest scruple of her excellence
But, like a thrifty goddess, she determines
Herself the glory of a creditor,
Both thanks and use.

(1.1.32–40)

Heaven and Nature do not give us virtues, as Hamlet would say, to "fust in us unused," but rather to be put in action, as if we were paying back a debt to Nature for the gifts she has given us. Moreover, the use of our virtues must be public—not for our own glory, but to set an example to others so they will use their virtues as well. Like a torch, a person who is publicly engaged in virtuous action lights the way for others to act virtuously.

Angelo and Isabella: Justice v. Mercy

In Vincentio's "absence," Angelo applies the law harshly. The first people to run afoul of a revived statute are Claudio and Julietta, who are betrothed to each other under a pre-contract of marriage that they have kept secret while attempting to gain the approval of Julietta's friends and relatives, who control her dowry. In England, a pre-contract was essentially an engagement that was legally binding. If a couple had sexual congress during the time of the pre-contract, they were deemed to have married each other at the time of intercourse. Claudio and Julietta have had sex, a crime punishable by death in Angelo's Vienna, but dealt with as a routine and fairly inconsequential lapse by the ecclesiastical courts of Shakespeare's England.

Lucio encounters his friend Claudio, who, under Angelo's instructions, is being paraded around town by the provost of the jail to demonstrate how the new regime will deal with crime. Claudio describes Angelo as one who is drunk with new power, applying laws that have not been used in nineteen years:

> . . . the new deputy now for the Duke—
> Whether it be the fault and glimpse of newness,
> Or whether that the body public be
> A horse whereon the governor doth ride,
> Who, newly in the seat, that it may know
> He can command, lets it straight feel the spur;
> Whether the tyranny be in his place,
> Or in his eminence that fills it up,
> I stagger in—but this new governor
> Awakes me all the enrolled penalties
> Which have, like unscour'd armour, hung by th' wall
> So long, that nineteen zodiacs have gone round,
> And none of them been worn; and, for a name
> Now puts the drowsy and neglected act
> Freshly on me: 'tis surely for a name.
>
> (1.2.146–60)

Claudio's only hope is clemency; he asks Lucio to find his sister, Isabella, who has just entered, as a novitiate, the Order of Clare, the most ascetic and strict order of Roman Catholic nuns. As Claudio puts it, Isabella has something in her that makes men want to do what she asks:

> Implore her, in my voice, that she make friends
> To the strict deputy: bid herself assay him.
> I have a great hope in that. For in her youth
> There is a prone and speechless dialect
> Such as move men; beside, she hath prosperous art
> When she will play with reason and discourse,
> And well she can persuade.
>
> (1.2.170–76)

When we first see Isabella, she is talking to one of the sisters of her order, inquiring as to whether the Order of Clare can be made even stricter than it is. This gives as broad a clue to Isabella's character as any single bit of information in the play; despite the rhetoric of mercy she will use with Angelo as she pleads for her brother's life, we find that Isabella, through most of the play, is as priggish and puritanical as Angelo. There is a coldness about her spirit that Lucio must dispel before Isabella can be an effective advocate for her brother. Indeed, Lucio's description of Angelo to Isabella could to some degree apply to her. According to Lucio, Angelo is a man who has never felt passion, a man less than human for he lacks the capacity to feel what others do; he is a robot lawyer:

> . . . Lord Angelo; a man whose blood—
> Is very snow broth; one who never feels
> The wanton stings and motions of the sense;
> But doth rebate and blunt his natural edge
> With profits of the mind, study, and fast.

(1.4.57–61)

Isabella seeks out a cloister; Angelo has cloistered himself in the midst of life.

Though the debate about justice and mercy that Angelo and Isabella will have in the second act is reminiscent of the trial scene in *The Merchant of Venice,* other issues make Shakespeare's review of that argument more complex. The law is in urgent need of enforcement in Vienna, and Angelo is acting as protector of the body politic, rather than the judge of a civil lawsuit brought for private gain. And the idea of executing someone for having premarital sex with a woman, though he love and fully intend to marry her, is somewhat more realistic than the flesh-bond story of *The Merchant of*

Venice; in fact, in the Puritan England of the mid-seventeenth century, statutes existed that would have punished Claudio's crime with death, though they were never enforced. To Shakespeare's audience such a sentence would have seemed utterly out of proportion to the crime, as it does to other characters in the play, such as Escalus, another judge, and to the provost of the jail, who hopes that Angelo will change Claudio's sentence. (Shakespeare and Anne Hathaway themselves would have been guilty of such a crime.) Applying a law so long out of date is akin to creating an *ex post facto* law, a point made by the most eminent judge of the time, Sir Francis Bacon:

> Specially in cases of Lawes Penall, they [judges] ought to have Care, that that which was meant for Terrour, be not turned into Rigour; and that they bring not upon the People, that Shower whereof the Scripture speaketh: . . . For Penall Lawes Pressed, are a Shower of Snares upon the People. Therefore, *let Penall Lawes, if they have been Sleepers of long, or if they be growne unfit for the present Time, be by Wise Judges confined in the Execution.* . . . Judges ought in Justice to remember Mercy; And to Cast a Severe Eye upon the Example, but a Mercifull Eye upon the Person. (italics added)[5]

Escalus brings up a third issue. If a judge is going to apply such a law, shouldn't he search himself for the same tendencies to err? Ask yourself, Escalus says to Angelo, whether "the working of your own affections," coupled with the opportunity to have your way, might not have caused you to err in the same way that Claudio has. Escalus's argument is taken straight from the Sermon on the Mount, that portion quoted at the beginning of this chapter, and it was applied by many writers to judges. The Puritan William Perkins, in his *Exposition of Christs Sermon in the Mount* (Cambridge, 1608), can be taken as representative:

> Consider how Christ would have all those which are to give judgment of the offences of others to be themselves without reproof or blame; else they are no fit persons to give censure of those that be under them. And therefore the Magistrate in the town and commonwealth . . . and every superior in his place must labour to be unblameable.[6]

Angelo is going to become even more blamable than Claudio, but unlike the duke, Angelo does not know himself at all, and he confidently tells Escalus it is one thing to be tempted and another to fall. Besides, the law is the law, and it must be applied by imperfect men. Still, Angelo acknowledges the correctness of Escalus's argument: if I ever break the law that Claudio broke, he says, "Let mine own judgment pattern out my death, / And nothing come in partial" (2.1.30–31). Angelo, like Shylock, articulates the ground rules for his own judgment, asking for the same measure of punishment, should he have illicit intercourse, as he has measured unto Claudio.

Isabella's argument to Angelo to spare her brother contains the most beautiful poetry in the play and recalls Portia's famous speech about mercy:

> No ceremony that to great ones longs,
> Not the king's crown, nor the deputed sword,
> The marshal's truncheon, nor the judge's robe,
> Become them with one half so good a grace
> As mercy does.

> (2.2.59–63)

Isabella then asks the same question as Escalus: Is Angelo measuring more punishment to Claudio than he would, under the same circumstances, measure to himself? Hasn't Angelo, in his desires, ever been guilty of Claudio's offense? "If he had been as you, and you as he, / You would have slipped like him, but he, like you / Would not have been so stern" (64–67).

Angelo takes no notice of this argument, so Isabella returns to Christian atonement:

> Why, all the souls that were, were forfeit once,
> And He that might the vantage best have took
> Found out the remedy. How would you be
> If He, which is the top of judgment, should
> But judge you as you are? O, think on that,
> And mercy then will breathe within your lips,
> Like man new made.
>
> (2.2.73–79)

Angelo has a reasonable response to Isabella's general argument: By rigorously applying the law, he shows mercy to the future victims of criminals who have not been adequately punished: "I show it [pity] most of all when I show justice; / For then I pity those I do not know, / Which a dismiss'd offense would after gall, / And do him right that, answering one foul wrong, / Lives not to act another" (2.2.101–05). As a general response to a general argument, Angelo's reply is logical; execute murderers so they do not murder again, thieves so they no longer steal. But how does the argument of special deterrence apply to the concrete case of Claudio and Julietta? Who is going to be saved from harm by executing Claudio? Won't such a sentence cause more trouble by leaving the pregnant Julietta and her future child without support? Angelo's argument might be that executing Claudio is a general deterrent rather than a specific one. Unwed mothers and illegitimate children are a drain on the state and a cause of social disorder. The best that could be said of Angelo's application of the law is that it eliminates potential "deadbeat dads" by scaring them away from sex, though whether it will do so in fact, whether any law attempting to regulate sex or passion can actually do so, is effectively questioned earlier by other characters in the play who we will hear from presently.

The contest between justice and mercy, articulated more sharply in *Measure for Measure* than in any other play by Shakespeare, was never resolved by the jurists of Shakespeare's England, and perhaps has not been resolved to this day, despite a judicial apparatus that now includes pre-sentencing reports by social workers and psychologists, the opportunity for victims to speak, and after sentencing, of parole boards to review. Every time someone is let out of prison and commits another crime, Angelo's words speak to us with great force, and lately such sentiments have inspired legislation like California's three strikes law.

Most Renaissance commentators on justice and mercy seem to regard these as absolute values, and although both are praised, Renaissance theologians spent little time examining their potential for conflict. Most theologians went as far as distinguishing private from state judgment, and no further: a Christian ought to privately forgive all wrongs, though as a judge he might have to publicly condemn. Yet, didn't God want mercy to play a part in the judgments of the state as well as those of private individuals?

According to William Perkins, in his *Treatise on Christian Equity and Moderation,* there are two kinds of bad judges, those who overemphasize mercy and those who overemphasize justice.[7] Duke Vincentio would be a good example of the first, Angelo the second.

> [Judges governed by mercy are] such men, as by a
> certain foolish kind of pity are so carried away, that
> would have nothing but *mercy, mercy,* and would . . .
> have the extremity of the law executed on no man.
> This is the high way to abolish laws, and consequently
> to pull down authority, and so in the end to open a
> door to all confusion, disorder, and to all
> licentiousness of life. But I need not say much herein,
> for there are but few that offend in this kind, man's
> nature being generally inclined rather to cruelty than
> to mercy.

Judges governed by justice are the more common.

> [These are] such men as have nothing in their mouths,
> but the *law,* the *law:* and *Justice, Justice:* in the
> meantime forgetting that Justice always shakes hands
> with her sister mercy, and that all laws allow a
> mitigation. . . . These men thereof, strike too precisely
> on their points, and the very tricks and trifles of the
> law, as (so the law be kept, and that in the very
> extremity of it) they care not, though equity were
> trodden under foot: and that law may reign on earth,
> and they by it: they care not, though mercy take her
> to her wings, and fly to heaven. These men (for all
> their goodly shews) are the decayers of our estate,
> and enemies of all good government.

Somehow, these two values have to be integrated.

> [Mercy and Justice] are the two pillars that uphold
> the throne of the Prince: as you cannot hold mercy,
> where Justice is banished, so cannot you keep Justice
> where mercy is exiled: and as mercy without Justice,
> is foolish pity, so Justice, without mercy, is cruelty.

Neither Perkins, nor anyone else, seems to have considered in any deep way just how these two competing but essen-

tial values are to be integrated, and Shakespeare, in the course of *Measure for Measure,* will offer no solution, though he will certainly sharpen the problem and thereby produce a more profound meditation on the topic, perhaps, than anything else written during his lifetime.

The issue of justice versus mercy is held in suspense, however, when judicial corruption enters as a complicating factor, reminding the audience, once again, of Matthew 7:1–5, quoted at the beginning of the chapter. Angelo develops an overwhelming lust for Isabella, whose arguments and "prone and speechless dialect" arouse passions in him that have slept for not only "nineteen zodiacs," but his entire life. Angelo does not know himself. Eros takes him unprepared, and having never experienced such passion, he has no defense against it. Angelo has suffered a surprise attack from a part of himself that he would have liked to believe did not exist. He tries to pray for help but can only think of Isabella, and ironically, her virtue is what has ensnared him. Perhaps Angelo's passion emerges from self-hatred. Isabella may be the sanctuary that Angelo would like to destroy because she represents his starved passion, the moral armor in which he has encased himself:

> Can it be
> That modesty may more betray our sense
> Than woman's lightness? Having waste ground
> enough,
> Shall we desire to raze the sanctuary
> And pitch our evils there? O fie, fie, fie!
> Dost thou desire her foully for those things
> That make her good? . . .
> . . . .
> O cunning enemy, that, to catch a saint,
> With saints dost bait thy hook! Most dangerous
> Is that temptation that doth goad us on

> To sin in loving virtue. Never could the strumpet
> With all her double vigor, art and nature,
> Once stir my temper: but this virtuous maid
> Subdues me quite.

(2.2.168–75; 180–86)

Angelo admits that he now has no moral authority to judge Claudio—since the beam of his lust is so much worse than the mote of Claudio's slip with his fiancée—and Angelo cannot gain control over himself. He tells Isabella that he will free her brother in exchange for a one-night stand. This sin is worse than Claudio's, of course, for Angelo has no intention to marry Isabella, but just wants to slake his lust for her: And Angelo's sin leads to worse consequences: fornication, attempted murder, slander, and perjury.

Escalus: The Pattern of the Good Judge

In the second act of *Measure for Measure*, Shakespeare introduces Escalus as a pattern of the good judge. Escalus displays the qualities of patience, attention, efficiency, moderation, and self-knowledge that Angelo lacks. His very name implies his function in the play, suggesting "scale"—both in the sense of "scales of justice" and "a just balance"—which implies that he knows the proper relationship between justice and mercy. This makes him not only a foil for Angelo, but as we will see, the duke as well. Escalus, unlike Angelo, realizes that not all crimes are equally pernicious, and that punishment should be scaled to the severity of the crime. Escalus's ability and Angelo's inability to see gradations are contrasted in the first lines of act 2, scene 1, as Escalus argues that Claudio's punishment should be reduced:

Angelo: We must not make a scarecrow of the law,
            Setting it up to fear the birds of prey,

> And let it keep one shape till custom make it
> Their perch and not their terror.

Escalus: Ay, but yet
> Let us be keen, and rather cut a little,
> Then fall, and bruise to death.

(2.1.1–6)

Angelo is unable to see that deterrence may be accomplished by a lesser response than the imposition of utter terror. And one of the psychological reasons for Angelo's inability to understand what constitutes the appropriate punishment stems from a lack of self-knowledge, for he tells Escalus that if he offended as Claudio has, he would have the same punishment meted to himself. Ironically, Escalus contrasts Claudio's actual slip with a potential for sin that Angelo is about to discover in himself:

> Well, heaven forgive him [Claudio]; and forgive us all.
> Some rise by sin, and some by virtue fall:
> Some run from breaks of ice and answer none,
> And some condemned for a fault alone.

(2.1.37–40)

In the trial of Pompey Bum (a pimp) and Froth (a potential customer), which occupies the central portion of this scene, Escalus demonstrates his superiority to Angelo as a judge. Here, Shakespeare presents a mimetic re-creation of a rather mundane trial. Escalus and Angelo are forced to confront obstacles to judgment that can be observed in any present-day small claims court: witnesses who cannot or will not communicate, or who are biased and unreliable; the continual assertion of hearsay and rumor as fact; and the simple boredom on the part of judges that can lead to bad results.

In "Of Judicature," Bacon emphasizes the ethical necessity for a judge to be a patient and perceptive listener:

> Patience and Gravitie of Hearing, is an Essentiall
> Part of Justice; And an Over-speaking *Judge* is no
> *well tuned Cymball*. It is no Grace to a Judge, first to
> finde that, which hee might have heard, in due time,
> from the Barre; or to shew Quicknesse of Conceit in
> cutting off Evidence or Counsell too short; Or to
> prevent Information, by Questions though Pertinent.
> The Parts of a *Judge* in Hearing are Foure: To direct
> the Evidence; To Moderate Length, Repetition, or
> Impertinency of Speech; To Recapitulate, Select, and
> Collate, the Materiall Points of that, which hath beene
> said; And to give the Rule of Sentence. Whatever is
> above these, is too much; And proceedeth, Either of
> Glory and willingnesse to Speake, Or of Impatience
> to Heare; Or of Shortnesse of Memories; Or of Want
> to a Staid and Equall Attention.[8]

By Bacon's criteria, Angelo is a failure as a judge. His
response to the verbal meandering of Shakespeare's typically
dim-witted constable, Elbow, is to lose patience before the
case has even begun. Like Constable Dogberry in *Much Ado
about Nothing*, Elbow is a prolific generator of malapropisms.
Angelo begins with impatience: "How now sir! What's your
name? And what's the matter?" (2.1.45). When Elbow accuses
the defendants—who have apparently mistaken his wife for a
prostitute—he tells Angelo they are two of the most notorious
"benefactors" in the community. At this point, Angelo goes
from confusion to pettish irascibility: "Benefactors? Well, what
benefactors are they? / Are they not malefactors?" (2.1.51–
52). This small exchange demonstrates that Angelo has little
understanding of the people whom he is to govern, or their
language, and that he is so thoroughly lacking in a sense of

humor that, indeed, he is unbalanced. Everything is deadly
earnest to Angelo, his approach inflexible. Lacking patience
and understanding, Angelo is able to accomplish little as a
judge. Because he has placed himself so far above people like
Elbow, he is unable to communicate with them, therefore finding it impossible to "direct the Evidence: To Moderate Length,
Repetition, or Impertinency of Speech."

In contrast, Escalus's dry comment, "This comes off well,
here's a wise officer," indicates that he can distance himself
from the courtroom activity and achieve the more detached,
even "playful" perspective of a theatergoer. Escalus appreciates the humor in Elbow and his case. His later line to Angelo,
in reference to Elbow's language, "Do you hear how he mis-
places?" is a gentle lesson in patience to Angelo.

The trial, a blizzard of malapropisms, continues in a
Groucho Marx vein with essentially no progress. Angelo is
unable to determine even the nature of the charges. Finally
he loses patience entirely and simply abdicates as judge, demonstrating his "impatience to Heare," and "Want of a Staid
and Equall Attention." He leaves Escalus to do the judicial
donkey work, saying:

> This will last out a night in Russia
> When nights are longest there. I'll take my leave,
> And leave you to the hearing of the cause;
> Hoping you'll find good cause to whip them all.

> (2.1.133–36)

This lack of judicial self-restraint is typical of Angelo, and it
parallels his unrestrained punishment of even minor criminals and his fear of "liberty." Angelo projects his own internal
struggle against desire onto the body politic of Vienna. But
Escalus, who can exercise self-restraint, does not find cause

"to whip them all." His speedy resolution of the case, once Angelo is gone, hints that Escalus has reservations about Angelo's ability as a judge—and that he, perhaps, is happy to have let the case drag on until Angelo left so that he himself could make the final decision.

Knowing he will get little if any reliable testimony, either from Elbow or the defendants, Escalus refers to the only objective evidence he has: Froth's face. As Pompey proclaims, "I'll be supposed [deposed] upon a book, his face is the worst / thing about him.—Good, then: if his face be the / worst thing about him, how could Master Froth do / the constable's wife any harm?" (2.1.153–56). This may seem a slim basis for judgment, but Elbow, as prosecutor, certainly has not proven his case, and the presumption of innocence holds. Froth and Pompey are released with warnings. "Master Froth, I would not have you acquainted with tapsters; they will draw you Master Froth" (201–02).

The trial of Pompey and Froth is one of Shakespeare's best scenes of low comedy and puts the difficulty of controlling sexual passion through law, and the possibility of Angelo's fall (which has not yet occurred), squarely before the audience. When Escalus lets Pompey and Froth go, he warns Pompey that prostitution is now illegal in Vienna, and they have this exchange:

Pompey:	Does your worship mean to geld and splay all the youth of the city?
Escalus:	No, Pompey.
Pompey:	Truly sir, in my poor opinion, they will to't then. If your worship will take order for the drabs and the knaves, you need not fear the bawds.
Escalus:	There is pretty orders beginning, I can tell you. It is but heading and hanging.

Pompey: If you head and hang all that offend that way but
            for ten year together, you'll be glad to give out a
            commission for more heads: if this law hold in
            Vienna ten year, I'll rent the fairest house in it
            After three pence a bay.

                                              (2.1.227–39)

Though Pompey's predictions of the depopulation of Vienna
and its ensuing economic collapse may seem comically exag-
gerated, the fall of Angelo, coming hard on the heels of this
prophecy, confirms Pompey's down to earth understanding of
human nature.

   After Escalus decides the case, the scene continues to
more firmly establish him as an exemplar of the good judge.
Realizing Elbow's incompetence as a constable, Escalus seeks
to replace him. However, Escalus does this in a way that demonstrates his respect, kindness, and psychological acuity. He
stresses Elbow's length of service by making an intentional
mistake that elicits a comment from Elbow himself about how
long he has served. Then Escalus stresses the frustrations of
being a constable and puts himself on Elbow's side, making
his replacement seem like a favor:

Escalus: Come hither to me, Master Elbow: come hither,
            Master constable; How long have you been in this
            place of constable?
Elbow: Seven year and a half, sir.
Escalus: I thought, by the readiness in the office, you had
            continued in it some time.—You say, seven years
            together?
Elbow: And a half, sir
Escalus: Alas, it hath been great pains to you: they do you
            wrong to put you so oft upon't. Are there not men
            in your ward sufficient to serve it?

                                              (2.1.254–64)

The scene concludes with a demonstration of Escalus's commitment to his job. Elbow is to bring him the names of six or seven of the "most sufficient men" of his parish so that Escalus can choose a better constable. Elbow is to bring the list to Escalus's house after dinner. (During the Tudor and Jacobean periods, courts met only in the morning.) Escalus, in other words, is a judge who is willing to do homework, and who cares enough about what he is doing to put himself out. As he exits, he is still pondering the problem of Claudio and the difficulty of balancing justice and mercy: "Mercy is not itself, that oft looks so; / Pardon is still the nurse of second woe. / But yet,—poor Claudio" (2.1.280–82).

Escalus continues to display a rational approach to sentencing in act 3, scene 2, where he is depicted in the process of sending Mistress Overdone to prison for prostitution. Where, in the judgment of Pompey and Froth, Escalus demonstrated that he knew the limits of severity, in his judgment of Overdone he demonstrates his understanding of the limits of mercy. Despite Mistress Overdone's reminder to Escalus that he has a reputation as a merciful man, in her case Escalus clearly realizes that mercy is not the solution: "Double and treble admonition, and still forfeit in / the same kind! This would make mercy swear and / play the tyrant" (187–89).

There is clearly nothing to be gained by extending mercy to "a bawd of eleven years' continuance." Escalus must respond with some kind of punishment. But, neither is there any indication that Mistress Overdone will be executed; Escalus merely says, "Go, away with her to prison." Upon hearing that one of Overdone's prostitutes, Kate Keepdown, has had a child by Lucio, and that Lucio had promised to marry her, Escalus orders Lucio to be called before him. Lucio has committed the same crime as Claudio, except that Lucio's is worse, for unlike Claudio he has no intention of marrying the mother of his child. Again, there is no indication that Escalus intends to punish this crime with death, and Escalus notes that he would save Claudio if Angelo did not stand in the way. Thus, when dealing with sexual offenders, Escalus tries to walk a middle path between extreme severity and extreme leniency, meting out punishments that seem appropriate to the crime, and then only after admonition has failed.

By the end of act 2, extreme examples of good and bad judges have been presented to the audience, and Vienna has been established as a realm of antithesis, where being and seeming do not coincide, justice and mercy are placed in opposition, and the rituals that support government and adjudication are ignored or abused. Escalus, although hindered by Angelo's severity and saddled with problems resulting from the duke's leniency, is working methodically and unobtrusively to establish a solid system of criminal justice in Vienna. But Escalus's lack of display can be seen as both a strength and a weakness. It is a strength because Escalus is more interested in making the right decision than in using his judgeship to gain a name, which is what Claudio accuses Angelo of doing. It is a weakness, by Renaissance standards, because hidden virtue has little ability to inspire. The laws not only need to be administered fairly, but that fairness must be seen, and there are few witnesses to the trials of Pompey, Froth, or Mistress Overdone. As Hermione notes in *A Winter's Tale*, "One good deed dying tongueless slaughters a thousand waiting upon that." The good deeds of judges must be perceived and celebrated so that more good judgments will follow.

Juggling Heads and Beds: The Duke's Extraordinary Powers and Improvisational Comedy

The duke, absent from the play since act 1, scene 3, returns as both an actor and playmaker in act 3, scene 1, where we see him in jail disguised as a friar and performing friarly offices as he helps to ready Claudio for execution. In having his duke adopt the disguise of a friar, Shakespeare is neither advocating sacrilegious fraud nor inviting condemnation of the duke as such. Rather, Vincentio's disguise emblematizes the relation of earthly authority to God. As critic William Lawrence explains, "The Duke . . . combines the functions both of State and Church in his person. As Duke, he is supreme ruler of Vienna, who returns at the end to straighten out the tangles of the action and dispense justice to all. In his disguise as Friar, he represents the wisdom and adroitness of the Church, in directing courses of action and advising stratagems so that good may come out of evil."[9]

A duke, a king, or any ruler was considered by the people of Renaissance England to be an image of God, though, of course, not divine. Rulers are called gods in Psalm 82: 6–7, though they are men: "I have said, Ye are gods, and ye all are children of the most High. / But ye shall die as a man, & ye princes, shall fall like others." Princes act as God's deputies, "Ruling, Judging, and Punishing in God's stead, and so deserving God's name here on earth," according to Thomas Bilson in *A Sermon Preached at Westminister before the King and Queenes Majesties, at their Coronations* (1603).[10] In *Magistrates Scripture* (1590), Henry Smith says that the prince is "like a great Image of God, the magistrates like little Images of God," appointed to "rule as he would rule, judge as he would judge, correct as he would correct, reward as he would reward."[11] In *Measure for Measure*, the duke sees everything, hears everything, manages everything, moving like Providence through the state and the lives of the other characters, a fact that Angelo recognizes in the final moments of the play when he tells Vincentio, "I perceive your Grace, like power divine, / Hath looked upon my passes" (5.1.367–68).

Vincentio has been criticized for his deceptiveness, and he certainly is deceptive, as we will see. But the way the duke uses his power throughout the play must be understood within the Renaissance theory that rulers were God's substitutes, and hence had a great deal of leeway in their methods. In this capacity, rulers had four privileges, as explained by Marie Elizabeth Pope in "The Renaissance Background of *Measure for Measure.*"[12] The first was "sanctity of person," which meant that the anointed prince could neither be physically attacked nor verbally abused. (This must be kept in mind when evaluating the duke's treatment of Lucio, later in the play.) The second was that the prince had "sovereignty of power." All men had to obey him except with regard to commands that "directly contradicted God's ordinances." The third privilege was the right to enforce the law. The fourth privilege will be of particular concern to us throughout the rest of the play:

> Finally, the ruler has the privilege of using extraordinary means. . . . [though] this certainly does not imply that he is entitled to deceive, betray and commit perjury in the manner recommended by Machiavelli, but only, in the words of William Willymat, that
>
>> Kings, Princes, and governors do oftentimes to use diverse causes to disguise their purposes with pretences and colours of other matters, so that the end of their drifts and secret purposes are not right seen into nor understood at the first, this to be lawful the word of God doth not deny.
>
> He then cites the examples of Solomon ordering the child divided; Jehu pretending he would serve Baal, when by the subtlety he really intended to destroy the servants of Baal (II Kings x); and the Emperor Constantius threatening to persecute the

> Christians when all he actually meant to do was by
> this stratagem to separate the sheep from the goats.[13]

Vincentio partly deceives Angelo about why he appoints him deputy and with regard to where he is going. He also disguises himself as a friar. And this is just the beginning. But his use of cunning is legitimate.

At the beginning of act 3, when we see "Friar" Vincentio with Claudio, he is acting as religious advisor and prince, seeing that the law is justly executed, for it is part of justice that condemned men be given the chance to ready their souls for the coming judgment of God. Claudio must be brought to the proper state of contrition for his sins before he can die well, and it is a matter of state concern that he have the proper opportunity and religious counseling to ready himself. Thus, the state's right and duty to execute criminals must wait upon the church's duty (as we shall see most obviously in the coming case of Barnardine) to minister to the soul. The duke-friar, understanding Claudio's fear of death, advises Claudio to quit clinging to life so that he is prepared to face God in the afterlife. He does this not through biblical arguments, but through philosophical arguments, easily derived from the Stoics and Epicureans but put to use for Christian purposes, advocating a renunciation of the world that leads to spiritual freedom:

> Be absolute for death: either death or life
> Shall thereby be the sweeter. Reason thus with life:
> If I do lose thee, I do lose a thing
> That none but fools would keep. A breath thou art,
> Servile to all the skyey influences
> That dost this habitation where thou keep'st
> Hourly afflict. Merely, thou art Death's fool;
> For him thou labour'st by thy flight to shun,
> And yet run'st toward him still. . . .

> . . . If thou art rich, thou'rt poor;
> For, like an ass whose back with ingots bows,
> Thou beart'st thy heavy riches but a journey,
> And Death unloads thee. Friend hast thou none;
> For thine own bowels which do call thee sire,
> The mere effusion of thy proper loins,
> Do curse the gout, serpigo, and the rheum
> For ending thee no sooner. . . .

(3.1.5–32)

Reminiscent of Hamlet's "To be or not to be" soliloquy, this speech is such a *tour de force* that we are convinced of Claudio's sincerity and steadfastness when he says, "I humbly thank you. / To sue to live, I find I seek to die, / And seeking death, find life. Let it come on" (3.1.42–44). However, after the duke leaves and Isabella enters, Claudio displays an all-too-human collapse of resolve when he finds out Isabella has a chance to save him. The duke, hidden, overhears their conversation. When Isabella inquires as to whether Claudio is ready to die, her brother first responds heroically, "I will encounter darkness as a bride, / And hug it in mine arms" (3.1.83–84). This pleases Isabella, who praises her brother: "There spake my brother: there my father's grave / Did utter forth a voice." When Isabella discloses that she might save his life by giving herself to Angelo, Claudio, carried by the momentum of his sister's expectations and the duke's counsel, says, "Thou shalt not do't." But as the possibility of saving his life becomes more real, he tells Isabella, "Sure, it is no sin; / Or of the deadly seven it is the least" (109–10). Then, overcome by his fear of death and hell, he begs her to save his life:

> . . . to die, and go we not know where;
> To lie in cold obstruction, and to rot;
> This sensible warm motion to become
> A kneaded clod; and the delighted spirit

> To bath in fiery floods, or to reside
> In thrilling region of thick-ribbed ice;
> To be imprison'd in the viewless winds
> And blown with restless violence round about
> The pendent world: or to be worse than worst
> Of those that lawless and incertain thought
> Imagine howling,—'tis too horrible.
> The weariest and most loathed worldly life
> That age, ache, penury and imprisonment
> Can lay on nature, is a paradise
> To what we fear of death.

(3.1.117–31)

In this passage, Claudio appropriately associates himself and Julietta with Dante's Paolo and Francesca, who in *The Inferno* are blown about the uppermost region of hell by the winds of passion. Claudio's new hope to live undermines the friar-duke's work in bringing Claudio to a true state of contrition, governed by sorrow for his sins rather than terror at their consequences (which would constitute "attrition," a less effective act of repentance). Out of this terror, Claudio begs Isabella to save him:

> Sweet sister, let me live.
> What sin you do to save a brother's life,
> Nature dispenses with the deed so far
> That it becomes a virtue.

(3.1.132–35)

Necessity, Shakespeare suggests, is the mother of virtue. If you know death is inescapable, you can afford to be brave, but how many people would not make an ignoble request, beg fathers, mothers, sisters, or brothers to degrade themselves, if by doing so they could save their lives? Claudio is a man in most urgent need of grace.

At this point, Isabel could confront her brother's weakness with charity and truly minister to him. She could refuse to grant his request, but still try to comfort him: that would be a manifestation of love appropriate to a Christian novitiate of the Clares. Instead, she displays the vindictiveness of an Angelo, questioning her brother's paternity and virtually consigning him, in his state of despair, to hell:

> O, you beast!
> O faithless coward! O dishonest wretch!
> Wilt thou be made a man out of my vice?
> Is't not a kind of incest, to take life
> From thine own sister's shame? What should I think?
> Heaven shield my mother play'd my father fair:
> For such a warped slip of wilderness
> Ne'er issued from his blood. Take my defiance,
> Die, perish! Might but my bending down
> Reprieve thee from thy fate, it should proceed.
> I'll pray a thousand prayers for thy death;
> No word to save thee. . . .
> Thy sin's not accidental, but a trade;
> Mercy to thee would prove itself a bawd;
> 'Tis best that thou diest quickly.

(3.1.135–46; 148–50)

Isabella can argue the theory of mercy to Angelo chapter and verse, but when it comes time to actually put mercy into action, she out-Angelos Angelo. The duke steps in at this point to repair the damage to Claudio and to calm Isabella. He puts into action all of the trickery that his position as prince allows and all the plot machinery that will govern the rest of the play.

First he arranges the "bed trick." We learn that a woman named Mariana, formerly betrothed to Angelo, had been cast off by him when she lost her brother and her dowry in a shipwreck. Isabella is to meet with Angelo and agree to have sex with him, but in the lightless room where they meet, Mariana will actually take Isabella's place, and the sexual congress between Mariana and Angelo will result in legally binding marriage, which later will only have to be formalized. This, the duke says, will redress Angelo's callousness toward Mariana, who still loves him.

After Mariana and Isabel accomplish the bed trick, the duke fully expects Angelo to pardon Claudio, as promised. But once Angelo has had "Isabella," he is afraid his corruption will be exposed if Claudio lives, and Angelo issues an order for Claudio's swift beheading. This stuns Vincentio. He could confront Angelo at this point, but he wants to turn the tables on him publicly. So he decides to fake Claudio's death just as he has faked Isabella's intercourse with Angelo. Unfortunately, Angelo has commanded that Claudio's head be brought to him so that he can confirm the execution. How to come up with another head, and one sufficiently like Claudio's? The duke asks the provost if anyone else is up for execution and learns that a murderer named Barnardine has long been scheduled.

Barnardine, unfortunately, *refuses* to be executed. Like an actor refusing to deliver his lines, Barnardine refuses to play the part of executee, either in jail or on the scaffold. In a bit of Monty Pythonesque humor, he refuses to prepare his soul for death, and thus perpetually stays himself from execution. The provost describes Barnardine as "A man that apprehends death no more dreadfully / but as a drunken sleep; careless, reckless, and fear / less of what's past, present, or to come: insensible of / mortality, and desperately mortal" (4.2.140–43). Barnardine stays too drunk to repent, and therefore too drunk to execute.

When the duke tries to shrive Barnardine, he will have none of it. Barnardine says that the jailers can beat out his brains with billets, but he will not consent to die, and the duke reluctantly concludes that Barnardine cannot be executed: "Unfit to live or die! O gravel heart. / . . . to transport him in the mind he is / Were damnable" (4.3.63; 67–68). Barnardine, apparently, will live as long as his liquor supply-lines are open. No wonder the duke concludes, "He needs instruction." On stage, the way Barnardine's stubborn depravity defeats the overly scrupulous duke can be very funny.[14] (One cannot imagine an execution being held up in perpetuity for such reasons under the reign of Queen Elizabeth; however, under James I, it is almost believable that such a scene could occur and that Shakespeare would exploit its potential for humor, as we will see in the final section of this chapter.)

As the duke's plot is about to fall apart, the provost conveniently informs him that a prisoner named Ragozine, of Claudio's age—his beard and head of Claudio's color—has died of a fever. Death, the duke says, is a great disguiser. Ragozine's head goes to Angelo, Barnardine and Claudio are put in storage for later use, and the duke prepares for his "return" to Vienna.

The Theatricality of Trial and Execution in England, 1603

In order to fully understand the trials that Vincentio is about to stage in act 5, we must become familiar with the political use of trial, pardon, and execution at the time of Shakespeare's writing. Few events could serve this purpose better than the treason trials of Sir Walter Raleigh, Sir Griffin Markham, Lord Grey, and Lord Cobham, which occurred in late 1603 and may have inspired *Measure for Measure*, at least in part. Certainly these trials (and the pardons of the defendants, who were all convicted) are reminiscent of many of the play's episodes.

When *Measure for Measure* was first performed, perhaps in the summer of 1604, or perhaps for the king on St. Stephen's

Day, 1604, the memory of Sir Walter Raleigh's spectacular trial and the trials and dramatic last-minute pardons of Markham, Grey, and Cobham would have been quite fresh.[15] Given the importance of judgment and pardon in act 5 of *Measure for Measure,* and the propensity Shakespeare's audiences had for giving his plays topical interpretations,[16] it would have been unusual if the events of the preceding fall did not influence the audience's response. Considering, in addition, the massive sale of James's *Basilikon Doron,* which takes the administration of justice as a central theme, the uneasy curiosity of the English about their new king's attitude toward the English common law, and James's active role in "staging" the pardons of Cobham, Markham, and Grey, *Measure for Measure* could have provided a fictional nexus that allowed audiences to interrogate and interpret these recent judicial events in a variety of ways.

Raleigh, Markham, Grey, and Cobham were arrested for treason in late 1603, not long after James's coronation. Raleigh was accused of using Cobham to get 600,000 crowns from the archduke of Austria to be used for fomenting rebellion, killing the king and "his cubs," putting Arabella Stuart on the throne, and bringing about peace with Spain and tolerance of the Catholic religion. Raleigh's indictment specified his involvement in "the Main Plot," which was connected with a second plot, the "Bye Plot." Though Raleigh was not accused of involvement in the "Bye Plot," it influenced his trial. The chief conspirators in the "Bye Plot" were two Catholic priests, Clerke and Watson; Griffin Markham, George Brooke, the brother of Lord Cobham; and Anthony Copley. (Rather optimistically, the Bye-Plotters had planned to seize the king and talk him into a policy of tolerance toward Catholics.)

At the time of his arrest, Raleigh was not a popular man. Many thought he was an atheist, and his pride had never en-

deared him to courtiers or the common people.[17] Raleigh had
openly gloated over Essex's downfall, and, as Robert Lacey
notes, "the ordinary people of London were delighted to see
him threatened with the same fate to which they believed he
had driven Essex."[18] When Raleigh was tried on November
17, 1603, the theaters had been closed for several months due
to a plague that was killing approximately two thousand Lon-
doners per week. Still, great crowds turned out to jeer him on
his way from the Tower of London to Winchester. Sir William
Waad, who was charged with getting Raleigh to Winchester
alive, testified, "It was had or nab whether Sir Walter Raleigh
should have been brought alive through such multitudes of
unruly people as did exclaim again him. He that had seen it
would not think there had been any sickness in London."[19]
Raleigh's defense did not gain him an acquittal (a virtual impossibility in treason trials), but it did swing public opinion
violently in his favor. Although the jury deliberated for only a
quarter of an hour before finding him guilty, the London public judged otherwise.

In his trial, Raleigh took the part of a single man, courageously standing against judges and prosecutors determined
to find him guilty from the start, enlisting the jury's aid "not-
withstanding any violent impression of power and authority to
the contrary." Sir Edward Coke, one of the most brutal and
unscrupulous prosecutors in English legal history, was at his
most vitriolic, and provided an excellent foil for Raleigh.

Virtually the only evidence against Raleigh was the examination of Lord Cobham, wherein Cobham had accused
Raleigh of participation in the Main Plot. Cobham himself
had retracted and then reasserted this accusation several times.
When the examination was read in court, Raleigh asked to
see it (a request that was routinely denied to criminal defendants, including Raleigh) and again took the opportunity to

enlist the jury's aid: "Let me see the Accusation: This is absolutely all the Evidence can be brought against me; poor shifts! You Gentlemen of the jury, I pray you understand this. This is that which must either condemn, or give me life; which must free me, or send my wife and children to Beg their bread about the streets."[20]

Developments in the trial magnified the impression of unfair treatment Raleigh wanted to convey to the jury. He was denied (again, typically) the right to cross-examine the witnesses against him, which was particularly damaging in application to Cobham. And Coke became so offensive that he was even upbraided by Robert Cecil, one of the judges.[21]

Near the end of the trial, Raleigh produced a surprise worthy of any fictional lawyer: a letter from Cobham in which Cobham had yet again retracted his charges against Raleigh. Raleigh gave it to Cecil to authenticate and read, both because Cecil was familiar with Cobham's handwriting and, undoubtedly, because Raleigh wanted to place in the jurors' minds the image of Lord Cecil testifying on his behalf. The letter reads:

> Seeing myself so near my end, for the discharge of my own conscience, and freeing myself from your blood, which else will cry vengeance against me; I protest upon my salvation I never practiced with Spain by your procurement; God so comfort me in this my affliction, as you are a true subject, for any thing that I know. I will say as Daniel, Purus sum à sanguine hujus. So God have mercy upon my soul, as I know no Treason by you.[22]

The letter should have resulted in an acquittal, since it definitively established that Cobham was an utterly unreliable witness either for or against Raleigh; instead, the jury returned a verdict of guilty. Raleigh maintained his composure through the reading of the standard sentence for traitors and felons:

> Since you have been found guilty of these horrible Treasons, the judgment of this court is, That you shall be had from hence to the place whence you came, there to remain until the day of execution; and from thence you shall be drawn upon a hurdle through the open streets to the place of execution, there to be hanged and cut down alive, and your body shall be opened, your heart and bowels plucked out, and your privy members cut off, and thrown into the fire before your eyes; then your head to be stricken off from your body, and your body shall be divided into four quarters, to be disposed of at the king's pleasure: and God have mercy on your soul.[23]

Although convicted, Raleigh became, in one day, "a symbol of the innocent man abused by harsh, unjust laws and wicked, time-serving men."[24] Greenblatt quotes one of the spectators at the trial, Dudley Carleton, on the magnificence of Raleigh's performance:

> Sir Walter Raleigh served for a whole act, and played all the parts himself. . . . He answered with that temper, wit, learning, courage, and judgment, that, save it went with the hazard of his life, it was the happiest day that ever he spent. And so well he shifted all advantages that were taken against him, that were not . . . an ill name half hanged, in the opinion of all men, he had been acquitted.[25]

Raleigh's alleged accomplices, Cobham, Markham, and Grey, were convicted of treason in separate trials. At this point the new king, James I, steps (like Duke Vincentio) into the picture as actor, director, and playwright. The reversal of public opinion in Raleigh's favor apparently took James by surprise. Rather than eliminating an ambitious, dissatisfied, and potentially dangerous courtier from Elizabeth's regime, he had created a public hero. Most of the Privy Council interceded on Raleigh's behalf. Raleigh's wife begged for the life of her husband. The queen interceded for Raleigh. And Raleigh, in a manner that some historians have found pathetic, pleaded for mercy.[26] In response the king ordered the bishop of Winchester to attend Raleigh and "to prepare him for death."[27]

The adverse reaction to Raleigh's conviction was exacerbated by public dis-ease over the executions of several other plotters. Watson and Clerke, the priests involved in the "Bye-Plot," were executed in early December at Winchester, and the ever-present Dudley Carleton noted that both Watson and Clerke were cut down while alive, and the sentence for treason carried out in all its horrid precision. One observer noted that this was done "to the great discontent of the people who now think that matters were not so heinous as were made show of."[28] George Brooke went to execution on December 6. "The executioner held up Brooke's severed head and cried 'God save the king!'" But the cry was not seconded, Carleton notes, "by the voice of any one man but the sheriff."[29]

Cobham, Markham, and Grey were to be executed on December 10 and Raleigh on December 13, 1603. In a letter to Henry IV dated December 8, the resident French Ambassador de Beaumont describes James's apparent irresolution about whether to extend pardons to the remaining conspirators. "The lords of the council joined in opinion and advice to the king, now in the beginning of his reign, to show as well examples of mercy as severity, and to gain the title of *Clemens* as well as *Justus*."[30] James appeared to be unmoved, but this, apparently, was a bit of acting, for by December 7, James had

formulated what Edward Edwards describes as "a comedy, of
which the principal scenes were to be enacted upon the scaffold at Winchester, whilst a by-scene or two were intended to
enliven the Court itself at Wilton."[31]

Though James pretended to be perplexed about whether
he should extend mercy, he had already decided to pardon
Markham, Cobham, and Grey. James appeared to be balancing the interests of justice and mercy, that apparent dichotomy
which is the thematic core of *Measure for Measure*. He had
taken pains to assign each of the condemned men a priest to
help prepare him for death, and these priests regularly re-
ported to James on the spiritual progress of their charges. By
December 8, however, James was merely feigning confusion.
For on the previous day he had already made the decision to
pardon Markham, Cobham, and Grey, but had told no one.
According to Beaumont, in a letter dated December 8:

> The King has been occupied for some days past, in
> hearing and considering the indictments and trials;
> having ordered, for the satisfaction of his conscience,
> that the whole should be reported to him, point by
> point, to the end that he might fully inform himself
> of the matter. The motives to mercy, and the reasons
> which urge a strict execution of law, have kept him
> long in perplexity. [Despite this, however] the King
> has now resolved that they shall all die; and has
> signed the needful warrants.[32]

The divines assigned to the prisoners were instructed to
tell them that pardons would not be granted. On the day before George Brooke's execution, Patrick Galloway, one of the
Scottish chaplains who had accompanied the king to England,
apparently sensing what he thought was the royal mood,
preached a sermon before the court in which clemency to traitors was described as sinful. The king rejected petitions of

mercy, telling his councilors they would have done better to plead for the due course of law. Yet on December 7, James had drawn a warrant, addressed to the sheriff of Hampshire, for the stay of the executions. He told no one about the warrant, and on the following day he signed the death warrants for Cobham, Markham, and Grey, sending them to the sheriff later that night. The executions were to take place on Friday the 10th. On December 9, James confided his secret to a Scottish page, John Gibb. Everyone else was taken in: Beaumont, the Privy Council, James's chaplains, the public, the prisoners, and the prisoners' families.

On the day of the executions there was a large crowd, and Raleigh, whose window commanded a view of the scaffold, could see everything. Markham was to be the first to die, Grey second, and Cobham last. But Markham was not ready to die; his preparation had been interrupted when friends at court had raised his hopes of a pardon; "When he reached the scaffold, he complained that he had been deluded with hopes, and brought to his fate unprepared. . . . [H]e took sorrowful leave of his friends and lookers-on; knelt down in prayer; and had just made himself ready for the execution, when a commotion was observed in the crowd."[33]

The commotion was the king's messenger, fighting his way through the crush, barely in time to stop the ax from falling. James had planned for a dramatic last-second entry by the messenger, but, by accident, the messenger had been delayed and very nearly arrived too late. After speaking with the messenger, the sheriff turned toward Markham: "You say you are ill prepared to die; you shall have two hours respite."

Markham was led from the scaffold and locked in a great hall, known locally as Arthur's Hall. Next, Grey was brought from his chamber to the scaffold, knowing nothing of what had passed. He addressed the crowd, made a long prayer, prepared to die, and was interrupted by the sheriff. The king, he was told, had decided to change the order of execution. Cobham was to die before Grey. A bewildered Grey was also led from the scaffold to Arthur's Hall. Dudley Carleton commented, "His going away seemed more strange unto him than his coming thither; for he had no more hope given him than an hour's respite. Neither could any man yet dive into the mysteries of this strange proceeding."[34]

Finally, Cobham was brought from his chamber; he reached the scaffold, likewise said a prayer and took leave of the crowd, and likewise was balked by the sheriff, who informed him that something yet was to be done. Markham and Grey, who were, as far as Cobham knew, dead, were brought from Arthur's Hall onto the scaffold and were read a speech, apparently drafted by James, consisting entirely of questions: "'Are not your offences heinous? Have you not been justly tried, and lawfully condemned? Is not each of you subject to due execution, now to be performed?' Each of them, it is said, confessed that it was so. 'Then,' continued Tichborne [the sheriff] 'see the mercy of your Prince, who of himself hath sent hither a countermand, and hath given you your lives!'"[35]

Dudley Carleton writes, "There was no need to beg a *plaudite* from the audience for it was given with such hues and cries, that it went down from the castle and into the town and there began afresh."[36] Thus, the theatricality of Raleigh's sensational treason trial was rivaled by James's production on the scaffold at Winchester. After the commutation of their executions, Markham, Grey, and Cobham were shortly pardoned. This proved to be extremely popular; Raleigh's execution was delayed indefinitely, with the possibility that the stay would bloom into a full pardon.

The similarity of these events to some of the scenes we have examined in *Measure for Measure* may have already struck the reader. As James, head of the English Church and sovereign, had sent churchmen to prepare the plotters for death, and had read their reports and kept daily track of the "spiritual progress" of the condemned men, so Shakespeare's duke, as Friar Lodowick, prepares Claudio for death and keeps track of his progress toward contrition. As Markham's preparation had been interrupted when friends at court had raised his hopes of a pardon, so Claudio's preparation for death is interrupted by hope that Isabella can buy his pardon. Once Claudio finds that Isabella will not save him by giving herself to Angelo, and his hopes for life, like Markham's, are consequently shattered, it becomes possible for him to make an act of contrition; and, like Markham, Claudio gets a respite to prepare himself. But these preliminary correspondences would scarcely be worth mentioning were it not for the strong continuance of this pattern in the last act.

The Theatricality of Trial and Execution in Duke Vincentio's Vienna

It remains for the duke, in act 5, to bring synthesis and harmony out of chaos by creating a ritual of justice. He needs to make an effective statement to the people of Vienna that his own authority will be reaffirmed, vice discovered and rejected, virtue revealed and glorified, status assigned according to dessert, and the ship of state set on a new course. Vincentio attempts to accomplish this through a highly dramatic trial—a comic crucible out of which the new society of Vienna is to be formed. The public morality play that he produces during the final scene of *Measure for Measure* powerfully emphasizes the ritual aspect of criminal trial and demonstrates Vincentio's determination to "stage himself to the people's eyes" and take the reins of government more firmly in hand. Occurring within the context of another ceremonial occasion—the "return" of the duke as ruler—the trial provides a framework for revelation, judgment, intercession, and, finally, forgiveness.

The success of Vincentio's trial depends largely on Isabella. For her own sake, and for the duke to make his point to the body politic, Isabella has to extend forgiveness to Angelo. She must do this because forgiveness has played no real part in her life. She is a Christian in theory, but in fact she is as rule bound as a New Testament pharisee. She needs to learn to forgive, and Vienna must see her act of forgiveness so that the value of mercy—within a justice system that enforces the law—may be affirmed. Isabella's act of forgiveness can only display exceptional virtue if she truly believes Claudio to be dead. Thus, for Vincentio's production to succeed, he must lie to Isabella about her brother's death and perpetuate the lie even after Angelo's confession until the time for Isabella's apotheosis has come. The revelation and glorification of unfeigned virtue, in the character of Isabella, is as important to the health of the body politic as the revelation and punishment of Angelo's vice. Isabella's request that Angelo be pardoned must rise so far above self-interest and the human desire for revenge that it leaves the Viennese stunned.

The final act begins with the duke entering Vienna, and for the first time in the play "staging himself to the people's eyes," mingling with them to create "an example of humanity and munificence."[37] The highly choreographed welcome given to him on his return, with leading citizens meeting him at the city gate, trumpeters sounding his entrance, and a procession through the streets, is remarkably similar to that given English assize judges, as they toured their circuits.[38] Vincentio emphasizes his reassertion of authority by requiring Angelo and Escalus to meet him at the gates of the city and return their commissions to him. With Angelo on one hand and Escalus on the other, Vincentio proceeds through the streets of Vienna, emphasizing that power is centralized in his person and that his judges are his appendages.

In addition, Vincentio issues a proclamation that "if any crave redress of injustice, they should exhibit their petitions [to the duke] in the street," giving Isabella her opportunity to bring charges against Angelo and also underscoring the duke's return as a new beginning. The trial begins when Isabella kneels before the duke (whom she does not recognize as Friar Lodowick) and issues her complaint:

> O worthy prince, dishonor not your eye
> By throwing it on any other object,
> Till you have heard me in my true complaint,
> And give me justice! Justice! Justice! Justice!
>
> (5.1.23–26)

The duke invites Isabella to relate her grievances, and after much interruption, she tells the story that Angelo believes to be true and that Isabella knows to be partly false—that she gave her body to Angelo for his promise to spare her brother:

> He would not, but by gift of my chaste body
> To his concupiscible intemperate lust,
> Release my brother; and after much debatement,
> My sisterly remorse confutes mine honor,
> And I did yield to him. But the next morn betimes,
> His purpose surfeiting, he sends a warrant
> For my poor brother's head.
>
> (5.1.100–06)

The duke responds to Isabella's accusation by accusing her of conspiring against Angelo; then he commits an obvious breach of even Renaissance due process by allowing Angelo to judge his own case. This unorthodox move accomplishes

several things. It heightens Isabella's courageousness; the duke
puts her in the position of helpless defendant beset by accusers, with no friend in sight, and Angelo in his position as powerful judge. It gives Angelo a chance to repent and confess—
or damn himself even further by committing in public an act
of judicial corruption as filthy as the one he has committed in
private. And, with Angelo now acting as judge, the duke gives
himself time to exit, change costume, and participate in the
trial as Friar Lodowick.

Isabella and Friar Lodowick appear emblematically as
Christian figures in their roles as novitiate and monk, and the
trial, in many respects, sets forth a ritual reenactment of Christ's
passion. Both Isabella and Friar Lodowick find themselves
before a corrupt judge, as Christ did before Caiaphas. Isabella
is betrayed, and Lodowick is slandered and abused by Lucio,
a type of Judas and the angry crowd, all in one. When all
seems lost, Lucio unfrocks Friar Lodowick, revealing the duke
and, in a sense, resurrecting him. The tables turn; the pros-
ecuted triumph, and Angelo and Lucio find themselves defendants. Lodowick the friar becomes Vincentio (meaning "vic-
tor"), the judge. The duke's sudden transformation, his omni-
scient knowledge of Angelo's wrongdoing, his control of events,
and his theatricality establish his god-like credibility in the
eyes of the populace; even Angelo confesses to Vincentio as if
he were God:

> O my dread lord,
> I should be guiltier than my guiltiness
> To think I can be undiscernible,
> When I perceive your Grace, like power divine,
> Hath looked upon my passes. Then, good prince,
> No longer session hold upon my shame,
> But let my trial be mine own confession.

(5.1. 364–70)

First, the duke orders Angelo to marry Mariana; although they are legally bound to each other, the public ceremony must be performed. He continues with the fiction that Claudio is dead, telling Isabella an outright lie because he wants to test her ability to forgive:

> Your brother's death, I know, sits at your heart:
> And you may marvel why I obscur'd myself,
> Labouring to save his life, and would not rather
> Make rash remonstrance of my hidden power
> Than let him so be lost. O most kind maid,
> It was the swift celerity of his death,
> Which I did think with slower foot came on,
> That brain'd my purpose.

(5.1.387–94)

After he has given Isabella every reason to hate Angelo, he then orders Angelo's execution, seemingly fulfilling the three general functions of criminal punishment: purification of the body politic by the public revelation and extirpation of vice, retribution, and the deterrence of future criminal activity.[39] But purgation is only a partial remedy for Vienna's moral lassitude. If vice is to be publicly purged, then virtue needs to be publicly celebrated, so that not only a morality of duty is encouraged, but also a morality of aspiration.[40] To accomplish this, the duke has deliberately contrived a situation in which Isabella can become such an exemplar. However, though ceremonies may be forced on people, the expression of virtue must be the result of free will, and therefore the duke is not completely in control of Isabella's actions. All Vincentio can do is to set the stage, by bringing her into contact with Mariana and by making her believe that Angelo's order for the execution of Claudio has been carried out.

When Mariana's pleas to Vincentio for the pardon of Angelo are unavailing, she asks Isabella to intercede—to "lend" her knees. To emphasize the unearthly character of what Isabella is about to do, the duke sets forth the most probable human reaction to Mariana's plea:

> Against all sense you do importune her.
> Should she kneel down in mercy of this fact,
> Her brother's ghost his paved bed would break,
> And take her hence in horror.
>
> (5.1.431–34)

Isabella, however, fulfills all of the duke's unstated expectations. In the dramatic apex of the play, Isabella kneels and, motivated by sympathy for Mariana, pleads that Angelo be pardoned:

> Most bounteous sir:
> Look, if it please you, on this man condemn'd
> As if my brother liv'd. I partly think
> A due sincerity governed his deeds
> Till he did look on me. Since it is so,
> Let him not die.
>
> (5.1.441–46)

These lines accomplish the apotheosis of Isabel. In asking mercy for Angelo, the "murderer" of her brother, the man who has done everything in his power to rape her, Isabella becomes "a thing enskied and sainted," making mythic truth of Lucio's earthly cynicism. It is after this that the duke reveals the living Claudio to Isabella.

Isabella's act of forgiveness completes a rite of passage begun in act 1, when she is preparing to enter the Order of St. Clare. At that point, she was an immature Christian, a girl;

but in her act of forgiveness, Isabella touches the essence of Christianity and becomes a woman. Mariana has become her truest sister and has pulled Isabella away from the Clares into the secular world of marriage and sex. When the duke proposes to her at the end of the play, there are no lines from Isabella, no stage directions indicating what she will do, but the dramatic trajectory Shakespeare has set for her makes her undoubted acceptance (given the play is a comedy) logical, if a bit sudden.[41] Isabella, we must assume, has learned that there are Christian vocations in the wide world as well as in cloisters. (However, many famous critics have found the marriage of Vincentio and Isabella not only improbable but repulsive. See endnote 39.)

Lucio is sentenced to be whipped and hung for slandering the duke. From our perspective, this seems like another case in which the punishment exceeds the crime, but in slandering the duke, Lucio has committed a direct attack on the sanctity of the anointed prince and the law as enforced in Vienna. For the judicial system to work, the integrity of judges must be preserved, which means that hidden corruption, such as Angelo's, must be exposed, and real integrity must not be damaged by slander. For the law to order society, it must not only be fair, but be perceived to be fair. Lucio's lies are a direct attack on political stability.

At the end of the play, the duke not only pardons Angelo and Claudio, but Lucio and Barnardine as well. Lucio is forced to marry Kate Keepdown. As he is packed off stage he begs to be executed instead: "Marrying a punk [prostitute], my lord, is pressing to death, / Whipping, and hanging." This "shotgun" marriage undoubtedly got a good laugh from Shakespeare's audience, but one has to wonder whether the duke is doing Kate Keepdown a favor. Given Vincentio's declaration at the beginning of the play about the need for law

enforcement, this ending has given critics trouble since the
time of Coleridge.[42] Doesn't the ending simply undo everything the duke sets out to accomplish at the beginning of the
play? Aren't the forced marriages at the end of the play likely
to produce more unhappy results, even more crime? These
are hard questions, for if Shakespeare has once again shown
us the value of mercy and forgiveness, he has not shown, in
any convincing way, how these values are to be incorporated
by a secular state that needs to protect itself against criminal
conduct. Has the play failed to address the very issues it raises
at its beginning?

First, let us consider the pardons. The duke's pardon of
Angelo is particularly troublesome, not only because of
Angelo's immorality, but because it is highly doubtful that
Angelo has committed a crime. This, I believe, becomes obvious as the play moves toward conclusion and serves as a final
irony about how wide the gap can be between true justice and
mere legality. Isabella is the one who puts forth the argument
that Angelo has not broken the law, and she makes perfect
legal sense:[43]

> My brother had but justice,
> In that he did the thing for which he died:
> For Angelo,
> His act did not o'ertake his bad intent,
> And must be buried but as an intent
> That perish'd by the way. Thoughts are no subjects;
> Intents, but merely thoughts.

(5.1.446–52)

Isabella's rationality distinguishes her from any other character in the final scene. The duke's performance—his double
return, at the gate of the city and again when Lucio reveals
him under "Lodowick's hood"—is so powerful and surprising

that it seems to preclude rational examination of the guilt or innocence of anyone he later pardons. Yet, the members of the audience, many of whom would have been ardent playgoers from the Inns of Court, may very well have probed more deeply into the duke's subsequent adjudications and found much to question. Indeed, Isabella's speech seems to beg for such questioning.

To commit a crime, as Isabella points out, one must *intend* to commit a criminal act and then *commit* the act, i. e., the act must "o'ertake [the] bad intent." Act and intention must coincide, and both must be proven to establish a crime. This is the law today, and it was the law during the time of Elizabeth I and James I. An objectively innocent act, even though accompanied by evil intent, cannot be regarded as a crime. Thus, consider the following examples from a law school textbook: "A soldier during battle shoots and kills an enemy soldier believing that his victim is his own sergeant. A man has sexual intercourse with a woman over the age of consent, though he believes that she is underage. A man deliberately shoots and kills the deceased, unaware that at the very instant the deceased was about to kill him." In all these cases an evil intention is present, but the actor committed no crime because his actions were not illegal. This principle reaches back to the beginnings of English common law.[44] The same analysis would have been available during the period in which *Measure for Measure* was produced, and it seems unlikely that those in the audience who had legal training would have missed it, given the very direct way in which Isabella raises the argument (and the fact that the duke never offers a counterargument.)

As Isabella notes, in the case of Angelo, the element of illegal action is missing. What is Angelo to be executed for? The murder of Claudio? Even if Claudio were dead, which, of course, he is not, Claudio would merely have received what had been coming to him under a literal application of the law. Angelo may have enforced the law for the wrong reasons—but that is no crime: laws are to be enforced. Angelo had the *right* to execute Claudio for fornication. Therefore, Claudio's "death" cannot form the basis for a criminal judgment against Angelo.

Is Angelo to be executed for the attempted seduction of Isabella? Though he wanted to seduce her, and thought he had seduced her, he never actually committed the act. He wound up in bed with Mariana.

Does Angelo's liaison with Mariana, then, constitute the crime of fornication? In other words, did the duke's bed trick result in an illegal act? This is much more ambiguous and has resulted in a spate of articles on the pre-contracts in *Measure for Measure*, trying to distinguish Claudio's case from Angelo's. (These modern literary musings—which are beyond the scope of this book—might well have been mind-boggling to a Jacobean attorney.[45]) Shakespeare's point, I believe, is simply that Angelo and Mariana *have* committed the same crime as Claudio and Julietta, but ironically, it is the one crime that Angelo cannot be charged with because the duke would be guilty as an accomplice.

But can Angelo be held guilty for *attempting* to commit the murder of Claudio or fornication with Isabella? Again, the answer is no, for at the time of Shakespeare, the criminal law of "attempts" was virtually nonexistent. That Angelo could even have been charged with such a crime would not have occurred to Shakespeare or his audience.

Although the argument I am presenting about Angelo's technical guiltlessness may seem overly ingenious, the script of the play itself indicates that Vincentio not only understands Isabella's argument, but feels its force. Vincentio never contradicts what Isabella says, but because of the persuasiveness of her argument, backpedals into another charge:

> Your suit's unprofitable. Stand up, I say.
> I have bethought me of another fault.
> Provost, how came it Claudio was beheaded
> At an unusual hour?

> (5.1.453–56)

It is hard to believe that the beheading of Claudio at "an unusual hour" by private message would be a capital crime, Angelo having complete sovereignty in Vincentio's absence. And once Claudio is revealed, his head yet on his shoulders, Angelo cannot be convicted of this crime anyway. The duke's description of Angelo's reaction when Claudio is uncowled provides further support: "By this Lord Angelo perceives he's safe; / Methinks I see a quickening in his eye" (5.1.492–93).

These words could indicate that Angelo now at least has the hope of presenting a defense. It is important to note that these lines occur before the duke's line: "I find an apt remission in myself," which is usually interpreted as a pardon of Angelo. But Angelo has done nothing for which a legal pardon is required, and the line may not be addressed to Angelo at all but to Lucio, for the duke is turning his attention toward Lucio, and the line could simply indicate that Vincentio, despite his inclinations toward clemency, will not pardon Lucio: "I find an apt remission in myself. / And yet here's one [Lucio] in place I cannot pardon" (5.1.496–97).

Lucio's pardon is also problematic. Vienna's raconteur at large, he recognizes no responsibility to anyone. Although he urges Isabella to come to Claudio's aid, he is quite willing to tesify—and falsely—against her in act 5, simply because, like any ham actor, he craves an audience. Though he had promised to marry Kate Keepdown, he has refused to honor the promise. Shakespeare and the duke seem to have given Lucio what he deserves, though the question remains whether they have given Kate Keepdown what she deserves.

Another difficulty for critics has been the duke's use of forced marriage as a solution to sexual license. Angelo and Lucio are both coerced into marrying women they obviously do not love. The multiple marriages at the end of this play little resemble the happy marriages at the end of such romantic comedies as *Much Ado about Nothing, A Midsummer Night's Dream,* or *As You Like It.* Will forcing people to marry promote the institution, or cause more disharmony and more adultery?

The duke's pardon of Barnardine, an unrepentant murderer, is perhaps the most problematic of all his decrees. Barnardine is the most subversive character in the play—the one who most consistently refuses to play the socially assigned role of a repentant man on his way to execution. Ironically, Barnardine's refusal to play that part has kept him alive for years. He cannot be executed because he does not fit into the standard script for executions. Barnardine's absolute refusal to be the scapegoat of the judicial system or the church poses a threat to the duke's new society, and from Vincentio's point of view, Barnardine "wants advice." Someone needs to "persuade this rude wretch willingly to die," or else the *performance* of execution—and therefore the message that accompanies it—will be thwarted. Vincentio turns Barnardine over to Friar Thomas for education.

Audience unwillingness to see Barnardine executed disrupts the theater of execution, for it puts the audience on the side of a criminal who refuses to take the process seriously, and so draws the audience's attention to the theatricality of Elizabethan trial and punishment. James's interest in bringing Cobham, Markham, and Grey to the proper state of repentance was not motivated solely by concern for their religious welfare. The carefully controlled gallows spectacle of repentance by the three men was typical of what occurred at most executions: the condemned man admitted guilt, stated his acceptance of the verdict and the justness of the sentence, and pronounced his willingness to die. Thus, the condemned were forced into the role of legitimating their own executions. Barnardine, though, refuses to legitimate any part of the process, and enlists the audience's sympathy with the same blackly comic alternative. Barnardine's refusal to play a role, his stubborn silence, can become the foil by which the duke's final scene is revealed as theater, for there is nothing that shatters the "reality" of game more than the refusal to play—or pretend.

Let us return to the scaffold of Cobham, Markham, and Grey, and James's production of last-minute pardons. The reader may already have noted the similarity between Shakespeare's act 5 and James's act at Winchester. James's play featured his apparently strong denial of pleas for mercy by friends of Markham and Grey, Raleigh's wife, and in Raleigh's case, even the queen; Vincentio's trial features pleas for mercy by Mariana for the life of her husband Angelo, by Isabella for Angelo—and the apparently adamant refusal of the duke to listen to those pleas of mercy. James led Grey to believe that Markham had been executed and Cobham to believe that both Markham and Grey had been executed, so that bringing them together on the scaffold would not miss its full effect—"wherein Grey, Markham, and Cobham looked upon each other's faces, as if each had just risen from the dead."[46] The "resurrection" of Claudio enacts political theater similar in style and effect to the "resurrection" of the three alleged conspirators, who never expected to see each other again; and the pardons of Angelo, Lucio, Barnardine, and Claudio give a theatrical echo of the surprise pardons of Cobham, Markham, and Grey, and Raleigh's stay of execution. Finally, as James had kept his intention to commute the executions of Cobham, Markham, and Grey secret for three days, except from his page John Gibb, so Vincentio keeps Claudio's rescue secret from everyone but the provost of the jail. James was as willing to play with the emotions of the three men, their friends, and their families as Vincentio is ready to play with Isabella's by telling her Claudio is dead.

Given that only about six months had elapsed between the time of James's pardons and the opening of *Measure for Measure* in the summer of 1604, it seems unlikely that the audience would not have seen topical significance in the play. For some spectators these fictional events may have been a fictional recelebration of the pardons issued by James—for others, a fictional reexamination of those pardons, a reexamination that led not to closure but to further thought. Shakespeare's audience could not have known yet that the pardons of Cobham, Markham, and Grey were to establish a pattern. James I made particularly liberal use of the pardon power. C. H. Rolph, in *The Queen's Pardon*, states:

> In the sixteenth, seventeenth and eighteenth centuries the royal pardon was in fact being granted pretty freely, the Stuart Kings in particular placing reliance on the hot line by which they felt themselves to be connected with the Holy Ghost.[47]

The three pardons we see at the end of *Measure for Measure* not only reflected the past but set before audiences a type of political action that would continue.

Arguably, *Measure for Measure* reaches both the formal closure appropriate to comedy and an ending that is morally satisfying. The threat to the lives of Claudio, Barnardine, and

Angelo is averted. Escalus, who has come closer than any other judge in the play to steering a middle course between justice and mercy, will play an important part in the future government of Vienna. The duke tells him: "Thanks, good friend Escalus, for thy much goodness; / There's more behind that is more gratulate" (5.1.525–26). The duke, in making clandestine marriages public, and in enforcing contracts of marriage already made, reestablishes the order needed for a society to function, and the ceremonies required by the duke will help to ensure that Angelo and Lucio fulfill their spousal responsibilities. In the theatricality of the last trial, the duke has elevated virtue, extirpated vice, and reestablished his own authority in Vienna—and in the process provided examples of moral inspiration for his people.

However, *Measure for Measure* goes as unwillingly to its comic ending as Lucio to his marriage. A duke who starts out proclaiming his desire to restore law and order pardons everyone, even a convicted murderer, at the end of the play. The duke requires there to be two unhappy marriages—hardly a way of discouraging fornication. No one thanks Vincentio for any of this. Angelo, even after he is married, says he prefers execution than to living with his shame; Lucio claims he would rather be whipped and hung than forced to marry a "punk." One can only wonder whether anything of moral value has been accomplished and whether marriage, as comic closure, will lead to the rejuvenation of society or merely promote further decay.

The duke's theatricality also has its price: to display Isabella as a moral exemplar, he must lie to her about her brother's death and get her to commit perjury and slander herself in the process. The moral order that Vincentio seeks to establish is undercut by his actions in attempting to bring it about. Perhaps *Measure for Measure* succeeds as a play be-

cause it ultimately fails as a comedy. The uneasiness of critics about the marriages and pardons, and the sense that the
duke is merely repeating former mistakes, underscore the in-
transigence of the problem he would like to solve. There are
no easy rules for reconciling justice with mercy, and as Isaiah
Berlin notes, every choice may entail irreparable loss. The
duke's show trial, in which he stands for justice and Isabella
for mercy, yields to a marriage proposal in which justice and
mercy unite. But the pageantry of justice and mercy married
cannot substitute for rational enforcement of the law. What,
we are bound to ask as Shakespeare's play takes root in our
imagination, will be the future of justice in Vincentio's Vienna?
It is the very question with which Shakespeare started the
play.

The duke ends *Measure for Measure* with a promise to tell
how he has brought about the amazing trial of act 5: "So bring
us to our palace, where we'll show / What is yet behind, that's
meet you all should know." At the time when Markham was
ascending the scaffold at Winchester, James, in court at Wilton,
called together his privy council and favorite courtiers and
explained in great and confusing detail how he had brought
about the pardons of Markham, Grey, and Cobham, and how
he had commuted the death sentence for Raleigh. When his
councilors finally understood what he was getting at, James,
having ended his oration with "and therefore I have saved
them all," was treated to applause that progressed from his
person throughout the court. It was as difficult for James to
leave the glow of his production as it was for the previously
shy duke to leave his. Thus, theater enters the blood of the
sovereign and, through that, the body politic—and through
that, the theater.

Brethren, in the primitive Church there was a godly discipline, that, at the beginning of Lent, such persons as were notorious sinners were put to open penance and punishment in this world, that their souls might be saved in the day of the Lord, and that others admonished by their example might be more afraid to offend.

"A Commination against Sinners, with Certain Prayers to Be Used Divers Times in the Year,"
Book of Common Prayer, 1559

Man that is born of woman hath but a short time to live, and is full of misery. He cometh up and is cut down like a flower; he flieth as it were a shadow, and never continueth in one stay. In the midst of life we be in death: of whom may we seek for succor but of thee, O Lord, which for our sins justly art displeased. Yet, O Lord God most holy...deliver us not into the bitter pains of eternal death. Thou knowest, Lord, the secrets of our hearts, shut not up thy merciful eyes to our prayers: but spare us . . . thou most worthy judge eternal, suffer us not at our last hour for any pains of death to fall from thee.

"The Order of Burial of the Dead,"
Book of Common Prayer, 1559

5

Judgment and Grace: Women in Court in *A Winter's Tale* and *Henry VIII*

Shakespeare's late plays are listed in the First Folio as comedies, though today they are often called "tragicomedies," because, as the name suggests, they move from tragic beginnings to comic endings.[1] (The exception, *Henry VIII*, is listed with the histories, but it has many of the generic characteristics of tragicomedy.) Neville Coghill defined Shakespearean comedy as "a tale of trouble that turned to joy."[2] In the late comedies the journey from trouble to joy is harder to make and takes longer. The damage caused by sin and error is immense, and large expanses of time—fifteen years in *The Tempest*, sixteen in *The Winter's Tale*—must pass before happiness can be achieved. Healing and reconciliation require faith, hope, and great patience. The late plays escape being tragedies by emphasizing the sheer tenacity of human life and the transformative power of grace; despite the coldest winter of sin and blunder, spring will come.

The Winter's Tale, which fits squarely within the genre, is the story of King Leontes, who nearly destroys all he loves in an insane fit of jealousy; only after sixteen years of penance and mourning does he find forgiveness and new life. *Henry VIII* is a hybrid of history play and tragicomedy. Unlike Leontes, Henry seems untouched by conscience or injury. The embodiment of power, he strides like a force of nature through life, leaving the maimed behind him. Rather, it is Henry's greedy henchman Cardinal Wolsey who, like Leontes, eventually feels regret and the need for reconciliation.

Though the *The Winter's Tale* and *Henry VIII* are comparable on many grounds, the most striking is the situation of their queens, Hermione and Katherine of Aragon, both of whom must endure unjust trials brought against them by their husbands. These trials and judgments contrast with the divine judgments that later vindicate the queens, making them recipients and vehicles of heavenly grace. To understand the religious and judicial significance of these stories to Shakespeare's audience, some understanding of women's experience in English Renaissance courts is helpful, and the place to begin is one of Shakespeare's earlier trial scenes.

Women in Court in Renaissance England

> I do entreat your Grace to pardon me,
> I know not by what power I am made so bold,
> Nor how it may concern my modesty
> In such a presence here to plead my thoughts,
> But I beseech your Grace that I may know
> The worst that may befall me in this case,
> If I refuse to wed Demetrius.

These are Hermia's lines from act 1, scene 1, of *A Midsummer Night's Dream*. She has been produced in court by her father, Egeus, because she refuses to marry the man of his choice (Demetrius), rather than her own (Lysander). Hermia, apparently, does not trust her father, who has told her that Athenian law requires daughters to marry men of their father's choosing and that the penalty for disobedience is death. Hermia wants "Duke" Theseus, the judge, to give her a more official statement of the law. Her "bold" inquiry—itself a challenge to her father's honesty and a rebellion against his authority—is made with the sense that courtroom pleading and feminine modesty do not go together. In the Peter Hall film of the play, Hermia appropriately goes to her knees before Theseus at this point, not only to plead, but as a demonstration of her chagrin and a counterweight to her boldness.[3]

Had Hermia a husband or male relative to represent her, the issue of her modesty would not arise, but Lysander, who does not even have the legal status of a fiancé, is in no position to plead on Hermia's behalf, but only for his own right to woo and marry her. (He argues that his background is as noble as Demetrius's, that he is as rich as Demetrius, and that Hermia loves him, concluding: "Why should not I then prosecute *my* right?" [1.1.105]) So Hermia is in a bind. As a woman, she has little business representing herself in court, but to get justice (or, at least, what she wants) she must speak; the man who would most naturally represent a single woman—her father—stands in relation to her as plaintiff to defendant. Maybe, Hermia implies, this odd position of being an unrepresented woman gives her license to plead her thoughts. She does not acknowledge, after all, that her inquiry to Theseus does put her modesty in question. She merely says, "I know not how...it may concern my modesty."

Theseus tells Hermia the law does provide a third course. You may, he says, choose "to abjure forever the society of men," to become Diana's nun, and "be in shady cloister mew'd, / To live a barren sister all your life, / Chanting faint hymns to the cold fruitless moon" (1.1.71–73). In response, the generically plucky heroine of Shakespeare's romantic comedy emerges, colors flying:

> So will I grow, so live, so die, my lord,
> Ere I will yield my virgin patent up
> Unto his lordship whose unwished yoke
> My soul consents not to give sovereignty.

> (1.1.79–82)

Theseus, like a schoolmaster telling a young lady how to behave, advises Hermia, perhaps somewhat impatiently, which choice she ought to make: "For you, fair Hermia, look you arm yourself / To fit your fancies to your father's will." Of course, Hermia does nothing of the sort, and the glancing look that Shakespeare has taken toward women as defendants, and the propriety of their courtroom pleading, gives way in *A Midsummer Night's Dream* to the chaos of love potions and dark forests.

The same concerns for feminine modesty affect Isabella in *Measure for Measure* and partly explain her initial reluctance to plead for her brother Claudio. However, Shakespeare does not explicitly touch upon the conflict between feminine modesty and courtroom pleading until *The Winter's Tale* and *Henry VIII*, in which the difficult position of female defendants significantly heightens the pathos and dramatic impact of their trial scenes, giving Shakespeare two last opportunities to dramatize the short-comings of human justice.

Among literary historicists, the analysis of women's legal status in Renaissance England has been a province of feminist criticism that starts and stops with the common law, which gives a notoriously bleak picture of women's rights. At the foundation of the common law's treatment of women is the concept of *coverture*, which Blackstone, in his *Commentaries on the Laws of England* describes as follows:

> By marriage, the husband and wife are one person in the law: that is, the very being of legal existence of the woman is suspended during marriage, or at least is incorporated and consolidated into that of the husband: under whose wing, protection and cover, she performs everything; and is therefore called in our law French a *feme-covert*; it is said to be *covert-baron*, or under the protection and influence of her husband, her baron, or lord; and her condition during her marriage is called coverture.[4]

My law school property professor, Harry Cross, summarized this principle more succinctly: "At common law, husband and wife were one, and the husband was the one."

The common law concept of *coverture* derives from more inclusive religious and social views about marriage and can only be understood adequately in that context. Coverture not only attempts to circumscribe the right of married women to own property and to form contracts, but it also includes, by implication, the culture's idea of what marriage is and how it imposes reciprocal demands on husbands and wives. Among other things, coverture is the legal incarnation of two passages from the Bible that define the relationship between husband and wife:

> Have ye not read, that he which made them at the beginning made them male and female, and said, For this cause shall a man leave his father and mother, and cleave unto his wife: and they twain shall be one

flesh? Wherefore they are no more twain, but one flesh. Let no man therefore put asunder that, which God hath coupled together. (Matthew 19:4–6)

Wives, submit yourselves unto your husbands, as unto the Lord. For the husband is the wife's head, even as Christ is the head of the church . . . Therefore as the church is in subjection unto Christ, so let the wives be to their own husbands in everything. Husbands, love your wives, even as Christ loved the church, and gave himself for it. So ought men to love their wives as their own bodies. He that loveth his wife loveth himself, for no man yet hateth his own flesh. (Ephesians 5:22–39)

Certainly the men of early modern England—at least the churchmen whose words have been passed down to us in print—seem fonder of the first half of the passage from Ephesians than the second. These verses show that the full force of religion, and therefore, the culture, was behind coverture. It was not just a legal doctrine, but a powerful mindset backed by the most potent authority. In practice, if the force of coverture were challenged, and legal ways around coverture were developed, it was usually because husbands were acting in flagrantly abusive ways to their wives, or because economic considerations demanded more flexibility than a strict application of coverture allowed. As a symbolic force and general principle, however, coverture remained untouched in England during the Renaissance.

Coverture led to some peculiar legal reasoning in situations where husbands and wives had economic dealings with each other. For instance, a man could not give real property to his wife during marriage because they were one legal entity, and how could you give something to yourself? Historian Timothy Stretton, in *Women Waging Law in Elizabethan England*, gives a long catalog of coverture's consequences:

In marriage, the doctrine of coverture removed from the wife her very legal entity, making it impossible for married women, *femes covert*, to enter contracts or to assert their rights in court, except with consent and assistance of their husbands. A woman who married lost her surname, her right to choose where she lived, her right to legal protection against her husband (except in the most extreme cases) and her ability to own property. The moveable property (goods or chattels) she brought to marriage became her husband's forever. Control of any real property (land) she possessed, and the profits accruing from it, passed to her husband for the duration of the marriage. Property that fell in between, 'chattels real,' like leases, became a husband's during marriage, though if they remained intact at the conclusion of the marriage they returned to the wife or her heirs. A married woman could not independently inherit legacies, nor could she accept gifts, even from her husband. She could not make a will without her husband's agreement, and any existing will or testament became invalid on the day she married.[5]

William Blackstone's sanguine comment on these legal arrangements, which changed little until the nineteenth century, was that they created a favored class—women:

These are the chief legal effects of marriage during coverture; upon which we may observe, that even the disabilities, which the wife lies under, are for the most part intended for her protection and benefit. So great a favorite is the female sex of the laws of England.[6]

However, coverture did not so neatly or one-sidedly settle the legal status of women in early modern England. The Court of Common Pleas presided over the common law, and therefore the doctrine of coverture, but it was only one jurisdiction out of sixteen (according to one of the day's most eminent lawyers, Edward Coke). Other bodies of law, administered by other courts, provided women with a broad range of rights and remedies not recognized by the common law. These jurisdictions included courts of equity (Chancery and the Court of Requests), the ecclesiastical courts, manorial and borough courts (which administered customary law), and the separate courts of Lancaster and the Palatines of Chester and Durham.

Church courts allowed women to sue in their own names without their husbands and were a favorite venue for bringing actions of slander, especially in cases involving sexual reputation. Other courts recognized property rights that the common law did not. For instance, in London and York, under customary law, a widow was entitled to one-third of her husband's moveable goods if he had children and one-half if he had none, no matter what provisions he made in his will.[7] Though customary law greatly varied from one locality to another, most customary law gave widows the right (known as "freebench" or "widow's estate") to inherit from one-third to all of their husband's holdings. On some manors, a widow's estate in her husband's copyhold (essentially, his tenancy) was for life.

Under the common law, husband and wife could not sue each other—for how could one legal entity sue itself? Yet such suits were allowed in the Court of Requests, an equity court that handled small claims and domestic problems. (In fact, it seems that the concept of alimony was developed by the Court of Requests.[8]) Suits for maintenance, brought by wives against husbands, tended to occur after ecclesiastical courts had granted a separation of the two parties. There were, however, rare instances in which the court awarded maintenance even though a separation had not been granted.[9]

Courts of equity recognized many ways in which a woman could keep her property separated from her husband's. She could, for instance, place her property in trust for the duration of her marriage and make a will by which she could leave her separate property or a specified portion of joint property. She could use a marriage settlement or jointures to determine ownership of property during her marriage or to specify inheritance rights.

In summary, women had various rights recognized by various courts. But even at common law, women were not completely bereft. Single women and widows had the right to sue, contract, and write wills without restriction. Married women who outlived their husbands had dower rights (half the income of the husband's interest in lands during widowhood). In Tudor and Stuart England, women inherited through the common law 20 to 25 percent of the time, this occurring when there were no living brothers in the family to inherit.[10] Stretton notes that in many instances the common law courts provided women their best legal remedy:

> The common law's bad press arises from its restriction of women's rights in marriage and in inheritance. But . . . female litigants went to court over other matters besides marriage and inheritance. In many, perhaps most instances they pursued litigation not as women asserting women's rights, but as creditors, debtors, executrixes, administratrixes, lease-holders, tenants, midwives, servants or traders seeking redress for wrongs. In these guises the common law courts were often the most helpful organs of justice for women, more helpful at times than equity courts.[11]

Thus, women not only had rights but often pursued them at court, during the period of Shakespeare's life, and in ever-increasing numbers. During Elizabeth's reign, women appeared in a quarter of all suits commenced in Chancery, and this proportion rose to 40 percent during the reign of James I. During Elizabeth's reign, in the Court of Requests women appeared as plaintiffs in 20 percent of the cases, and as defendants in 16 percent.[12] In the consistory court of York, women brought 51 percent of the defamation actions during the 1590s, and in the London consistory court from 1572 to 1640 they brought between 70 and 75 percent of the defamation cases.[13]

Whether women should go to court at all, or how they should behave if they had no male to guide them, no doubt became topics of increasing controversy because of the increasing number of female litigants. Stretton notes:

> Women's legal options were considerable, and their access to litigation improved substantially with the growth of the central justice system between the accession of Elizabeth I and the demise of Charles I. The numbers of women who participated in litigation increased at a rate that outstripped increases in population. In church courts, Chancery, Request, and the major common law courts, women, like men, were availing themselves of institutional justice in numbers which approach or exceed modern levels of participation in the legal process. This meant more women traveling to court and more women defending their honour and protecting their property, but it also meant more wives publicly challenging their husbands, more women fighting contests against men, and, for a while at least, more poor women challenging their richer neighbors.[14]

Certainly not all of the women who appeared in court showed Hermia's concern with how it might reflect on their modesty. During a Star Chamber proceeding, Judge Thomas Egerton became so incensed at a plaintiff's wife, who would not stop haranguing the court, even at noon recess, that he ordered her "whipped and made to confess her fault" and fined her husband twenty pounds "for the better government of his wife."[15] Egerton wanted to bar the personal appearance of women in Star Chamber, but his colleagues, perhaps conscious of the income produced by female litigants, would not go along with his motion. Judge Anthony Benn complained about witless and clamorous women in Chancery, advocating that they "be shutt out of all courts." Stretton explains that "Benn and Egerton did not express a desire to deny women rights, but they wished to exclude them from the courtroom and prevent them arguing their cases or responding to accusations, in person. What concerned them was the deportment of women in court."[16] Female conduct in court was just a special instance of a concern with female conduct generally, and it reflects a cultural stereotype that divided women into two categories: modest and immodest. Bishop Aylmer gives flesh to this dichotomy in a sermon before Elizabeth:

> Some of them [women] are wiser, better learned, discreeter, and more constant than a number of men, but another and worse sort of them, and the most part, are fond, foolish, wanton, flibbergibs, tattlers, triflers, wavering, witless, without council, feeble, careless, rash, proud, dainty, nice, talebearers, eavesdroppers, rumour-raisers, evil-tongues, worse-minded, and in every way doltified with the dregs of the devil's dunghill.[17]

A woman's modesty was largely concerned with her sexual reputation, and any kind of immodesty, including importunate speech, was taken to imply sexual looseness. "Modesty" and sexual probity are so closely related in some lines of Shakespeare that they are nearly synonymous. Take, for instance, Demetrius's lines to Helena in *A Midsummer Night's Dream* as, lovesick, she pursues him in the wood outside of Athens: "You do impeach your modesty too much / To leave the city and commit yourself / Into the hands of one who loves you not, / To trust the opportunity of night / and the ill counsel of a desert place / With the rich worth of your virginity" (2.1.214–19).

For women to go to law in the large central courts, which were male and public, went against the grain of cultural concerns for female modesty and controlled speech. Pleading in court at all seemed to many commentators immodest because it took women outside their natural sphere of influence—the home—and exceeded their capacities. The reason women were given away by men in marriage, according to Richard Hooker, was that it reminded them of their natural disabilities and duties: "It putteth women in minde of a dutie, whereunto the verie imbecillitie of their nature and sexe doth bind them, namely, to bee always directed, guided and ordered by others . . . ."[18] Thomas Smith, in *The Commonwealth of England*, asserted that nature made women "to keep home and nourish their family and children, and not to meddle with matters abroad."[19]

A lawsuit is a battle performed in public and would thus certainly qualify as meddling in "matters abroad." Juan Luis Vives, Katherine of Aragon's good friend and counselor, advises women in his book *A Very Fruteful and Pleasant Boke Calyd the Instruction of a Christen Woman* that they should "ever use the counsayle" of trustworthy men, and "shulde ever be under the rule of their fathers and brotherne and huysbands, and kynsmen." With regard to the law, he quotes Cato: "an honest wife shulde be ignorant, what lawes be made or annulled in her countrey, or what is done amonge men of lawe in the courte."[20]

But what if extreme conditions forced a woman to go to court? Commentators acknowledged that the concerns of justice could outweigh those of modesty. Certainly lawyers did not mind collecting fees from women, and they unsurprisingly supported the right of women to bring suits. Latimer and Vives urged that if women were forced into court, they put their trust in Christ, and their views were echoed in 1631 by Richard Braithwait:

> If you have businesse with the Judge of any Court, and you much feare the power of your adversary, imploy all your care to this end, that your faith may be grounded in those promises of Christ: Your Lord maketh intercession for you, rendring right judgment to the Orphane, and righteousnesse unto the widow.[21]

Stretton summarizes the viewpoint of the conduct-book writers on how a woman should represent herself in court, and how it concerned her modesty, as follows:

> Vives reflected that when a widow approached "feble" attorneys, her cause "shalbe so moche more recommended unto them, the lesse that she recommendeth it. And her cause shalbe more like to be good, whom men think so good and virtuous, that she wyll neither aske nor hold that is nat her own." If women had to go to law, they should stand "humble and lowely" behind their male attorneys and hope that male judges would show them sympathy. In this view less was more and silence was golden, for "she that is bablyng, and busy, and troublous must nedes wery men, and make them to loth her, and hindreth her of the succour that I spake of." And innocent woman could speak out in the pursuit of justice in the manner of the importunate widow in Luke 18.[22]

The ideal female litigant, then, had to walk a tightrope strung between her right to obtain justice and the need to conserve her modesty. A woman who was too modest ran the risk of not getting her story across, but a woman who was immodest ran the risk of undermining the credibility of her testimony, since immodesty reflected deeper problems with her sexual integrity and honesty. Thus, a woman unrepresented by an attorney or other male was usually caught in a Catch 22. But, as they gained in sophistication, women often pled their own "imbecilitie" and humbleness to advantage, as we shall see in the case of Katherine of Aragon.

Given the impediments of women who went to court, if a dramatist wanted to portray the most defenseless and hence pathetic defendant on trial, it would be a woman who was abandoned by the men about her, a *feme-covert* who, accused by her husband, is forced to defend herself as a *feme-sole*, a woman whose modesty is, in effect, impeached by the husband who has placed her in court. Hermione of *The Winter's Tale* and Katherine of Aragon of *Henry VIII* are both placed in this position. The challenge they face in defending themselves reflects the power of coverture as an idea and the real dilemmas faced by women in contemporary English courts. The women in these plays don't seek to evade the consequences of coverture but to assert them. They are married women who have fulfilled their obligations as wives and now plead that their husbands fulfill theirs by extending to them the "cover" of marriage, rather than denying it. The ability of women to stand up and defend themselves in court would not have been novel, but watching Shakespeare's two queens do it, while retaining their modesty, would have tapped a vein of popular interest and created high drama.

The Winter's Tale: Hermione and Leontes

At the beginning of *The Winter's Tale,* Shakespeare introduces King Leontes of Sicilia, a man who is a good and rational ruler, loving to both his wife and his best friend, Polixenes, the king of Bohemia. Leontes and Polixenes were childhood friends, and as children, according to Polixenes, possessed a virtually prelapsarian innocence. He describes it to Hermione, Leontes' queen:

> We were as twinn'd lambs that did frisk i' th'sun,
> And bleat the one at th' other: what we chang'd
> Was innocence for innocence: we knew not
> The doctrine of ill-doing, nor dream'd
> That any did. Had we pursu'd that life,
> And our weak spirits ne'er been higher rear'd
> With stronger blood, we should have answer'd heaven
> Boldy 'not guilty', the imposition clear'd
> Hereditary ours.
>
> (1.2.67–74)

Thus Polixenes claims that had he and Leontes not lost their innocence—through their awakened sexual desire, Polixenes intimates—they could have justly answered God that they were clear even of original sin. (Though the play takes place in pagan times, statements such as this give it a Christian moral and spiritual orientation.) When Polixenes tells his friend that he must return to Bohemia, Leontes commands his wife Hermione to persuade Polixenes to stay longer, though he has already stayed nine months. Hermione, nine months pregnant, does what her husband asks, and out of the blue Leontes becomes convinced that she is bearing Polixenes' child.

Shakespeare makes little attempt to account for the origin of Leontes' jealousy. Perhaps Leontes has overheard and misconstrued the last lines of Hermione's response to Polixenes' speech, in which she pokes fun at the idea that she or Polixenes' queen were responsible for their husbands' fall from innocence:

> Th' offences we have made you do, we'll answer,
> If you first sinn'd with us, and that with us
> You did continue fault, and that you slipp'd not
> With any but with us.

(1.2.83–86)

Perhaps Leontes believes that Hermione is using the royal "we," and thus referring to herself alone as a cause of sin in Polixenes. Yet, these few lines, even if heard out of context, provide no rational excuse for Leontes' jealousy, and none other is given. Similarly, Shakespeare provides little cause for Iago's hatred of Othello or Othello's easily awakened jealousy of Desdemona. Shakespeare is seldom concerned with the psychological origins of evil. His approach is Augustinian; sin, by its nature, is irrational, a choosing of the worst over the best. It is the result of a love and attachment which, turned from God, has fixed on less worthy objects. Ultimately no accounting for such error is possible, beyond the corruption of the human intellect through Adam's fall. Shakespeare's audience came to the theater with this understanding and needed no further explanation. It almost certainly never occurred to Shakespeare to give one.

Leontes, whose jealousy grows at a fearsome rate, asks his advisor, Camillo, to help him kill Polixenes, but Camillo, knowing that Leontes has become irrational, tries to reason with him. Camillo fails, however, and sees that reason cannot reach Leontes; therefore, Camillo helps Polixenes escape, and Hermione is left behind to face her husband's wrath. Leontes puts her on trial for treason and adultery. One of his courtiers, Antigonus, tells him, "I wish, my liege, / You had only in your silent judgement tried it, / Without more overture," for merely by voicing his suspicions, Leontes does terrible damage to Hermione. He compounds this by separating Hermione from her son, Mamillius, and imprisoning her.

Abandoned by Leontes' court, Hermione has no one to defend her until her friend, Paulina, takes it upon herself to be Hermione's advocate. Shakespeare never portrays a professional lawyer defending a client. *The Winter's Tale* is the only play in which one character, trying to establish another's innocence, engages in lawyer-like advocacy. In this aspect, *The Winter's Tale* is closer to modern courtroom drama than any other of Shakespeare's plays. The audience already understands that Leontes is in the grip of insane jealousy. The question is whether anyone can make him see reality before he takes irreparable action.

Paulina is just the type of importunate woman who would have appalled the conduct-book writers and inspired Justice Egerton to ban women from personal court appearances. With all the men cowed by Leontes, Paulina produces the king's new daughter in court, urging the baby's resemblance to Leontes as proof of Hermione's faithfulness. Paulina's advocacy saves Hermione, for a time, from having to defend herself, and it probably injected some humor into the play for the Globe audience, demonstrating both the need for women to be clamorous on occasion and the wilting effect such behavior could have on men. The courtiers are afraid to cross Leontes, but they have no relish to tangle with Paulina either, and she calls them cowards: "Fear you his tyrannous passion more, alas / Than the queen's life?"

It is comic that Antigonus, Paulina's husband, cannot "rule" her, and that Leontes, who keeps telling him to make her shut up, threatens to hang Antigonus for being unable to do what Leontes cannot. Getting wives to hold their tongues apparently is not so easy, and Antigonus comments, "Hang all the husbands / That cannot do that feat, you'll leave yourself / Hardly one subject" (2.3.109–11). Antigonus, of course, is in the same position as the husband who was fined twenty pounds by Egerton for not being able to rule his wife. He is powerless to stop Paulina's domestic and political insurrection. But he would not do it if he could. He is proud of her: "When she will take the rein I let her run; / *She will not stumble* (2.3.51–52; italics added).

The way power was divided in a Renaissance marriage does not correspond to current academic stereotypes and misconceptions about patriarchy or English law, but rather to the temperaments and capacities of individual husbands and wives. (This remains a fact of daily life that has not penetrated feminist criticism, though Socrates certainly understood it, as did Chaucer.) Paulina makes it clear that she obeys her husband, "in every good thing."[23] But he cannot rule her to a course of dishonor: "From all dishonesty he can [rule me]: in this— / Unless he take the course that you have done, / Commit me for committing honour" (2.3.47–49). In other words, if Antigonus disgraces himself, as Leontes has done, he will not even be able to rule Paulina in good things. Wives only have the obligation to follow honorable men who make morally upright decisions.

Paulina is the only one of Leontes' subjects who is doing her duty as a courtier ought, giving wise, if ill-received, counsel. She is the female doppelganger of *King Lear*'s Kent. It is only because women are taken less seriously than men that Paulina is allowed to plague Leontes as long as she does. In this way, her sex works both for and against her. The tongue-lashing she gives Leontes may be discounted by him and his court as female meddling (though not altogether), but at least she gets the chance to give it, and this is one of the reasons that her mission to Leontes is, as she tells Hermione's jailor, an "office [that] becomes a woman best." She tells Leontes that she comes to him with words medicinal, to purge him from the humor that has possessed him, and he reacts to her with an excess of anger and loathing that indicates fear. Being put to one's purgation with "words medicinal" is not a comfortable experience, and one of the play's comic ironies is that Leontes will soon yield himself up to this "callet" for sixteen years of purgation.

Enraged by Paulina's intervention, Leontes orders Antigonus to carry Hermione's "female bastard" to "some remote and desert place quite out of our dominions" and to "leave it (without more mercy) to its own protection / And favor of the climate." Antigonus departs on this mission, though before picking up Hermione's child, Paulina warns him, "For ever / Unvenerable be thy hands, if thou / Tak'st up the princess, by that forced baseness / Which he has put upon 't" (2.3.76–79).

Though the charges against Hermione recall more closely those against Anne Bullen [Boleyn] and Katherine Howard, Hermione's fictional appearance in court bears a striking resemblance to that of Katherine of Aragon's, since both women will seek to reawaken their husband's commitment to marriage, and hence coverture, and because both women realize that, given the charges against them and the bias of the court, they cannot get a fair trial. Hermione argues that being placed on trial by her husband, the man who ought to know her best, has so put her integrity into question that she cannot hope to testify effectively in her own behalf. Who would believe her word against her husband's?

> Since what I am to say, must be but that
> Which contradicts my accusation, and

> The testimony on my part, no other
> But what comes from myself, it shall scarce boot me
> To say 'not guilty': mine integrity,
> Being counted falsehood, shall, as I express it,
> Be so receiv'd.
>
> (3.2.22–28)

Hermione attempts to awaken the memory of the king to her virtuous life as his queen—to reposition herself as a wife still under her husband's "cover":

> . . . You, my lord, best know
> (Who least will seem to do so) my past life
> Hath been as continent, as chaste, as true,
> As I am now unhappy; which is more
> Than history can pattern, though devis'd
> And play'd to take spectators. For behold me,
> A fellow of the royal bed, which owe
> A moiety of the throne, a great king's daughter,
> The mother to a hopeful prince, here standing
> To prate and talk for life and honour 'fore
> Who please to come and hear.
>
> (3.2.32–42)

By putting Hermione on trial, Leontes has made her an object of public display and has forced her to defend herself—a position that for Hermione is as unnatural as her husband's conduct. She presents the extreme case that the conduct-book writers cannot deal with, a wife who has been denied cover by her husband, has no male counsel, and is humiliated by being made a public spectacle, "To prate and talk for life and honour 'fore / Who please to come and hear." Her situation is so bizarre, Hermione says, that there is no historical example for it, even in a history designed and "played to take spectators." Even Shakespearean history plays, she seems to assert, could not furnish such an example. Yet the very play she is in gives this the lie, as does the story of Katherine of Aragon in *Henry VIII*. Indeed, in this little bit of meta-dramatic comedy, Shakespeare's Hermione seems to be throwing down the gauntlet to her author, daring him to write *Henry VIII*.

Hermione reminds Leontes she is "a great king's daughter," which has the double effect of invoking her nobility and harkening back to their wedding ceremony, in which she went from her father's cover to that of her husband. The implication is that Leontes has not only failed in his duties to Hermione, but to her father as well. She also invokes coverture when she reminds Leontes he was "the crown and comfort of [her] life." Coverture gone, separated from her children, the only aspect of royal identity Hermione has left is her honor, a quality that can only be recognized by a higher court—that of Apollo.

In *The Winter's Tale*, only the words of the women, Hermione and Paulina, are backed by Apollo. A horrible divine intervention occurs during the trial of Hermione, one that costs Hermione's son, Mamillius, his life; imposes sixteen years of separation between Leontes, Hermione, and their daughter; and kills Antigonus. The oracle proclaims:

> Hermione is chaste; Polixenes, blameless; Ca-
> millo a true subject; Leontes a jealous tyrant; his
> innocent babe truly begotten; and the king shall live
> without an heir, if that which is lost be not
> found.

(3.2.132–36)

Leontes blasphemes against the oracle of Apollo, saying, "There is no truth at all in the oracle." Leontes' son Mamillius dies immediately, and soon after Paulina reports that Hermione has died of grief. Until Leontes' daughter is recovered, Leontes shall have no heir.

Antigonus, without knowledge of the disaster at home, carries out his orders. He leaves the baby, whom he has named "Perdita," or "lost one," on the seashore of Bohemia with a box containing gold, jewels, and a letter explaining the baby's background.[24] Immediately after, Shakespeare follows with his most famous stage direction: "Exit, pursued by bear." Antigonus is duly dismembered and eaten, off-stage, and the ship that delivered him is swallowed by the sea.

Out of this Shakespeare, manages a happy ending. Perdita and the box are rescued by a shepherd and his son. She grows into a beautiful sixteen-year-old girl, with whom Florizel, King Polixenes' son, falls in love. Polixenes, impressed with Perdita but not her apparent humble origins, tries to block his son's marriage. Aided by Camillo, who wants to return home, the young couple flees to Sicily. Polixenes and Camillo follow. There Perdita's identity is discovered, and Leontes, having gained a son-in-law who, in a sense, substitutes for Mamillius, regains his family—with one great exception, Hermione. Paulina, however, who has functioned as the king's spiritual advisor since the day of his blasphemy, has a final card to play. She produces a statue of Hermione, miraculous in its likeness, especially because the sculptor has imagined Hermione sixteen years older than when she died. When the statue moves, the audience, having accepted the conventions of magic and fantasy appropriate to the play, is suspended between belief in a magical statue and a suspicion that Hermione has been in hiding with Paulina for these sixteen years. But this is a simulated resurrection; Hermione is indeed alive. She has separated herself from Leontes to fulfill the oracle by denying Leontes an heir until Perdita could be found.

The happy ending makes clear heaven's forgiveness of Leontes. His sincere penance, in proportion to his sin, makes way for the recovery of "that which was lost": Perdita and his own soul. In most Protestant denominations, the belief that faith alone, *sola fide*, justifies the soul before God tends to preclude a doctrine of penitential action, which smacks of working one's way to heaven. The Anglican church, however, remained close to Roman Catholic orthodoxy in its practices regarding penance. The ecclesiastical courts of England assigned penance for various sexual offenses, encouraged penitential actions by whole families on Shrove Tuesday, and allowed confession to a priest on a voluntary basis. (Under Elizabeth I, the position of the Anglican church regarding confession was that none must, all could, and some ought.) After hearing confessions, Anglican priests often would assign some kind of penance as a token of the sinner's forgiveness.

The point of penance, in both the Anglican and Roman Catholic churches was, and still is, to reorient the sinner toward God. Penance was not a way of atoning for one's sins, which had already been accomplished by grace through the death and resurrection of Christ, but a discipline that helped conform the soul to the will of God. The rationale, as stated in the current Roman Catholic Catechism, was as much a part of Catholic doctrine four hundred years ago as it is today:

> Many sins wrong our neighbor. . . . But sin also injures and weakens the sinner himself, as well as his relationships with God and neighbor. Absolution takes away sin, but it does not remedy all the disorders sin has caused. Raised up from sin, the sinner must still recover his full spiritual health by doing something more to make amends for the sin: he must "make satisfaction for" or "expiate" his sins. This satisfaction is also called "penance."
>
> The *penance* the confessor imposes must take into account the penitent's personal situation and must seek his spiritual good. It must correspond as far as possible with the gravity and nature of the sins

committed. It can consist of prayer, an offering, works
of mercy, service of neighbor, voluntary self-denial,
sacrifices, and above all the patient acceptance of
the cross we must bear. Such penances help configure
us to Christ, who alone expiated our sins once for all
. . . .[25]

Paulina, who functions as Leontes' personal confessor, at
first asserts that what he has done is beyond forgiveness; no
amount of repentance will be enough:

> O thou tyrant!
> Do not repent these things, for they are heavier
> Than all thy woes can stir: therefore betake thee
> To nothing but despair. A thousand knees
> Ten thousand years together, naked, fasting,
> Upon a barren mountain, and still winter
> In storm perpetual, could not move the gods . . .
>
> (3.2.207–13)

This seems utterly heartless, and is certainly born of intense
anger and despair; yet Paulina's voice has to compete with
others in the court who would try to let Leontes off easily, and
Leontes ought not be comforted until he feels the full impact
of what he has done. He chooses Paulina, who more than anyone has spoken the truth, to be his leader in sorrow. He imposes penance on himself, but makes Paulina his spiritual
administrator:

> Prithee, bring me
> To the dead bodies of my queen and son:
> One grave shall be for both: upon them shall
> The causes of their death appear, unto
> Our shame perpetual. Once a day I'll visit
> The chapel where they lie, and tears shed there
> Shall be my recreation. So long as nature

> Will bear up with this exercise, so long
> I daily vow to use it. Come, and lead me
> To these sorrows.
>
> (3.2.234–43)

Since part of Leontes' sin stems from pride—the worry that as a cuckold, he'll be a laughingstock—and part from shaming Hermione, publishing what he has done on the tomb of his wife and son is an appropriate penance; likewise, his failure to listen to those who tried to dissuade him from prosecuting Hermione will be repaid by Paulina's daily reminders of what he has done. Understandably, Leontes' courtiers want him to forgive himself and remarry. It would seem to be better for the kingdom to have an heir. After sixteen years of this penitential regimen have passed, Cleomenes tries to convince Leontes that he has done enough, that his sorrow has made up for his sin:

> Sir, you have done enough, and have perform'd
> A saint-like sorrow: no fault could you make,
> Which you have not redeem'd; indeed, paid down
> More penitence than done trespass: at the last,
> Do as the heavens have done, forget your evil;
> With them, forgive yourself.
>
> (5.1.1–6)

Cleomenes speech is wrongheaded in two ways. Penitential actions do not erase sin. They are for the good of the sinner, but have nothing to do with justification, which is a matter of grace. Second, the pagan conventions that Shakespeare has established continue to hold. There is no way to tell whether "the heavens" have forgotten Leontes' trespass until Perdita is found, and Paulina will not have Leontes remarry until the "dead" Hermione breathes. You killed her, she reminds

Leontes, constantly and brutally. However, the workings of grace, and therefore forgiveness, are woven into the fabric of this pre-Christian yet Christian play from the beginning. The word "grace," including its plural form, occurs twelve times in *The Winter's Tale*, and "gracious" occurs three times, making it a significant linguistic theme in the play. Most of these occurrences allude to the spiritual meaning of "grace" as a gratuitous gift of divine aid. Grace as a measure of divine blessings received (as in "full of grace") is often directly meant or punned upon. Leontes' forgiveness is the result of grace freely given, not of penitence.

The recovery of Perdita is a gift, grace working through Providence, as is the "resurrection" of Hermione, which as an analog of Christ's resurrection manifests grace. When Hermione is imprisoned, she says it is for her "better grace," indicating that trouble can sometimes be to a person's spiritual benefit. It may have recalled to Shakespeare's audience Romans 28:8: "we know that all things work together for the best unto them that love God, even to them that are called of his purpose." Falls can be fortunate and without suffering there can be no redemption, for as Portia says in *The Merchant of Venice*, "nothing is known without respect" to something else; only by contrast with evil do we know good. Commenting on the reunion of Perdita and Leontes, a gentleman comments, "Every wink of an eye, some new grace will be born," which as Roy Battenhouse points out, echoes St. Paul regarding the grace of resurrection: "In the twinkling of an eye, we shall be changed" (1 Corinthians 15:52).[26] And before Paulina is about to unveil Hermione as statue, she tells Leontes cryptically, "it is a surplus of your grace," the grace accorded to Leontes from heaven, which is about to effect the recovery of Hermione. Perdita kneels before the statue because she would like to believe she is receiving her mother's blessing, and when

Paulina tells Leontes she can make the statue move, she says, "It is requir'd / You do awake your faith." When the statue moves, and Hermione is seen to be alive, her first action is to grant her daughter's request: "You gods, look down / And from your sacred vials pour your graces / Upon my daughter's head!" (5.3.121–23). Hermione's blessing is a prayer that Perdita be anointed with sanctifying grace as received in baptism, which brings the soul into communion with God and enables it to act with love. The point of Christ's resurrection is that it releases such grace.

Virgil's Fourth Eclogue was taken by the Christian humanists of the Renaissance as a pagan prefiguring of Christ's coming. With *The Winter's Tale*, Shakespeare creates, after the fact, his own pagan prefiguring of Christ's resurrection. A winter's tale is an old tale, as old as death in winter and rebirth in spring. For Shakespeare's audience, *The Winter's Tale*, though wrapped in pagan garb, told the oldest, most important story of all, and one in which they themselves still participated.

Henry VIII: Wolsey and Katherine

Generically, *Henry VIII* is an unusual play. Like Shakespeare's first three plays, *Henry VI Parts 1, 2,* and *3, Henry VIII* has little connective tissue, but is rather a set of episodes, of which there are four, occurring in chronological order: the fall, trial, and execution of the Duke of Buckingham, ca. 1521; the trial and house arrest of Katherine of Aragon; Cardinal Wolsey's fall from power as Henry's chancellor; and the trial and rescue by Henry of Archbishop Cranmer on the same day on which Elizabeth I is born, September 7, 1533. Thematically, the play resembles *The Winter's Tale* in that it deals with suffering, reconciliation, and redemption; theatrically, it contains masque-like elements that make it comparable to *The Tem-*

pest. Our focus is on Henry's "Great Matter"—the annulment of his marriage to Katherine of Aragon—and the way in which Katherine and Wolsey face divine judgment. But to provide a context, we need to examine the first episode about Buckingham and the last about Cranmer, both of which illustrate corrupt judgment during the reign of Henry VIII.

The play begins not long after King Henry, aged 30, has signed a peace treaty with the French king, Francis I, at the Val d'Or in France. Historically, the English people had great hopes for Henry, and Shakespeare captures some of their enthusiasm in the first scene, in which Norfolk describes the commemoration of the peace treaty at "The Field of the Cloth of Gold." Norfolk tells Buckingham, who was pointedly absent, that he has missed the view of much earthly glory, each day of celebration topping what preceded, "To-day, the French, / All clinquant all in gold, like heathen gods / Shone down the English; and to-morrow they / Made Britain India: every man that stood / Show'd like a mine" (1.1.18–22).

The English traditionally admitted to stodgy, phlegmatic dispositions, but they also considered themselves tenacious and honest. They typically thought the French their opposites: vain and mercurial, affected in speech and dress. However, at the Field of the Cloth of Gold the English character seems to become French. Norfolk's comparison of the French to heathen gods applies as well to the English, who attempted to outdo the French in pomp and display. The duke of Buckingham criticizes this spectacle, describing its destructive cost to the realm, and all for a treaty that has already failed.[27] Buckingham refers to the ceremonies and tournaments as "fierce vanities," which have driven some of the nobility close to bankruptcy. He blames these useless expenditures on the king's minister, Wolsey, who Buckingham believes has been bribed by Katherine's nephew, the Holy Roman Emperor,

Charles I, to advise Henry to break the peace treaty shortly after its adoption.

Wolsey, who had become Henry's chancellor and a cardinal in 1515, was a man of boundless ambition who wanted to use Henry as his instrument to become pope. Henry was content to delegate most of his governing power to Wolsey, making him, for most practical purposes, the most powerful man in England. When Buckingham accuses Wolsey of treasonous activity, Buckingham's friends warn him that Wolsey is too powerful to challenge. Buckingham's arrest immediately follows his accusation of Wolsey, and he knows he is as good as dead: "It will help me nothing to plead my innocence, for that dye is on me which makes my whit'st part black" (1.1.208–09). Wolsey is the dye. Henry pronounces Buckingham's death even before trial: "A giant traitor," he calls him, ensuring that no one will dare find Buckingham innocent.

Buckingham's trial is reminiscent of the rigged trials Shakespeare depicts in *Henry VI, Part 2* and *Richard III*. Buckingham is soon convicted of treason by the report of a bribed witness and executed. His last words support Norfolk's characterization of the festivities at the Field of the Cloth of Gold as heathenish:

> I have this day receiv'd a traitor's judgment,
> And by that name must die; yet heaven bear witness,
> And if I have a conscience, let it sink me,
> Even as the axe falls, if I be not faithful.
> The law I bear no malice for my death,
> 'T has done upon the premises but justice:
> *But those that sought it I could wish more Christians.*
>
> (2.1.58–64; italics added)

Given the circumstances of Buckingham's last words, Shakespeare's audience would have given them great credit.

People going to the block tried to "die well," forgiving, seeking forgiveness, and telling the truth. When Sir Thomas Lovell, accompanying Buckingham to execution, asks his forgiveness, Buckingham replies:

> Sir Thomas Lovell, I as free forgive you
> As I would be forgiven: I forgive all.
> There cannot be those numberless offences
> 'Gainst me that I cannot take peace with: no black
>   envy
> Shall make my grave. Commend me to his grace,
> And if he speaks of Buckingham, pray tell him
> You met him half in heaven: my vows and prayers
> Yet are the king's, and till my soul forsake
> Shall cry blessings on him.
>
>   (2.1.82–90)

Those who Buckingham would have wished more Christian, who have angled for his life, are most clearly Wolsey and possibly Henry, though the audience will have to become better acquainted with Shakespeare's stage king before they can make a confident judgment that Buckingham is right. Buckingham's death becomes the foil for those of Katherine and Wolsey. It sets the standard for a good death and shows how the world appears to those about to enter eternity.

Some commentators see *Henry VIII* as the story of a young, naïve king, who trustingly puts his faith in Wolsey (the advisor he inherited from his father), is duped by Wolsey during the first years of his reign, makes a mistake about Buckingham, and then comes to a maturity of judgment that is the undoing of Wolsey and the beginning of just rule. Certainly, this is not the historical Henry, and, I would argue, it is not Shakespeare's. As Battenhouse indicates, Shakespeare is writing in the tradition of *De Casibus* tragedy, which portrays the downfall of great and ambitious men; this genre is based on Christian tradition and the *Consolatio* of Boethius.[28] Wolsey sets forth the play's theme when near the end of his life he says, "Vain pomp and glory of this world, I hate ye!" Henry's court is the seat of vanity and Henry himself has an insatiable appetite for glory and sensual pleasure.

The destructiveness and injustice Henry is ready to countenance to get what he wants are illustrated mainly through the three trials of the play, all of which are "rigged," either by Henry or with his consent, and in each instance Henry's self-interest or vindictiveness plays a part. Buckingham's trial serves as prologue to the diagnostic episode, Henry's infatuation with Anne Boleyn and infidelity to his wife, Katherine.

Shakespeare establishes early in the play that Katherine has the best interests of her husband and of England at heart. We first see her as a petitioner for the realm, begging her husband to abolish taxes (currently set at the rate of one-sixth of each taxpayer's "substance") that she blames Wolsey for exacting. We next see her pleading for Buckingham; she points out that the main witness against him, his surveyor, is biased, Buckingham having sacked the man because of the complaints of his tenants. Knowing Wolsey's determination to get Buckingham, she says, "My learn'd lord cardinal, / Deliver all with charity" (1.2.144–45), and she tells the surveyor to "take good heed / You charge not in your spleen a noble person / And spoil your nobler soul" (1.2.173–75). Though Katherine is able to bring about a change of policy regarding the taxes (she successfully shows how dangerously unpopular they are), she can do nothing for Buckingham, and ends her intervention with "God mend all," leaving the audience to decide who needs mending. Katherine is clearly set up as the opposite of Wolsey, and as the play proceeds, of her husband.

The episode of Buckingham's arrest shortly precedes

Henry's meeting Anne Boleyn at a dinner given by Wolsey. Henry dances with Anne, and his first words to her are: "The fairest hand I ever touch'd: O beauty, / Till now I never knew thee" (1.4.75–76). Shortly after this, Wolsey becomes precisely as valuable to Henry as he is effective in procuring the annulment of Henry's marriage to Katherine.

Henry's loyalty to anyone in the play begins and ends with their utility to him. This is pointedly dramatized at the end of the play in the plot against Henry's cleric, Archbishop Cranmer. Cranmer, who had granted an annulment to Henry in May 1533, has aroused the envy of Stephen Gardiner, the bishop of Winchester. Gardiner's plan, backed by other members of the King's Council, is to accuse Cranmer of treason and have him executed. Cranmer is in much the same position as Buckingham, except that in this instance Henry saves the accused rather than aiding in his destruction. Before meeting with his council, Henry gives Cranmer a lesson in practical politics and the courtroom. Without his intervention as king, Henry tells Cranmer, Cranmer's judicial murder is virtually assured; judicial verdicts reflect not honest judgment based on fact, but the king's will:

>   Know you not
> How your state stands i'th'world, with the whole
>   world?
> Your enemies are many, and not small; their practices
> Must bear the same proportion, and not ever
> The justice and the truth o'th'question carries
> The due o'th'verdict with it: at what ease
> Might corrupt minds procure knaves as corrupt
> To swear against you? such things have been done.
>
>   (5.1.126–34)

To Buckingham, for instance, such things have been done, but Henry makes it clear to the terrified Cranmer that he need only fear the verdict of one person in the realm, and that is Henry, who supersedes all courts: "Thy truth and thy integrity is rooted / In us thy friend" (5.1.114–15), "They [the Privy Council, which also served as a court] shall no more prevail than *we* give way to" (5.1.143; italics added). Cranmer has proven a useful servant to Henry, who wants to keep him. Henry's analysis comes as no surprise to the audience, which has already seen Henry's manipulation of Katherine's trial, which occurs in the second act.

Historians attribute Henry VIII's desire to annul his marriage with Katherine to three things: (1) Katherine's failure, after twenty years of effort, to bear him a son; (2) his conscience, which was troubled by the fact that he had married his brother's wife, an act contrary to one interpretation of two verses from Leviticus (Leviticus 20:21, "And if a man shall take his brother's wife, it is an unclean thing . . . they shall be childless"; and Leviticus 18:16: "Thou shalt not uncover the nakedness of thy brother's wife: it is thy brother's nakedness."); and, (3) his infatuation with Anne Boleyn. Shakespeare puts forth all of these theories to his audience. The order in which these factors impinged on Henry's mind, or the weight he gave to each, is a matter of controversy. Pope Clement VII, virtually a prisoner of Katherine's nephew, Charles I, was not in a position to grant Henry's request for an annulment, and thus, what might have been resolved by a rather routine papal dispensation led to Henry's break from Rome, the annulment of his marriage to Katherine, and the English Reformation.

When Shakespeare's Norfolk asks the Lord Chamberlain why there are rumors of "separation" between Henry and Katherine, he replies "It seems the marriage with his brother's wife / Has crept too near his conscience" (2.2.16–17).

Shakespeare does not delve into the theological intricacies of this problem, but his audience may have realized Henry's argument was weak, even on the basis of Leviticus, which, according to the weight of authority, not only failed to support, but actually undermined Henry's action for an annulment.[29] Given the fact that Henry had a papal dispensation to marry Katherine, obtained just in case such questions arose, and given Katherine's claim that her marriage to the young prince, Henry's older brother Arthur, was never consummated (which was probable, due to their youth and the quickness with which Arthur Tudor's fatal illness followed their marriage), Henry's arguments for annulment were thin indeed.

Norfolk's statement about Henry's conscience being troubled is undercut severely by Suffolk's immediate aside to the audience: "No, his conscience / Has crept too near another lady" (2.2.17–18). Shakespeare's audience would have credited Suffolk's assertion on the basis of history and because of the stage convention that asides are often meant to give reliable inside information. Both Suffolk and Norfolk recognize that divorcing Katherine would be a travesty, but Norfolk blames it on the cardinal alone:

> He dives into the king's soul, and there scatters
> Dangers, doubts, wringing of the conscience,
> Fears and despairs, and all these for his marriage:
> And out of all these, to restore the king,
> He counsels a divorce, a loss of her
> That like a jewel has hung twenty years
> About his neck, yet never lost her luster;
> Of her that loves him with that excellence
> That angels love good men with; even of her
> That when the greatest stroke of fortune falls
> Will bless the king.

> (2.2.26–36)

The last line and a half recalls the "stroke" of Buckingham's execution, thus linking Katherine's destruction to his, but the audience will find that Norfolk's blame of Wolsey is wide of the mark. Henry's eager progress in his love affair with Anne is obvious. And if Wolsey wants an annulment of Henry's marriage, it is not to promote the Anne Boleyn affair, for Wolsey declares his intention to bring about a marriage that is more practical politically: "It shall be to the Duchess of Alençon, / The French king's sister; he shall marry her. / Anne Bullen? no; I'll no Anne Bullens for him, / There's more in't than fair visage" (3.2.85–88).

But Henry's desire is unshakeable after his first dance with Anne. He makes her marchioness of Pembroke before the annulment proceedings even begin and gives her a living of one thousand pounds per year to boot.[30] At the end of the first day of the trial, after Katherine gives Henry's progress toward divorce a major setback, he reveals his real feelings to the audience in an aside that confirms Suffolk: "These cardinals trifle with me: I abhor / This dilatory sloth and tricks of Rome." He simply wants his divorce as quickly as possible. Wolsey will fall because he cannot get it for him.

The history of Henry's "Great Matter," his divorce of Katherine, is a fascinating tale of desire, politics, and danger. Shakespeare tries to give his audience a sense of Katherine's personal story with two highly dramatic scenes, the first being her one and only day in court, the second her approach to death. Katherine's brilliant performance in court assures that Henry will not get his divorce quickly.

Holinshed's account suggests that during the annulment trial, Katherine might have been following the conduct-book advice of her good friend Vives, using her modesty as a weapon.[31] Holinshed's Katherine displays innocence under attack as well as a humility and unwillingness to proceed with-

out male counsel that the conduct-book writers urged upon
women throughout the Renaissance. Shakespeare follows
Holinshed's account of Katherine's speech very closely, the
main difference being that Shakespeare gives Katherine four
more short but fiery pieces of dialogue aimed at Cardinal
Wolsey, which she prefaces with "my drops of tears / I'll turn
to sparks of fire" (2.4.70–71).

Katherine's first courtroom speech, directed only to Henry,
follows. The stage directions are important and follow
Holinshed's description of Katherine's action when she is called
into court. The similarity to Hermione's courtroom speeches
is striking:

> The Queen makes no answer,
> rises out of her chair, goes about the court,
> comes to the King, and kneels at his feet:
> then speaks.

> Sir, I desire you do me right and justice,
> And to bestow your pity on me; for
> I am a most poor woman, and a stranger,
> Born out of your dominions: having here
> No judge indifferent, nor no more assurance
> Of equal friendship and proceeding. Alas sir,
> In what have I offended you? What cause
> Hath my behaviour given to your displeasure,
> That thus you should proceed to put me off,
> And take your good grace from me? Heaven witness,
> I have been to you a true and humble wife,
> At all times to your will conformable,
> Ever in fear to kindle your dislike,
> Yea, subject to your countenance, glad or sorry
> As I saw it inclin'd. When was the hour
> I ever contradicted your desire
> Or made it not mine too? . . .

> . . . Sir, call to mind
> That I have been your wife, in this obedience
> Upward to twenty years, and have been blest
> With many children by you. If in the course
> And process of this time you can report,
> And prove it too, against mine honour aught,
> My bond to wedlock, or my love and duty
> Against your sacred person; in God's name
> Turn me away, and let the foul'st contempt
> Shut door upon me, and so give me up
> To the sharp'st kind of justice. Please you, sir,
> The king your father was reputed for
> A prince most prudent, of an excellent
> And unmatch'd wit and judgment: Ferdinand
> My father, King of Spain, was reckon'd one
> The wisest prince that there had reign'd by many
> A year before. It is not to be question'd
> That they had gathered a wise council to them
> Of every realm, that did debate this business,
> Who deem'd our marriage lawful: wherefore I humbly
> Beseech you sir, to spare me till I may
> Be by my friends in Spain advis'd, whose counsel
> I will implore.

(2.4.11–26; 32–54)

Katherine tries to transform the nature of the court proceeding from a legal to an intimately personal one by talking to Henry as wife to husband, as if no one else were present in the courtroom, though of course she understands the dramatic effect of what she is doing. By refusing to cast herself as anything but a good and loyal wife, Katherine applies great pressure on Henry to act in kind as a husband.

Like Hermione, Katherine stresses that she is the daughter of a great king, and she is a foreigner who can count on no help from her family but is forced, as Blanche DuBois might say, to rely on the kindness of strangers. Like Hermione,

Katherine recalls her humility, her isolation, and her honorable conduct as Henry's wife. Both women assert that they have borne their husbands' children, have been true to their wedding vows, and that now it is time for their husbands to be true to theirs.

Katherine protects her modesty during the rest of the lengthy trial by throwing herself on her husband's mercy and then refusing to attend additional court sessions, although she absents herself in defiance of the court's order to return. As a woman who should be protected by her husband she is out of place in court. She adopts the role that Vives urges, that of the widow of Luke 18. Like Hermione, she points out the bias of the judges while at the same time asserting her status as Henry's loyal wife, a woman still under Henry's "cover." She lists a perfect record of wifely conduct, alluding to twenty years of nearly constant pregnancy. All this is, in effect, an assertion of coverture. Katherine's statement, "I have to you been a true and humble wife / always to your will conformable" is a plea to Henry to recognize his duty to cover his wife and shield her from harm, which he cannot act on without dismissing the entire proceeding.

Katherine's reference to the determination by both Henry's father and her own that her marriage to Henry was valid—that, in a sense, she was given away by two men—stresses her own modesty. It also recalls Hooker's explanation of why men give away women in marriage, and at the same time places two male opinions against Henry's. It is interesting that Shakespeare's source, Holinshed, and therefore Shakespeare also, does not report the two most telling sentences of Katherine's speech: "And when ye had me at the first, I take God to be my judge, I was a true maid, without touch of man. And whether this be true or no, I put it to your conscience."[32] That is, Katherine's marriage to Henry is valid because her marriage to his older brother, Arthur, was never consummated. Henry's pangs of conscience about marrying his brother's wife are beside the point because there never was a marriage, which Henry well knows. This was Katherine's courtroom bombshell, and it is not surprising that a Tudor chronicler, not wanting to offend the queen by insulting her father, would leave it out, and Shakespeare probably never had knowledge of it. Katherine certainly is not how she describes herself to Wolsey, "a simple woman, much too weak / T'oppose your cunning."

Both Hermione and Katherine challenge their courts because they know they cannot get a fair trial, and this is Katherine's main motive in walking out. Katherine tells Wolsey, who along with Cardinal Campeius is her judge:

> I do believe
> (Induc'd by potent circumstances) that
> You are mine enemy, and make my challenge.
> You shall not be my judge. . . .
> ....
> I do refuse you for my judge, and here
> Before you all, appeal unto the Pope,
> To bring my whole cause 'fore his holiness
> And to be judg'd by him.

> (2.4.73–76; 116–19)

After Katherine leaves the courtroom (despite calls by the bailiff for her to return), Henry praises her at length, but he is just trying to save face. What we might have taken for sincerity is undermined by his aside, in which he complains of the cardinals' lack of effectiveness in bringing the trial to successful conclusion. Historically, although Katherine was finally the loser, her comportment brought her great support. With the help of Charles I, Eustache Chapuys (the Imperial Ambassador), and some courageous Englishmen, she held off the divorce action for six years. Her intellect was superior to Henry's. Even her enemy, Thomas Cromwell, said that "Nature had wronged the Queen in not making her a man."[33]

Katherine saw herself not only as fighting to retain her marriage, but to keep England Catholic and to save her husband's soul. During her protracted battle she played the modesty card many times, and it had the effect Vives predicted: it made men want to come to her rescue. For a period of time, when discontentment with Henry VIII and Anne Boleyn was at its height, Katherine might have led a successful Catholic rebellion against Henry. But Eustache Chapuys could never convince her to do it. Her conscience would not let her precipitate a civil war in England, whose people she had come to love. And she had hope for Henry, almost to the end.

Katherine's old enemy, Wolsey, dies before she does, stripped of his chancellorship for failing to obtain the divorce Henry so wanted. Wolsey looks back over a life of ambitious power-brokering and manipulation, and realizes it was all for nothing. Near death, he almost gives way to despair: "Had I but serv'd my God with half the zeal / I serv'd my king, he would not in mine age / Have left me naked to mine enemies" (3.2.455–57). With Wolsey's admission of nakedness, Shakespeare reintroduces the idea of coverture as "cover," but he expands it to include the human race in its relationship to God. Wolsey's longing for a divine cover of protection is analogous to that which women, in theory, were entitled from their husbands.

If what Wolsey means by cover is divine consolation and hope for a better life in heaven, he has indeed changed from the ambitious materialist he was. If he is thinking of cover in a more worldly sense—that those true to God will have some sort of special protection on earth—his assertion is falsified by Katherine's experience, since she gets no justice from Henry. But even Wolsey, the most blatant villain of the play, recovers himself at the end, and Katherine's man Griffith reports that he has "died well":

> About the hour of eight, which he himself
> Foretold should be his last, full of repentance,
> Continual meditations, tears and sorrows,
> He gave his honours to the world again,
> His blessed part to heaven, and slept in peace. . . .
> ....
> His overthrow heap'd happiness upon him,
> For then, and not till then, he felt himself,
> And found the blessedness of being little;
> And to add greater honours to his age
> Than man could give him, he died fearing God.
>
> (4.2.26–30; 64–68)

Katherine, who is ill, finds Griffith's account of her old enemy comforting. And seeing Katherine following in the footsteps of Buckingham and Wolsey, perhaps Shakespeare's audience felt a sense of the absurd importance men place on career and prestige.

Katherine is the only character Shakespeare depicts as being accepted into heaven. This occurs in Katherine's dream, which is staged while she sleeps, but there is no reason to doubt the dream as promise. Six "personages" in white robes, "wearing on their heads garlands of bays, and golden vizards on their faces, branches of bays or palm in their hands," bow to her and take turns holding an extra garland over her head. Still sleeping, Katherine makes signs of rejoicing and holds her hands to heaven, but she wakes with a sense of loss: "Spirits of peace, where are ye? are ye all gone? / And leave me here in wretchedness behind ye?" (4.2.83–84). She asks Griffith:

> Saw you not even now a blessed troop
> Invite me to a banquet, whose bright faces
> Cast thousand beams upon me, like the sun?
> They brought me garlands, Griffith, which I feel
> I am not worthy yet to wear; I shall, *assuredly.*
>
> (4.2.87–92; italics added)

Katherine lived until 1536, dying less than six months before Anne Boleyn was executed. Shakespeare chooses to end his play with the redemptive birth and christening of Elizabeth, who performs much the same function as Perdita in *The Winter's Tale.* Cranmer prophesies Elizabeth will be the queen who unites England in greatness, the royal infant who promises "a thousand thousand blessings upon this land . . . the happiness of England." Anne's displacement of Katherine, seen in historical perspective, turns out to issue in a blessing.

The divine sanction that Katherine is given by her dream is succeeded by one even more powerful and surprising—the explicit approval of her author, an honor that Shakespeare bestowed on *none* of his other creations. If the play gets applause, the epilogue says, it will most likely come from women, in appreciation of Katherine:

> . . . I fear
> All the expected good w'are like to hear
> For this play at this time is only in
> The merciful construction of good women,
> For *such a one we show'd 'em.* . .
>
> (Epilogue, 7–11; italics added)

One has to wonder what Shakespeare thought about the Reformation, and whether his religious bent was not more Catholic than Protestant. Were Elizabeth and England's emergence as a great power worth the Reformation? Perhaps Shakespeare, comparing trees in winter to cloisters, "where late the sweet birds sang," had his doubts. His plays reflect the understanding of both Catholics and Protestants that nothing which happened was outside of God's providential design. While *The Winter's Tale* and *Henry VIII* bear out Shakespeare's description of man as a "giddy thing" (Benedick's phrase from *Much Ado about Nothing*), their heroines, Hermione and Katherine, remain figures of steadfast integrity, the beneficiaries of God's cover if not of their husbands'.

No man has a right to lead such a life of contemplation as to forget in his own case the service due his neighbor; nor has any man a right to be so immersed in active life as to neglect the contemplation of God."

St. Augustine,
The City of God, XIX, 18

Every action of yours, every thought, should be those of one who expects to die before the day is out. . . . If you aren't fit to face death today, it's very unlikely you will be tomorrow.

Thomas à Kempis,
The Imitation of Christ

6

The Tempest: Judgment and Divine Providence

It is impossible, in the field of Shakespeare studies, to find a more corrupt and politically motivated body of criticism than that which has been attached to *The Tempest*. For new historicists and cultural materialists, the hero of the play, Prospero, has become a model for everything wrong with Western culture. To them, he is a colonial imperialist, a slave owner (and a cruel one, to boot), a misogynist—in short, one who takes a nasty pleasure in exerting power and control over everything around him. By implication, much of the mud thrown at Prospero sticks to Shakespeare. Political and feminist critics tend to be poor readers of literature, and therefore, even the play's most obvious themes and ideas get lost in the cacophony.[1]

The Tempest, however, is one of Shakespeare's most humane plays, and like *The Merchant of Venice* and *Measure for*

Measure, it takes its core ideals from the Sermon on the Mount and situates them in a dangerous, Machiavellian world. *The Tempest* is about a man who makes grave political and personal mistakes but has one last chance, near the end of his life, to repair the damage he has done. The play is about temperance, the exercise and relinquishment of power, and forgiveness. Finally, it is about the judgment that Prospero, the former duke of Milan, metes unto his enemies, knowing that someday he must come to judgment himself.

Prospero's misfortune is that he has the introverted and reclusive temperament of a scholar, fine in itself, but, when taken to the extreme, unsuitable in a political leader. Prospero's mistake, much like Duke Vincentio's in *Measure for Measure*, is in giving full reign to his scholarly tendencies rather than performing his duties as duke. Eventually, Prospero is rousted out of his library and overthrown by his brother. But in effect, he had abdicated long before.

The play begins with a tempest twelve years after Prospero's deposition, a tempest in which we meet Prospero's main opponents: his brother, Antonio; Alonso, the king of Naples; and Sebastian, the king's brother. We also meet the king's counselor and Prospero's former benefactor, Gonzalo. All are returning to Italy from northern Africa, where the king's daughter, Claribel, has unwillingly married the king of Tunis. Their ship, caught in the storm, threatens to founder. They do not know yet—and neither does the audience—that the storm has been called up by Prospero, who, marooned with his daughter on a nearby island, has become a powerful sorcerer.

As is often the case with Shakespeare's opening scenes, this one broaches many of the issues to be developed during the play. As the sailors try to save the ship, the royal party panics, interfering with the crew. The boatswain orders the king and his followers to get below, and Gonzalo, offended by the man's insolence, asks him to be patient. The boatswain replies, "What care these roarers for the name of king?" Imminent drowning makes all men equal, and there are none aboard "that I love more than myself," the boatswain says, a sentiment that will be put into action by several survivors of the storm. The issue of legitimate authority is raised, ironically, by the boatswain's reference to Gonzalo's lack of such: "You are a counselor; if you can command these elements to silence and work the peace of the present, we will not hand a rope more; use your authority." Gonzalo cannot do this, but Prospero, who created the storm, can. Finally, the element of fate is introduced, for Gonzalo takes hope in the boatswain: the ship will survive the storm, he rationalizes, because the boatswain was born to hang. "Stand fast, good Fate," Gonzalo says, "to his hanging: make the rope of his destiny our cable." The scene presents a microcosm of judgment day, its inescapability, the equality of souls before God, and judgment as man's fate, the culmination of history and fulfillment of God's providential plan.[2] What happens on the island will recapitulate the action of this scene, and the last speech of the mariners, "All lost, to prayers, to prayers," will resonate with the epilogue, Prospero's last speech.

When Prospero's daughter, Miranda, sees the ship, she believes it has been dashed to pieces. "Miranda" derives from the word "admiration," which we would translate as "wonder." She is a wonder in herself, but more importantly, she has a great capacity for wonder and empathy. Fifteen years old, she has spent the past twelve on the island with her father. She has no experience of the human race; she is fresh, defenseless, and innocent. Yet she seems to have inherited her father's capacity for command (and anger), and she has acquired from him a sophisticated education. But in the first scene, she is full of sympathetic concern for the people on

board the ship and begs her father, if he has caused the storm,
to make it stop:

> . . . O, I have suffered
> With those that I saw suffer! a brave vessel,
> (Who had, no doubt, some noble creature in her,)
> Dash'd all to pieces. O, the cry did knock
> Against my very heart! Poor souls, they perish'd!
> Had I been any god of power, I would
> Have sunk the sea within the earth, or ere
> It should the good ship so have swallow'd, and
> The fraughting souls within her.

(1.2.5–14)

Miranda, throughout the play, is the voice of awe and sympathy. But here she also shows a fine diplomatic tact. In referring to what she would do if she were "any god of power" she
is indirectly addressing her father and perhaps even criticizing him a little, but in her oblique way she is a perfectly tact-
ful Renaissance daughter. Miranda's description of the people
on board as "poor souls" and "fraughting souls" poses the
central question of the plot—what will be the fate of these
souls? The religious connotation is part of her meaning and
becomes more important as the play progresses. Miranda further suggests a comparison of the tempest to doomsday, "The
sky, it seems, would pour down stinking pitch, / But that the
sea, mounting to th' welkin's cheek, / Dashes the fire out"
(1.2.3–5). For the men on the boat, the world has been reduced to a chaotic mixture of water, air, and—courtesy of
Prospero's spirit-servant, Ariel—Saint Elmo's fire. The sea
threatens to smash the ship against the sky, but its passengers
will be spit up, on land, for Prospero to judge.

Prospero's History and Fortune's Celestial Clock

The Tempest, Harold Bloom declares, is "fundamentally plot-less," and though he exaggerates somewhat, most of its plot is given to us as narrative in act 1, scene 2, in which Prospero tells Miranda her origins.[3] After assuring her that the people on board the ship are safe, Prospero begins his long *protasis,* broken intermittently by questions and exclamations from Miranda, explaining to her who she is and how they came to be on the island. Though Miranda has asked about her origins before, Prospero has always said, "Stay, not yet." Now Prospero begins by trying to awaken her memory, for it is the course of history that Prospero wants to correct, and the wrong turn happened twelve years earlier, in "the dark backward and abysm of time" (1.2.50).

Twelve years earlier, Prospero, the duke of Milan, "rapt in secret studies" and not wanting to be bothered with administrative chores, had put his brother, Antonio, in charge of Milan's government. Antonio took to the job with such alacrity that he began to conceive of himself as the duke, and the courtiers of Milan, recognizing who had the power to give or deny them what they wanted, began to think the same. Antonio, Prospero explains,

> Being once perfected how to grant suits,
> How to deny them, who t'advance, and who
> To trash for over-topping, new created
> The creatures that were mine, I say, or chang'd 'em,
> Or else new form'd 'em; having both the key
> Of officer and office, set all hearts i' th' state
> To what tune pleas'd his ear . . .
>
> (1.2.79–85)

Prospero has been seen by many critics as dictatorial, but he recognizes that his failure to exert control over the ambi-

tious people in his realm resulted in his deposition, and sometimes this motivates his forceful treatment of Ariel and Caliban
(his two strange servants), the people from the ship, and even
his daughter. In the dangerous world of Italian politics,
Prospero's great failure, to himself and his countrymen, was
his *unwillingness* to exercise power.

Prospero realizes that this failure was not only a political
blunder but morally wrong in that it tempted his brother to
sin. Prospero himself was much too immersed in the knowledge and power magic might give him:

> I, thus neglecting worldly ends, all dedicated
> To closeness and the bettering of my mind
> ....
> ... in my false brother
> Awak'd an evil nature; and my trust,
> Like a good parent, did beget of him
> A falsehood in its contrary, as great
> As my trust was; which had indeed no limit.
>
> (1.2.89–90; 92–96)

Antonio, thinking his brother ill-suited for government
and wanting to be "Absolute Milan" himself, made an alliance with Prospero's "enemy... inveterate," the king of Naples.
"One midnight" he opened the gates of Milan to the Neapoli-
tans, who captured Prospero and his three-year-old daughter,
Miranda, and after taking them to sea, set them adrift:

> ... they hurried us aboard a bark,
> Bore us some leagues to sea; where they prepared
> A rotten carcass of a butt, not rigg'd,
> Nor tackle, sail, nor mast; the very rats
> Instinctively have quit it.
>
> (1.2.144–48)

Before Prospero and Miranda were put to drift, however, they were helped by the very man who had been charged with putting them to sea, Gonzalo, who not only gave them food and clothing, but volumes from Prospero's library, which, Prospero says, he prized "above his dukedom." Unrigged, the boat could not be steered, a detail that allows Shakespeare to emphasize that Prospero and Miranda are in the hands of Providence.[4] Now, twelve years later, Prospero has the chance to confront his enemies and escape the island:

> By accident most strange, bountiful Fortune,
> (Now my dear lady) hath mine enemies
> Brought to this shore; and by my prescience
> I find my zenith doth depend upon
> A most auspicious star, whose influence
> If now I court not, but omit, my fortunes
> Will ever after droop.

(1.2.178–84)

Prospero has until "six," the couple of hours in which the play takes place, to put things right. He sees himself not working against Providence but with it. *The Tempest* is the only play in which Shakespeare observes the unities of time, place, and action.[5] Fortune has given Prospero a very limited time to accomplish what he wants. He works against the clock of the zodiac, and in harmony with the favorable position of one star, which, for a few hours only, will enable him to recover Milan. Critics of Prospero's strong-arm tactics, who apply our notions of egalitarianism to the sixteenth century, are being both ahistorical and naïve. Prospero must be all attention to the task at hand or lose his chance to get himself and Miranda off the island. He must hurry, and this leaves him little choice but to be hamfisted, at times, even with his daughter and Ariel, the spirit he loves.

Most of the royal entourage make it ashore together. These include King Alonso of Naples, Antonio, Sebastian, Gonzalo, and a few other courtiers. Prospero sees to it that Alonso's son Ferdinand swims to shore separately, and his father fears that he is drowned. In addition, two people Prospero has never met are washed up on the island: these are the low comedians of the play, Stephano, Alonso's drunken butler, and Trinculo, Alonso's court jester.

On the island, Gonzalo finds that his garments, and those of the others, are "as fresh as when we put them on first in Afric," as if they were "new dyed than stained with salt water." The cleansing of the men's clothing is an obvious analogy to the cleansing of the soul through baptism, though in these men such purification has yet to occur. This small miracle is a hint from Prospero to the men about their need to repent so that forgiveness and purification will follow. Gonzalo's words would have reminded playgoers of Isaiah 1:18–20, which sets forth the two courses these men may take and foreshadows what will happen when Prospero lays an imaginary banquet before them: "Though your sins were as crimson, they shall be made white as snow: though they were red like scarlet, they shall be as wool. / If ye consent and obey, ye shall eat the good things of the land. / But if ye refuse and be rebellious, ye shall be devoured with the sword: for the mouth of the Lord hath spoken it."

Prospero's intentions for the "shipwrecked" men are not at all clear to the audience, and perhaps not entirely to Prospero himself. After twelve years, Prospero's enemies are at his mercy, but what will he do with them? He has two clear objectives. One is to marry his daughter to Ferdinand and, through this political marriage, to end the hostility between King Alonso and himself. The second is to bring the royal castaways to some kind of judgment and perhaps to awaken in them some sense of remorse by putting them in the position that Prospero himself was in twelve years earlier. To this end Prospero employs Ariel, "an airy spirit," to bedevil them. Prospero's manipulation of the castaways, aimed at bringing them to sorrow and repentance, is complicated by two plot elements reminiscent of Prospero's overthrow: Sebastian, the king's brother, and Antonio plot to kill King Alonso; and the two clowns, Stephano and Trinculo, conspire with Caliban to murder Prospero and become kings of the island. The latter conspiracy becomes the low comic parody of the former, and both challenge Prospero to be more alert than when he was duke.

Prospero and His Servants, Ariel and Caliban

Prospero has been portrayed by so many recent critics as a proto-Western imperialist, slave owner, and exploiter of native populations that it is necessary to examine his two servants, Caliban and Ariel, and their relationship to Prospero. Caliban, whose name is a near-anagram of "cannibal," is the offspring of Sycorax, a witch who, born in Algiers, was marooned on the island by her countrymen, as Prospero puts it, "For mischiefs manifold, and sorceries terrible / To enter human hearing" (1.2.264–65). We do not know for sure who Caliban's father was, but Prospero, whether seriously or out of spite, tells Caliban he was "got by the devil himself / Upon thy wicked dam" (1.2.321–22). We learn that the pregnant Sycorax was brought to the island about twelve years before Prospero and Miranda landed, making Caliban twenty-four on the day of the tempest. There are also indications that Caliban is not quite human; Trinculo, at first, mistakes him for a fish, and not a fresh one. Prospero describes him as "A freckled whelp, hag-born—not honour'd with / A human shape" (1.2.283–84). Harold Bloom notes that the relationship between Prospero and Caliban is more that of father and son than master and slave[6] and indeed, it starts out that way, according to Caliban's own description:

> When thou cam'st first,
> Thou strok'st me and made much of me; wouldst give
> me
> Water with berries in't; and teach me how
> To name the bigger light, and how the less,
> That burn by day and night: and then I loved thee,
> And show'd thee all the qualities o'th' isle,
> The fresh springs, brine pits, barren place and fertile:
>
> (1.2.332–38)

Miranda even helped with Caliban's education:

> I pitied thee,
> Took pains to make thee speak, taught thee each hour
> One thing or other: when thou didst not, savage,
> Know thine own meaning, but wouldst gabble like
> A thing most brutish, I endow'd thy purposes
> With words that made them known.
>
> (1.2.355–60)

Caliban, however, is not quite civilized. In the play he represents natural man, and not the "noble savage" imagined by Montaigne in his essay "Of Cannibals," which Shakespeare used as a source. Rather than being a noble savage, free from the corrupting influence of civilization, Caliban is natural man in the worst sense, fallen into sin but unredeemed, controlled by passion rather than reason and lacking the inhibitions that make civilization possible. His outward form, part bestial, emblematizes passion's control over reason, and yet he will be shown to be more reasonable than either of the two men (Stephano and Trinculo) he falls in with later in the play. Prospero despairingly describes Caliban as one

> . . . on whose nature
> Nurture can never stick; on whom my pains,
> Humanely taken, all, all lost, quite lost;
> And as with age his body uglier grows,
> So his mind cankers.

(4.1.188–92)

Caliban is Shakespeare's rebuttal to Montaigne, a refutation of the notion that were it not for "civilization," man would retain his Edenic character. Shakespeare holds to the doctrine of original sin, that is, the teaching that man has an ingrained tendency toward evil from birth. (To show that "civilized" people can be as bad or worse than natural man—their sophistication aiding their cunning—Shakespeare gives us Antonio and Sebastian.) Caliban's happy home life with Prospero and Miranda comes to an end before the play begins when he tries to rape Miranda. "O ho, O ho!" Caliban tells Prospero, "would't had been done! Thou didst prevent me; I had peopled else this isle with Calibans" (1.2.351–53). Thus, when the play begins, we see Prospero using Caliban for manual labor. But Prospero's anger toward Caliban reveals a deep frustration with the failure that he and Caliban share: Caliban, it seems, cannot change, and there is nothing that Prospero, for all his magic, can do to change him.

Though Caliban has only about one hundred lines in the play, Shakespeare is still able to give his character some complexity. Even Caliban appreciates the beauty and mystery of the island. The innocence and wonder with which he describes it to Stephano and Trinculo make us feel that he is potentially redeemable, as Prospero must have initially thought. When Stephano and Trinculo hear Ariel, invisible, playing a tabor and pipe, Caliban reassures them about the sound:

> Be not afeard; the isle is full of noises,
> Sounds and sweet airs, that give delight, and hurt not.
> Sometimes a thousand twangling instruments
> Will hum about mine ears; and sometime voices,
> That, if I then had wak'd after long sleep,
> Will make me sleep again: and then, in dreaming,
> The clouds methought would open and show riches
> Ready to drop upon me; that, when I waked
> I cried to dream again.

(3.2.133–41)

What riches could Caliban be wanting? He knows little of what civilization calls wealth. Perhaps Caliban yearns for grace—indeed, at the end of the play, he says he will seek it.

Ariel, "an airy spirit," is governed by air and fire. He is mercurial, quick, and essentially ecstatic. Ariel wants to be free, needs to be free as part of his essential nature. Prospero discovered Ariel imprisoned by Sycorax, who "in her most immitigable rage" had cast Ariel into a cloven pine where he painfully remained, groaning, for twelve years. Prospero freed him, but apparently under the condition that Ariel be his servant for a set term, which will end before the play ends. Because of this, Prospero is sometimes accused by his critics of unjustly taking Ariel as his slave. But given the initial situation from which Prospero rescued Ariel, it does not seem completely unjust that he demand some service in return, especially when his daughter's future depends on Ariel's help. Prospero does upbraid Ariel at the beginning of the play for asking for freedom, but in his defense we must note that Prospero wants Ariel to concentrate on the tasks at hand. At the same time, Prospero is very fond of Ariel, referring to him as "my bird" and "my dainty Ariel." When Ariel asks Prospero, "Do you love me, master? No?" Prospero replies "Dearly, my delicate Ariel." He never goes back on his word to free the spirit, and Ariel's joy, as his freedom approaches, accelerates and energizes the later part of the play. Prospero's release of Ariel corresponds poignantly with his giving of Miranda to Ferdinand: ". . . my dainty Ariel! I shall miss thee; / But yet thou shalt have freedom" (5.1.95–96).

To characterize Prospero as a prototype of the colonizing, new-world slave owner is to read into the play a meaning and an analogy that simply are not there. Prospero has been cast up, against his desire, on an island not in the Caribbean but somewhere in the Mediterranean, between Africa and Italy. He does not want to stay on the island, but uses all his power to escape. Neither Caliban nor Ariel are "natives" of the place in any but the most superficial sense: Caliban was brought to the island in his mother's womb, and Ariel is a spirit of no particular place who simply happens to be imprisoned there. When Prospero gets the chance, he will leave immediately. Though the play does not directly tell us of his fate, it is unlikely that Caliban would want to be left on the island alone, having become too civilized to enjoy permanent solitary confinement on even a beautiful island.

The New Conspiracies

During the second act, Shakespeare introduces two new conspiracies that are in effect reiterations of the plot that succeeded against Prospero in Milan. These plots demonstrate that the villains of the play have not improved with time. The evil embodied in Antonio, Sebastian, and Caliban becomes increasingly palpable throughout the play, a device Shakespeare uses to set up the last act, in which they are judged.

The most serious plot is on the life of Alonso. With the exception of Antonio and Ferdinand, the king's followers are all put to sleep by Ariel. Prospero is testing Antonio to find out whether he is still the opportunistic power-monger of twelve years before. In act 2, scene 1, Antonio offers to kill Alonso while he sleeps, suggesting that Sebastian slay Gonzalo. In a trenchant comment on courtly loyalty, Antonio advises Sebastian that he need not worry about the rest: "They'll take suggestion as a cat laps milk; / They'll tell the clock to any business that / We say befits the hour" (2.1.284–85). Though Sebastian is cautious, Antonio convinces him, and Sebastian promises that in return for Antonio's help, Milan will no longer have to pay tribute to Naples. Antonio, who is obviously Sebastian's superior in cunning, probably has the future deposition of Sebastian in mind.

The murder of Alonso is presented as a logical continuation of Antonio's evil, beginning against his own brother in Milan; Sebastian takes it so: "Thy case, dear friend, / Shall be my precedent: as thou got'st Milan, / I'll come by Naples" (2.1.285–87).

As Antonio and Sebastian, their swords drawn, are about to commit the murders, Ariel awakens the sleepers, and the two have to concoct a story about protecting the king from wild beasts. Ariel explains, "My master through his Art foresees the danger / That you, [Gonzalo] his friend, are in; and sends me forth— / For else his project dies,—to keep them living" (2.1. 292–94). Ariel will thwart all plans of assassination thereafter.

The comic counterparts of Antonio and Sebastian are represented by the bumbling and drunken Trinculo and Stephano. When Caliban meets Stephano, who has salvaged a butt of "celestial liquor" from the ship, Stephano offers him a swig from the bottle, saying "kiss the book" but substituting the bottle for the Bible. Sensual pleasure thereby displaces God as Stephano's master, and Caliban, thinking Stephano is the man in the moon, exchanges Stephano for Prospero as his master: "I will kiss thy foot. Prithee be my god." Caliban's only demand in exchange for his promise of servitude is that Stephano kill Prospero. Caliban suggests a variety of methods: drive a nail through his head, "brain him . . . with a log / Batter his skull, or paunch him with a stake, / Or cut his wezand with thy knife" (3.2.86–89). The comic plot comes closest to succeeding because it is the one Prospero gives the least attention; he nearly repeats the mistake which lost him Milan, becoming so immersed in magic that he fails to keep an eye on the threat.

Temperance and the Marriage of Ferdinand and Miranda

Prospero's plans for the future, which include the recovery of his dukedom and the establishment of peace with Naples, depend on the marriage of Ferdinand and Miranda, which will create a political alliance between Milan and Naples and make Prospero's heirs future kings and queens. Ariel leads Ferdinand from the "wreck," as Ferdinand believes, to the cave of Prospero, where Miranda, having never seen a man other than her father, at first takes him for a spirit and, on cue, falls in love with him. Ferdinand, grieving over the loss of his father, who he thinks is drowned, wastes no time falling in love with Miranda, who he proclaims will be "Queen of Naples." This begins a perfunctory romantic comedy, in which Prospero deliberately takes on the ancient role of the patriarch who stands in the way of true love. He accuses Ferdinand of being a "traitor," whatever that might mean in such a situation:

> I'll manacle thy neck and feet together:
> Sea-water shalt thou drink; thy food shall be
> The fresh-brook mussels, withered roots, and husks
> Wherein the acorn is cradled.

> (1.2.464–67)

Miranda passionately objects. Prospero sets Ferdinand to work hauling wood, but not for long. Prospero is only playing the difficult father to make Miranda more valuable in Ferdinand's eyes. Prospero explains in an aside: "They are both in either's pow'rs: but this swift business / I must uneasy make, lest too light winning / Make the prize light" (1.2.453–55).

When this very short comedy of thwarted love is ended, Prospero arranges a celebration of the young couple's engagement. He calls on various spirits, led by Ariel, to perform a masque, which celebrates both chastity and marriage. Of the three major examples of Prospero's magical skill—the tempest, the illusionary feast that he dangles before Alonso and his followers, and the masque—this last would have been the most spectacular in performance at the Globe, involving elaborate stage machinery to produce a descending goddess, Juno.

Masques, a form of highly stylized drama, were essentially invented by Ben Jonson and stage designer Inigo Jones for the purpose of celebrating royal power. Initially commissioned by and performed for James I, they often involved members of the royal household as well as professional actors. Stephen Orgel, an authority on the masque, explains that it "undertakes to lead the court to its ideal self through a combination of satire, exhortation, and praise."[7] The genre influenced popular drama in the latter part of Shakespeare's career, and masques were eventually commissioned by important members of the nobility such as the earl of Bridgewater, for whom John Milton wrote the masque *Comus* for the festivities that presented Bridgewater's daughter Alice.

Prospero creates his masque through magic, calling on Ariel and other spirits to take the parts of Juno, Ceres, and Iris, and on several "nymphs" and "reapers," who celebrate the marriage to come. Prospero's warning to Ferdinand not to have sex with Miranda before their wedding serves as a prologue to, and explanation of, the masque:

> Then, as my gift, and thine own acquisition
> Worthily purchas'd, take my daughter: but
> If thou dost break her virgin-knot before
> All sanctimonious ceremonies may
> With full and holy rite be minister'd,
> No sweet aspersion shall the heavens let fall
> To make this contract grow; but barren hate,
> Sour-ey'd disdain and discord shall bestrew
> The union of your bed with weeds so loathly
> That you shall hate it both.

(4.1.13–22)

What follows is a celebration of the fertility and bountifulness of a happy marriage, one in which the female member, at least, has remained chaste.

The first character to enter is Iris the rainbow, Juno's messenger. The rainbow is the Old Testament symbol of God's covenant with man, but within the context of the play, Iris, in a typical Renaissance merger of classical and biblical elements, represents the covenant of marriage. Iris calls upon Ceres, the representative of fertility, who is described lavishly as a "most bounteous lady," the goddess of full harvest—"Of wheat, rye, barley, vetches, oats and peas"—and of rebirth and "spongy April." Ceres appears and Iris tells her that she has been summoned by Juno to celebrate a marriage. Ceres says she will attend only if Venus and her "waspish" son, Cupid, are excluded, for they were responsible for making Dis (Pluto) lust for her daughter Proserpina. Pluto and the underworld, in their barrenness and death, represent the opposite of the fecundity of Ceres and marital happiness. Ferdinand would be choosing the realm of Dis if he broke Miranda's "virgin knot" before marriage. Juno, the goddess of hearth and home—domestic happiness—arrives to bless the coming marriage, and it is celebrated, as is typical in Shakespeare's comedies, with a dance, this one between nymphs and reapers.

Why was chastity so important a virtue in Shakespeare's time? One answer is that a chaste daughter is an economic asset to her father. Prospero's demand that Ferdinand abstain from sex with Miranda is also a declaration that she is a virgin who will faithfully extend her future husband's bloodline rather than someone else's. Virgins commanded more on the marriage market. This was especially true among royal families or the high nobility, but also among shopkeepers with smaller dynastic dreams of their own. Marxist and feminist analyses, having grasped market conditions, usually stop at this point, but before we simply classify the virtue of chastity as a piece of the patriarchal economy, we should pay Shakespeare the respect of seriously considering Prospero's speech, which connects marital happiness to chastity.

As a culture, we have gone so far through and past the "sexual revolution" of the 1960s that current university students may wonder what there was to revolt against. Chastity, though making a comeback in some quarters, is therefore to most people today a quaint prejudice: when presented as a virtue, it elicits giggles. However, Prospero argues that chastity is the key element to happiness in marriage; he does not bother to explain why, because Shakespeare's audience needed no explanation. They understood that chastity was a part of temperance, the virtue of deferring short-term appetitive pleasure in favor of long-term happiness. The Renaissance recognized lack of temperance as self-destructive and, in the case of men, emasculating, for a life based on pleasure was inconsistent with the male duty of protecting and providing for wife and children. Bounty is associated with chastity, barrenness and death with sexual looseness. Jane Austen, living in an age when the virtue of chastity was still appreciated, gives her heroine Elizabeth Bennet a trenchant thought on why premarital sex between her sister Lydia and Wickham, with whom Lydia has eloped, bodes ill for their marriage: "How Wickham and Lydia were to be supported in tolerable independence, she could not imagine. But how little of permanent happiness could belong to a couple who were only brought together because their passions were stronger than their virtue, she could easily conjecture."[8] Premarital chastity indicates one's determination to commit to one person only, and with respect to marriage, is "an apprenticeship in fidelity."[9] Spiritually, it is the analog of God's fidelity to man.

Shakespeare allows his villains to demonstrate the results of intemperance. Impatience and lack of self-control make Sebastian an easy mark for Antonio, and both failings help to scuttle Caliban's plot against Prospero. For bait, Prospero has Ariel hang some of his clothing outside his cave. When Stephano, Trinculo, and Caliban approach the cave, the two Italians are so taken with the rich garments that they busy themselves with trying them on and haggling about who will get what rather than getting to the business of killing Prospero. Caliban knows this is a big mistake and shows more self-control than either of his masters: "What do you mean / To dote thus on such luggage? Let 't alone, / And do the murder first. / . . . We shall lose our time, / And all be turned to barnacles, or to apes / With foreheads villainous low." Prospero does in fact set a pack of spirits on them, all in the shape of hounds, who attack the villains and give them cramps and pinches. Stephano cries, "Every man shift for all the rest, and let no man take care for himself; for all is but fortune" (5.1.256–57). Stephano, of course, has meant to say "every man for himself, and devil take the hindmost," but, in the strain of the moment, he has reversed himself and ironically set forth the Christian paradigm of behavior. In this play, temperance and self-control are the defining marks of the truly civilized man.

Prospero's Judgment

The remainder of the play is about repentance and the limits of magic, for although Prospero can create tempests and illusions, cramp the muscles of his enemies, or make them fall asleep, he has no direct access to their hearts; he can only create situations and take actions that may lead Alonso, Antonio, and Sebastian to repent. Their wills remain their own. In this limitation, Prospero is like the three witches of Macbeth, who can plague a sailor with storms "sev'n-nights nine times nine," but who have no power to sink the sailor's ship or make him despair: "Though his bark cannot be lost, / Yet it shall be tempest tost." If the man hangs onto his courage and will, he will survive—unless a power higher than the witches or sorcerers decrees otherwise.

Prospero's method of eliciting repentance follows the biblical model. He preaches wrath to promote a sense of guilt, hoping that guilt will lead to sorrow and sorrow to true repentance. Though repentance founded on "attrition"—the sheer terror of divine punishment—was held to be acceptable to God, "contrition"—repentance motivated by genuine sorrow for one's sins—was better, for it acknowledged God's justice as well as his power. (Thus, we see Duke Vincentio in *Measure for Measure* trying to reason Claudio out of the fear of death so that he can make a true act of contrition.) Prospero would prefer that Alonso, Antonio, and Sebastian be truly sorry for what they have done to him and Miranda, for the sake of their "fraughting souls" as well as his own satisfaction, so he forces them into situations in which they are forced to experience what he and Miranda have experienced. This is not eye-for-an-eye vengeance, but an attempt to induce in the men some empathy for Prospero and Miranda's sufferings. First, the men are made to believe that they have been shipwrecked, as have been Prospero and Miranda. Because Miranda, then a three-year-old, would likely have died along with her father, Prospero plagues Alonso with the apparent death of his son Ferdinand. On the island, the castaways find no apparent sources of food or water, and they have no idea how they will sustain themselves—problems they knew Prospero and Miranda would confront if they survived drowning. To drive this point home, Prospero tantalizes the men with a banquet that vanishes when they attempt to eat it. Robert Gram Hunter likens the banquet to the sacrament of Holy Communion, from which "notorious and unrepentant sinners are traditionally excluded,"[10] referring to the following passage from the *Book of Common Prayer:*

> And if any of these [as do intend to be partakers of the Holy Communion] be an open and notorious evil liver, so that the congregation by him is offended, or have done any wrong to his neighbours by word or deed: The Curate having knowledge thereof, shall call him and advertise him, in any wise not to presume to the Lord's Table, until he have openly declared himself to have truly repented and amended his former naughty life, that the Congregation may thereby be satisfied, which afore were offended; and that *he have recompensed the parties he hath done wrong unto,* or at the least declare himself to be in full purpose so to do, as soon he conveniently may.[11] (italics added)

Clearly, none of the men is sorry for what they have done to Prospero and Miranda; Antonio and Sebastian only remember the coup as a precedent for murdering Alonso. Ariel, in the form of a harpy, removes the feast and pronounces the men's guilt, adding understanding to their suffering. The "Homily on Repentance,"[12] with which Shakespeare's audience would have been very familiar, lists four requirements of adequate repentance: contrition of heart, unfeigned confession and acknowledgment of sins, faith that God will pardon one's sins, and the amendment of one's life, which included a sincere attempt to make restitution for previous wrongdoing. Prospero will try to take Alonso and his men along this path. Ariel begins by trying to induce a true sense of guilt in the men:

> You are three men of sin, whom Destiny,—
> That hath to instrument this lower world
> And what is in't,—the never-surfeited sea
> Hath caus'd to belch up you; and on this island,
> Where man doth not inhabit,—you 'mongst men
> Being most unfit to live . . .
>
> . . . .
>
> For that's my business to you,—that you three
> From Milan did supplant good Prospero:
> Expos'd unto the sea, which hath requit it,
> Him and his innocent child: for which foul deed,
> The powers, delaying, not forgetting, have
> Incens'd the seas and shores, yea all the creatures
> Against your peace. Thee of thy son, Alonso,
> They have bereft; and do pronounce by me
> Ling'ring perdition—worse than any death
> Can be at once—shall step by step attend
> You and your ways; whose wraths to guard you
>   from,—
> Which here, in this most desolate isle, else falls
> Upon your heads,—is nothing but heart-sorrow,
> And a clear life ensuing.

>   (3.3.53–58; 69–82)

The only way to avoid the wrath of Fate (Shakespeare could not use the word "God" because the 1605 Statue of Abuses

forbade it to be said on stage) is through "heart's sorrow" and
a "clear [blameless] life ensuing," which restates the standard church doctrine of repentance. Ariel's pronoucement of
guilt drives the three men to desperation, though in different
ways. Antonio and Sebastian, with drawn swords, rush off stage
to fight legions of fiends; Alonso, believing that his sins have
caused Ferdinand's death, threatens suicide:

> O, it is monstrous, monstrous!
> Methought the billows spoke, and told me of it;
> The winds did sing it to me; and the thunder,
> That deep and dreadful organ-pipe, pronounc'd
> The name of Prosper: it did bass my trespass.
> Therefore my son i' th' ooze is bedded; and
> I'll seek him deeper than e'er plummet sounded,
> And with him there lie mudded.
>
> (3.3.95–102)

Gonzalo, fearing that the men will harm themselves, tells the
others to follow them. Gonzalo recognizes the guilt of the three,
but moreover, recognizes the spiritual corruption within them:

> All three of them are desperate: their great guilt,
> Like poison given to work a great time after,
> Now 'gins to bite the spirits. I do beseech you,
> That are of suppler joints, follow them swiftly,
> And hinder them from what this ecstasy
> May now provoke them to.
>
> (3.3.104–09)

At this point the play turns toward the comedy of forgiveness. The Bible passages discussed in previous chapters about
forgiving enemies all apply here, and to an older man like
Prospero, who is looking toward the grave, they are especially
forceful. Once Alonso feels the pain that Prospero has been

put through, Prospero perhaps recalls his own pain and begins to feel a bond with his enemy. Even Ariel, nimble, mercurial, and inhuman, can feel the spiritual pain of the shipwrecked men:

Ariel: The King,
              His brother, and yours, abide all three distracted,
              And the remainder mourning over them,
              Brimful of sorrow and dismay; but chiefly
              Him that you term'd, sir, "The good old lord,
                  Gonzalo";
              His tears run down his beard, like winter's drops
              From eaves of reeds. Your charm so strongly works
                  'em
              That if you now beheld them, your affections
              Would become tender.

Prospero: Dost thou think so, spirit?

Ariel: Mine would, sir, were I human.

Prospero: And mine shall.
              Hast thou, which art but air, a touch, a feeling
              Of their afflictions, and shall not myself,
              One of their kind, that relish all as sharply
              Passion as they, be kindlier mov'd than thou art?
              Though with their high wrongs I am struck to th'
                  quick,
              Yet with my nobler reason 'gainst my fury
              Do I take part: The rarer action is
              In virtue than in vengeance: they being penitent,
              The sole drift of my purpose doth extend
              Not a frown further.

                                              (5.1.11–30)

     Prospero has clearly made the Christian choice. His judg-
ment extends charity to others, as he hopes to attain it himself
at the moment of his death. Yet, as the play draws to a close,
Shakespeare raises doubts about whether Prospero's god-like

manipulation of events has led Alonso, Antonio, or Sebastian to sincere repentance, or whether Prospero's decision against vengeance rises to the level of forgiveness. Certainly the three "men of guilt" have been scared out of their wits and Alonso has been bludgeoned with the death of his son. If any of the three feels sorry for what he has done, it is surely Alonso, and when Prospero reveals Ferdinand and Miranda playing chess, and Alonso knows his son to be alive and in love with a beautiful and noble woman, his reconciliation with Prospero, through the marriage of their children, seems sure. Alonso takes all the steps of repentance, asking forgiveness of the one wronged and offering to make reparations. He tells Prospero: "Thy dukedom I resign, and do entreat / Thou pardon me my wrongs" (5.1.118–19). Alonso's transformation makes poetic truth of the song that Ariel sings to Ferdinand in act 1, which seemed to speak of Alonso's death but also foreshadowed his rebirth and transformation through the baptism of shipwreck:

> Full fadom five thy father lies;
> Of his bones are coral made;
> Those are pearls that were his eyes:
> Nothing of him that doth fade,
> But doth suffer a sea-change
> Into something rich and strange.

(1.2.399–403)

From Sebastian, however, Prospero gets only an antagonistic lie. When Prospero tells Sebastian and Antonio that he knows about their plot to kill Alonso, he says "But you, my brace of lords, were I so minded, / I here could pluck his highness' frown upon you, / And justify you traitors"; Sebastian's response is, "The devil speaks in him" (5.1.126–30). When Prospero forgives his brother, his speech strives toward forgiveness, but perhaps falls short:

> For you, most wicked sir, whom to call brother
> Would even infect my mouth, I do forgive
> Thy rankest fault,—all of them;—and require
> My dukedom of thee, which perforce, I know,
> Thou must restore.

> (5.1.130–34)

Antonio gives Prospero no thanks in reply and offers no apologies. He does not ask to be forgiven, and he has nothing to restore to Prospero, Alonso having returned the dukedom already. Antonio does not find his voice until Caliban, Stephano, and Trinculo appear on stage, and then it is only to throw a verbal barb at Caliban. There is nothing to indicate that either Antonio or Stephano are repentant. Grace does not reach them. Stephano and Trinculo wish only to be free of their cramps and are only as repentant as children who want to stop being spanked. But perhaps Caliban has learned something, for he recognizes his foolishness: "I'll be wise hereafter, / And seek for grace. What a thrice-double ass / Was I to take this drunkard for a god, / And worship this dull fool!" Perhaps Caliban's resolution to seek grace refers only to his asking Prospero's forgiveness, but we cannot be sure he does not refer to a higher source, and even if he does seek only Prospero's "grace," for Caliban that is a step in the right direction.

Gonzalo brings the idea of Providence back into the play at this point, and his summary has the elevation of a psalm:

> . . . look down you gods,
> And on this couple drop a blessed crown!
> For it is you that have chalk'd forth the way
> Which brought us hither. . . .

··

> Was Milan thrust from Milan, that his issue
> Should become Kings of Naples? O rejoice
> Beyond a common joy! and set it down
> With gold on lasting pillars: In one voyage
> Did Claribel her husband find at Tunis,
> And Ferdinand, her brother, found a wife
> Where he himself was lost, Prospero his dukedom
> In a poor isle, and all of us ourselves
> When no man was his own.

$$(5.1.201–04; 205–13)$$

Gonzalo's characteristic optimism leads him to overstatement, since there is little evidence that Antonio and Sebastian or Stephano and Trinculo have found their lost selves, the selves they could become if they allowed grace to enter their lives. But in Shakespeare's Christian view, which is certainly more Roman Catholic than Calvinist or Lutheran, every man's soul is his own;[13] free will remains intact, and no one is transformed who does not want to be.

Prospero: Renunciation and Responsibility

Prospero provides an example of how tenacious the faults embedded in temperament can be. For though he has had twelve years to brood upon his failings as a leader those failings still threaten to topple him, when, caught up in creating the marriage masque of Ferdinand and Miranda, he once again loses track of more imperative concerns. Surprised, and obviously vexed with himself as he calls an abrupt halt to the masque, Prospero realizes that absorption in magic could once again be his undoing, and in an aside says:

> I had forgot that foul conspiracy
> Of the beast Caliban and his confederates

Against my life: The minute of their plot
Is almost come.

(4.1.139–42)

Ferdinand, clearly surprised by Prospero's immediate about-face, says to Miranda, "This is strange: your father's in some passion / That works him strongly" (4.1.143–44). Miranda, who knows her irascible and sometimes impatient father, replies "Never till this day / Saw I him touch'd with anger, so distemper'd" (4.1.144–45). Prospero is clearly angry with himself. He already knows of the plot, but once again he has drifted off. In the beginning of the play, he noted that his library was a dukedom for him large enough, and thanks to Gonzalo he has had such a dukedom for twelve years. Ironically, being marooned has given Prospero just what he wanted; twelve years of study and teaching his daughter will have done little to change his bookish approach to the world.

Even at the beginning of the *The Tempest,* Prospero is thinking seriously about the limitations of magic and the changes he will have to make in himself if he returns to govern Milan. The speech that follows, a comment on the disappearance of the masque, has traditionally been taken as Shakespeare's valedictory to the theater, but within the context of the play it is a comment on the transience of life and the illusion of power, spoken by a man past middle age who knows his own death no longer lies far in the future:

Our revels now are ended. These our actors,
As I foretold you, were all spirits, and
Are melted into air, into thin air:
And, like the baseless fabric of this vision,
The cloud-capp'd towers, the gorgeous palaces,
The solemn temples, the great globe itself,
Yea, all which it inherit, shall dissolve,

And, like this insubstantial pageant faded,
Leave not a rack behind. We are such stuff
As dreams are made on; and our little life
Is rounded with a sleep.

(4.1.148–58)

Prospero realizes his pursuit of god-like power has amounted to very little. It was a dream, as was his life, and as was even "the great globe itself." He cannot make himself live forever, and what is worse, he cannot seem to make himself much better. In light of this, the catalog of his magical accomplishments seems lackluster:

Weak ministers though ye be—I have bedimm'd
The noontide sun, call'd forth the mutinous winds,
And 'twixt the green sea and the azur'd vault
Set roaring war: to the dread rattling thunder
Have I given fire, and rifted Jove's stout oak
With his own bolt; the strong-bas'd promontory
Have I made shake, and by the spurs plucked up
The pine and cedar: Graves at my command
Have wak'd their sleepers, op'd, and let 'em forth
By my so potent Art. But this rough magic
I here abjure; and when I have requir'd
Some heavenly music,—which even now I do,—
To work mine end upon their senses that
This airy charm is for, I'll break my staff,
Bury it certain fadoms in the earth,
And deeper than did ever plummet sound
I'll drown my book.

(5.1.41–57)

Perhaps these two speeches can be taken as Shakespeare's prescient comment, at the dawn of science, about the limitations of knowledge sought to serve human power. Prospero has even made the dead rise, a power attributed to some magicians during the Renaissance. But even if he can perform this feat as a mechanical contrivance, Prospero cannot affect the souls of the dead any more than he can his brother's. Power cannot improve the human heart. Antonio, Sebastian, Stephano, and Trinculo remain what they are, and the world remains what it is. When Miranda, amazed at the sight of Alonso and his entourage, says, "How beauteous mankind is! O brave new world / That has such people in it," her father comments dryly "'Tis new to *thee*." From the Christian perspective, there is no progress, or if there is any, it is fleeting and fragile; the world is never made over, and heaven does not appear on earth. What matters is the bond between the individual soul and God, and this is not affected by the accumulation of power or improvements in bodily health and creature comforts. No doubt there is a vast difference between the mindset of a medieval peasant or craftsman and that of a twenty-first century grocery clerk, but from a Christian point of view, what God requires from all three is the same. The sinfulness of human nature and the gift of salvation do not change over time.

The modern age began four hundred years ago with the rise of science. Thus, we now live in the age that Faustus and Prospero confronted at its inception. The streets of London no longer function as open sewers, and if the average human life span can be taken as a general indicator of well-being—thirty-five to forty in Shakespeare's day, compared with over seventy-six in contemporary America—then we are well off indeed. None of us would desire to inhabit Shakespeare's London, filled as it was with stench, filth, and infection, yet if there was an indicator of spiritual health, the citizens of ca. 1611 London, when *The Tempest* was first performed, might well surpass us, for they had few illusions about human weakness and mortality. Death was an unhidden and constant visi-

tor. To our forebears, the portal to eternity was wide open.
This spiritual element does not enter the play explicitly until
the epilogue, spoken by Prospero, who has buried his book
and scepter:

> Now I want
> Spirits to enforce, Art to enchant;
> And my ending is despair
> Unless I be reliev'd by prayer,
> Which pierces so that it assaults
> Mercy itself, and frees all faults.
>> As you from crimes would pardoned be,
>> Let your indulgence set me free.
>
> (Epilogue, 13–20)

The indulgence the actor asks for is, of course, applause.
But this epilogue is even more an extension of the play than is
usually the case with Shakespeare. It dilates an earlier line in
the act 5, when Prospero declares that upon his return to Milan,
"Every third thought shall be my grave" (5.1.311). And it recalls the line in the first scene when shipwreck is imminent:
"All lost! To prayers! To prayers!" Prospero cannot dispense
mercy, which covers all faults and crimes. He can only pray
for that; his magic will do him no good. He gives up his power
in a leap of faith, trusting himself to God. He frees Ariel, a
spirit he loves; he will give away his daughter to Ferdinand;
and he takes responsibility for Caliban: "This thing of darkness I acknowledge mine." Prospero is putting his affairs in
order, and everything that gives the illusion of human power
will only hinder him as he moves to his own judgment before
God and a transformation that finally cures self-idolatry.

A play in which the wicked prosper, and the virtuous miscarry, may doubtless be good, because it is a just representation of the common events of human life: but since all reasonable beings naturally love justice, I cannot easily be persuaded, that the observation of justice makes a play worse; or, that if other excellencies are equal, the audience will not always rise better pleased from the final triumph of persecuted virtue.

In the present case the public has decided. Cordelia, from the time of Tate, has always retired with victory and felicity. . . . I was many years ago shocked by Cordelia's death, that I know not whether I ever endured to read again the last scenes of the play till I undertook to revise them as an editor.

Samuel Johnson on *King Lear*

CONCLUSION

"Is this the promised end?"

If there is one Shakespeare play that might be put forth as a refutation of the main argument of this book, it is *King Lear*. I have contended all along that Shakespeare and his audience held in common the Christian belief that justice did exist in a world created by a just God who endowed human beings with an innate sense of right and wrong and the reasoning ability to extend and apply moral knowledge. The extension and application of moral knowledge in Shakespeare's society could most obviously be observed in Parliament and the judicial system. In Shakespeare's plays, we see it in his trial scenes, or perhaps in the fifth act of some tragedies in which "poetic justice" is meted out to the likes of Iago, Richard III, Macbeth, and in *Lear*, Edmund. Yet one of the most fascinating elements of the English Renaissance is the incongruity of elements that influenced art and society: Classical literary sources, imbued with an ethic of pagan heroism, competed with the very different ethic and stories of the Bible. A third element, which struck a popular chord, was Marlowe's incipient nihilism, as exhibited in such plays as *Tamburlaine, Parts 1* and *2*, and the *Jew of Malta;* and these, no doubt, owe a great debt to Machiavelli's *The Prince.* If one wanted to locate the religious and ethical content of Shakespeare's plays, these three coordinates—the Bible, classical literature, and the first glimmerings of modern nihilism—would be the most important. And of all Shakespeare's plays, it is *King Lear* that is tugged most strongly in a nihilistic direction.

The story of *King Lear* has many antecedents, all involving a king who has three sons or three daughters. The aged king, wanting to retire, decides to divide his kingdom among his three children (a ghastly idea from a Jacobean standpoint). He will keep some of the perks of kingship, such as a retinue of knights, and he intends to be maintained through the hospitality of his children. Of the three children, only the youngest is truly loyal to his (or her) father. The other two turn on the old man and reduce him to destitution, and in the end he is saved by his youngest child. Holinshed, one of Shakespeare's main sources, places the reign of Lear in 800 B.C., and Shakespeare's play seems vaguely set in pre-Christian days, though it has, like *The Winter's Tale,* many Christian references. In essence, we might say that Shakespeare's play really takes place in "mythic" time, outside of history.[1]

Shakespeare had several potential sources for Lear, including Holinshed and *The Mirrour for Magistrates* (1574), but for our purposes, two have special relevance. From an earlier dramatization of the Lear story, *The True Chronicle History of King Leir* (1605), he took the idea of the love contest with which *King Lear* begins. Goneril, Regan, and Cordelia are to compete with each other to say who loves Lear the most, and the one who makes the most impressive declaration of love will get a larger share of the kingdom for her dowry than her sisters. Cordelia, the youngest, says she cannot "heave her heart" into her mouth, and refuses to play the game, though she is the only daughter who truly loves her father. Her reward is banishment, after which Lear foolishly consigns himself to the care of Cordelia's older wolfish sisters, Goneril and Regan, who bar him from their homes and force him into destitution. In *Leir,* the king is rescued by his youngest daughter (Cordilla) and they live to see happier days, but in Shakespeare's *Lear,* Cordelia is hanged and Lear dies—apparently of heart failure—shortly thereafter.

Shakespeare got his idea for the subplot involving Gloucester, Edmund, and Edgar from Philip Sidney's *Arcadia* (1590). Edmund, as the bastard son of Gloucester, convinces his father that Edgar, the legitimate son, is plotting patricide. Easily duped, Gloucester seeks to capture and punish his truly faithful son Edgar, who flees for his life. For attempting to help Lear, Gloucester is later accused of treason by Regan's husband, the duke of Cornwall. Edmund not only informs on his father, but leaves him to his fate, knowing that Cornwall has something dreadful in store. Cornwall gouges out the old man's eyes. Later, in trial by combat, Edgar wounds Edmund mortally (Edmund is carried off stage, clinging to life). Gloucester dies, his heart bursting with passion when Edgar reveals himself as the loyal son. The major difference between Shakespeare's version and Sidney's is that in the latter, the two brothers are reconciled.

We get a sense of Shakespeare's intentions by noting how determinedly he swerves from the happier endings of his sources. Shakespeare clearly went out of his way to make *King Lear* not just tragic, but horrifically so. The blinding of

Gloucester, which occurs on stage, is perhaps the most excruciating scene Shakespeare ever wrote, and the ensuing carnage tops even that of *Hamlet*. A servant, appalled at what his master Cornwall is doing to Gloucester, gives Cornwall his death wound, and Regan kills the servant by stabbing him in the back. Edgar kills Oswald, one of Goneril's servants, and, finally, defeats Edmund in trial by combat. Gloucester dies offstage after his heart bursts. Goneril poisons her sister Regan out of jealousy for Edmund and then stabs herself to death when Edmund dies. The bodies of the two dead women are produced on stage. At this point, with the villains (and Gloucester) cleared from the boards, it would be easy for Shakespeare to follow his sources and give Lear and Cordelia a happy ending. Instead, Shakespeare makes a surprising move. Edmund has ordered that Cordelia and Lear be hanged, and before the order can be countermanded, Cordelia is executed. Lear carries her body on stage and dies at her side shortly afterward. "Is this the promised end?" asks Kent, Lear's faithful retainer. "Or image of that horror?" finishes Edgar. These are questions that many in Shakespeare's audience who were familiar with the traditional Lear stories, or the earlier *Leir*, might well have asked.

The mirror-like double plot of *King Lear* is another clue that Shakespeare's intention was to exhibit human depravity to an extent that far exceeded his previous work. Just as Lear casts off his loyal daughter Cordelia, Gloucester casts off his loyal son, Edgar; and just as Lear's ungrateful daughters seek to destroy him, Edmund seeks to destroy his father Gloucester. As A. C. Bradley notes, this does not just double the pain of *King Lear*, but suggests that there is a "malignant influence" in the land, and that what is happening in the households of Lear and Gloucester is no aberration.[2]

Ending *Lear* with the death of Cordelia proved so dis-

tasteful to later audiences that in 1681, Nahum Tate rewrote
the ending so that Lear and Cordelia survived, and Edgar
married Cordelia. This played as the standard stage version of
Lear until 1838. Audiences agreed with Samuel Johnson:
Shakespeare's original was just too hard to take.

With the flourishing of academic criticism in the twentieth century came two versions of *Lear*. The first, which held
sway from the beginning of the century to the mid-sixties, held
that Lear was a Christian play about pre-Christian times, in
which its audience, observing the play from a more informed
Christian viewpoint, would have seen much dramatic irony:
pre-Christians attempting to understand the world without the
benefit of Christian revelation. Later readings took *Lear*'s nihilistic element not as a subject of irony, but as a serious statement of universal meaninglessness. Nicholas Brooke argued
that the moral arguments and invocations of Edgar and Albany are undercut by the dramatic experience of the play:

> The final sense is that all moral structures, whether
> of natural order or Christian redemption, are
> invalidated by the naked fact of experience. The
> dramatic force of this rests on the human impulse to
> discover a pattern, a significance, by investigating
> nature. But nature itself finally frustrates that
> impulse; when Lear dies, the moral voices are
> silenced.[3]

This reading and subsequent productions of *Lear* were highly
influenced by existentialism and the Theater of the Absurd.
Peter Brook's film of *King Lear* (1970), with Paul Scofield in
the title role, is emblematic of this viewpoint, and owes much
to *Waiting for Godot*, though blood and misery replaces vaude-
ville as a way of passing the time until death. The Brook production is a good representative of the last thirty to forty years

of critical thought about *Lear.*

But is the vision of *King Lear* really hopeless and nihilistic? Certainly, there is evidence in the play that can be marshaled in support of such an argument. A remarkably prescient Edmund seems to think the world works according to Darwinian principles. "Thou, Nature, art my goddess; to thy law / My services are bound" (1.2.1–2). For Edmund, nature is the realm of dog-eat-dog, and he believes he can get Edgar's inheritance because he is strong enough and ruthless enough to take it.

To the blinded Gloucester, the gods seem indifferent at best, and sadistic at worst. He says, "As flies to wanton boys are we to the gods, / They kill us for their sport." (4.1.38–39). The duke of Albany, Goneril's decent husband, appalled by what she and Regan have done to Lear, says:

> If that the heavens do not their visible spirits
> Send quickly down to tame these vile offences,
> It will come:
> Humanity must perforce prey on itself,
> Like monsters of the deep.

> (4.2.47–51)

Albany calls upon divine intervention many times in the play, as do others, such as the two servants who see Gloucester blinded. Referring to Regan and Cornwall, one exclaims, "I'll never care what wickedness I do / If this man come to good" (3.7.98–99); the other replies, "If she live long, / And in the end meet the old course of death, / Women will all turn monsters," implying that if there is no divine sanction against the wicked, people will infer that there are no gods, and do whatever they want. (As Dostoyevsky's Ivan Karamazov says, "If there is no God, everything is permitted.")

But does the action of the drama consistently support declarations of nihilism and undercut speeches that assert the existence of justice? The deaths of Cornwall, Goneril, Regan, and Edmund might indeed be chalked up to divine justice. Albany gives the gods credit when he hears of Cornwall's death: "This shows you are above, / You justicers, that these our nether crimes / So speedily can venge" (4.2.79–81). Albany's assessment is the same when Goneril kills Regan and then herself: "This judgment of the heavens that makes us tremble / Touches us not with pity" (5.3.230–31). Many critics, however, feel that these apparent instances of justice are erased dramatically by the deaths of Cordelia and Lear. Kent's line, "Is this the promised end?" elicits three syllables from Albany: "Fall, and cease," which Foakes glosses to mean "in general terms, 'Let everything come to ruin, and cease to be.'"[4] The final damage to the body politic is incalculable. Kent refuses to be king, and neither Albany nor Edgar seems to want the job. What, they might say, is the point?

The apparent absence of heavenly "justicers" in the final scene is paralleled by the absence, throughout the play, of any human institution for trying cases and dispensing justice. The only trial scene Shakespeare gives us is the product of Lear's deranged mind. In act 3, scene 6, Lear, deep in madness, imagines he arraigns Goneril and Regan. As Lear, Edgar, and the fool wait out the storm in a hovel, Lear seems to see a courtroom before him in which Goneril and Regan stand as defendants. The fool and Edgar, disguised as a madman, become Lear's co-adjudicators. As Lear gazes into this imagined scene, and begins to question "Goneril," the fool, looking in the direction of Lear's gaze, says to her, "Cry you mercy, I took you for a joint stool" (3.6.51). This is all that is left of institutional justice in the world of Lear—wish fulfillment. But even as wish fulfillment, Lear's dream goes astray, for the imaginary Goneril escapes the court: "Stop her there!" Lear

cries to the bailiff, "Arms, arms, sword, fire, corruption in the
place! / False justicer, why hast thou let her 'scape?" (3.6.53–
55). In the plays we have examined, Shakespeare shows how
judicial decision making can go astray, but in this scene the
very possibility of justice is rejected. Justice is not even vi-
able in the imagination.

But it is not only his desire to punish his daughters that
motivates Lear's trial. Lear also wants answers. How could
Goneril and Regan have become what they are? How could
they be so evil? How could the gods allow such evil to exist?
Lear says of his fellow judges, "Then let them anatomize Regan;
see what breeds / about her heart. Is there any cause in nature
that make / these hard hearts?" (3.6.73–75). This, of course,
is another statement of the play's central question, implied
every time someone invokes divine intervention or interprets
events as if such an intervention had occurred. Does God exist? Does he pay attention? Then why is there evil?[5]

Shakespeare, I believe, does suggest an answer to this
question, for it is in suffering the consequences of evil and his
own foolishness that Lear finally attains an understanding of
himself and his obligations to the rest of mankind. It is because Lear can find no justice for himself that he begins to
ask whether he has been just to others. Certainly he has not
been just to Cordelia, and the knowledge of this is at the root
of his madness. But Lear becomes aware of a far broader failure to the people of his kingdom. The first inklings of this
dereliction occur on the heath, in the storm, when Lear commits his first unselfish act: he offers shelter to the fool and
Kent before entering the hovel himself:

[To Kent]

> Prithee go in thyself, seek thine own ease.
> This tempest will not give me leave to ponder
> On things would hurt me more. . . .

[To the fool]

In boy, go first. You houseless poverty—
Nay, get thee in. I'll pray . . .

(3.4.23–27)

Lear's prayer is essentially for forgiveness for ignoring the poor people of his realm, all of whom will shortly be given dramatic representation through Edgar, as Tom of Bedlam. For us, Tom translates as the homeless schizophrenic, wandering the streets, conversing fiercely with invisible companions. But Lear is aware of these people before Tom appears, and he now feels their poverty and their mental afflictions.

[Lear kneels]

Poor naked wretches, wheresoe'er you are,
That bide the pelting of this pitiless storm,
How shall your houseless heads and unfed sides,
Your looped and windowed raggedness, defend you
From seasons such as these? O, I have ta'en
Too little care of this. Take physic, pomp,
Expose thyself to feel what wretches feel,
That thou mayst shake the superflux to them
And show the heavens more just.

(3.4.28–36)

When Lear meets Edgar, who is smeared with dirt and apparently mad, he attempts to give his clothing to the poor man, but the fool and Kent stop him: "Unaccommodated man is no more but such a poor, / bare, forked animal as thou art," he tells Edgar. "Off, off, you lendings: / come, unbutton here" (3.4.105–07). Lear has come a long way from the infantile old man who wanted to retire as king but keep the glory of office. At the beginning of the play, when Regan comments that Lear "hath ever but / slenderly known himself" (1.1.294–95), she must be credited with telling the truth, but by act 4, the de-

scription is no longer accurate. In looking back at life as a
king, Lear realizes that he was lied to from his earliest years,
was always told what he wanted to hear, and that it warped
him:

> They flattered
> me like a dog and told me I had the white hairs in my
> beard ere the black ones were there. To say "ay" and
>   "no"
> to everything that I said "ay" and "no" to was no good
> divinity. When the rain came to wet me once and the
> wind to make me chatter; when the thunder would not
> peace at my bidding, there I found 'em, there I smelt
> 'em out. Go to, they are not men o' their words: they
> told me I was everything; 'tis a lie, I am not ague-
>   proof.
>
> (4.6.96–104)

Lear's suffering is not useless. It finally makes him human.

Samuel Johnson characterized *King Lear* as "a play in
which the wicked prosper," but is there really any evidence to
support this view? Regan and Goneril are dead before they
have a chance to enjoy their inheritance. Edmund's prosper-
ity runs a very brief course before his brother kills him.
Cornwall is killed by his own servant just one instant after he
blinds Gloucester. And against this must be matched the good
that is demonstrated in the play. Cordelia and Kent remain
true to Lear, despite his rejection of them, as does Edgar to
Gloucester. Though Lear dies, he is forgiven by and reconciled to Cordelia first, as is Gloucester to Edgar. Through suffering, Lear is "redeemed" on the heath, or at least ennobled,
throwing off a childish egocentricity and finally thinking of
the needs of others. Denied justice himself, he comes to realize that he has been less than just to others.

King Lear does not refute a Christian view of the world any more than Job does. However, the effect of *Lear,* appropriate to a great play, is that it arouses a complicated response. Shakespeare strongly introduces nihilism as a possibility, a shadow that haunts our best hopes. We see this in most of Shakespeare's great tragedies. Hamlet continually doubts the meaningfulness of life. Macbeth sees life as "a tale told by an idiot, full of sound and fury, signifying nothing." The existence of a personal, loving God who gives meaning to life is not a foregone conclusion, and cannot be derived from the experience of daily life. If such were the case, there would be little need for injunctions to faithfulness, hope, and charity. Rather, it is because believers have doubts that these virtues are urged. *King Lear* honestly and openly portrays our reasons for doubt, but the steadfastness of Cordelia and the transformation of Lear give us better reasons to hope than to disbelieve. Evil is able to accomplish nothing in *King Lear.* The character defects of Lear and Gloucester let evil into the body politic. It exists parasitically on the good and is finally expelled, after much devastation all around. As in Shakespeare's last plays, the tragicomedies, the certainty that justice will prevail is not emphasized so much as the hope and faith that it will. And although hope and faith—along with charity—are Christian virtues, certainty never has been.

An Epilogue for Students

My original plan, when coming to the end of this book, was to top it off with a detailed polemic about what has gone wrong in the academy with Shakespeare studies. But good books have been published on the subject, and I found that after writing about the Christian dimension of judgment in Shakespeare's plays, such a task seemed unnecessary. Literature finally stands on its positive aesthetic and moral character. It defends itself to those who care about it, and for those who don't, no defense is convincing. I have had students who refused to find pleasure in *Treasure Island* because it was "misogynistic," who could not endure C. S. Lewis's *Tales of Narnia* because they were "sexist," *Heart of Darkness* because it was "imperialistic," *Huckleberry Finn* because it was "racist," and Shakespeare's plays because they were said to be all those things. Read these books with an open and receptive spirit, and then make your own decisions, but don't let other people's politics or resentments get between you and what you read.

You will be told, if you are a college English major, that understanding current "critical theory" is important because it will make you aware that all readings of a book are situated in one or another ideology or viewpoint, in one or another set of critical assumptions. This is true, but not a recent discovery, and we find this for ourselves whenever we discuss a book with any thoughtful person. Arguing about the meaning of books and their value is at least as old as Plato and Aristotle, and when we discuss books in any dorm-room or coffeeshop bull session we also discuss ourselves and our beliefs. There needs not come a ghost from purgatory or a critical theorist from France to tell us that reading is personal and influenced by our unique experience. Such discussions, into which we pour our thinking and passion, duplicate in a small way the activity of great critical readers, who, like Samuel Johnson, thrived long before academic literature departments were born.

It is also true that any *theory* about literature also contains values and assumptions, so that in applying to Shakespeare's plays and poetry the theories of deconstructionism, Marxist or new historicist determinism, or various versions of feminism, one simply bounces current ideologies off older ones. You don't *need* theory to understand Shakespeare, anymore than you need theory to understand theory. If you did need theory to understand theory, you would begin a regression from which there is no escape. What you do need in order to understand the older authors is some information about genre, historical context, and the explanatory footnotes for which we can be thankful to bygone philologists. You will become far more sophisticated about various ways of seeing the world by reading primary texts, from *The*

Communist Manifesto to *The Divine Comedy,* than by reading books on how to "demystify" these texts. Great works are great because they still gnaw into the very marrow of our culture. They are the great demystifiers, not only of their own times but of ours.

Current critical theory attacks traditional humanist beliefs about "transcendent truths" as superstitious mumbo-jumbo. Yet, the belief that there are no transcendent truths is itself metaphysical. The antihumanist position that there are no transcendent truths itself purports to be true under any and all circumstances, in any place, at any time—and therefore claims transcendence for itself. In other words, it is a claim that refutes itself. Since no metaphysical foundation can be established for the assumptions of deconstructionism, or Marxist or new historicist determinism, or their derivative feminist theories, a leap of faith is required to believe in them, just as if they were religions—which they are. If, through your own intellectual struggles, you come to understand the philosophical precariousness of theory, you may wonder whether a traditional religious view isn't truer, and whether it embraces more of your humanity than the gaggle of ephemeral religions that have settled into departments of literature. You may decide that Shakespeare has more heart and head than those critics who advertise themselves as his moral superiors. If you come to such views, don't be embarrassed about them or out of them. You will have earned your opinion and your heritage.

NOTES

Introduction: God and the Courts

1. As of February 2001.

2. See Scott Turow's fine novel about judicial corruption, *Personal Injuries*, which was informed by his own experience as a deputy U.S. attorney in Chicago.

3. Roland Mushat Frye, *Shakespeare and Christian Doctrine* (Princeton, N.J.: Princeton University Press, 1963), 63.

4. *Certain Sermons or Homilies Appointed to Be Read in Churches in the Time of Queen Elizabeth I* (1623; reprint, Gainesville, Fla.: Scholar's Facsimiles & Reprints, 1968).

5. John Fortescue, *On the Laws and Governance of England*, ed. Shelley Lockwood (Cambridge: Cambridge University Press, 1997), 7.

6. Ibid., 9–10. Luther and Calvin challenged the idea that law could be anything but secular, arguing that human laws were a product of man's corrupted will, and therefore subject to the same infections as any human institution. This is completely consistent with their theological positions that man is utterly depraved and can do nothing for himself, but is saved only by grace. Thus, the modern, secular understanding of law

has its birth in the Reformation. The Protestant understanding of law emerged in the sixteenth century and gathered momentum during the seventeenth; it did not, however, have a significant impact on English jurisprudence during Shakespeare's lifetime. The main difference between the Lutheran and Calvinist position and that of political theorists in England was not about whether human corruption affected the legal system. Both sides would have agreed about that. The dispute lay in what the judicial system could hope to be, its purposes and its origins. The English still felt that all legitimate human laws originated with God and that the judicial system had a religious function, which it should at least attempt to perform, despite its inevitable failings. Luther and Calvin would have disputed this.

7. Sir Thomas Smith, *De Republica Anglorum* (1565; reprint, Menston, England: The Scholar Press, Ltd., 1970), 47–48.

8. William Hughes, "The Diversity of Courts and Their Jurisdictions," in *The Mirrour of Justices* (1903; reprint, New York, August M. Kelley, 1968), 291.

9. Francis Bacon, *Essays* (Harmondsworth, England: Penguin Books, Ltd., 1985), 222.

10. Francis Bacon, *The Letters and Life of Francis Bacon*, ed. James Spedding, 7 vols. (London: Longmans, Green, Reader and Dyer, 1872), 6:303. To foster impartiality, assize judges could not be from the circuit where they did judicial business.

11. Sir Robert Phelps, reporting from the Committee of the Abuses in the Courts of Justice, in *Commons Debates 1621*, ed. Wallace Notestein et al., 7 vols. (New Haven, Conn.: Yale University Press, 1935), 2:239. Phelps says of Bacon: "It is a cause of great weight. It concerns every man here. For if the fountain be muddy, what will the streams be? If the great dispenser of the King's conscience be corrupt who can have any courage to plead before him?"

12. William Lambarde, *Archeion, or A Discourse upon the High Courts of Justice in England*, ed. Charles H. McIlwain and Paul L. Ward (1634; reprint, Cambridge, Mass.: Harvard University Press, 1957), 66. Lambarde (1536–1601) dedicated a manuscript of *Archeion* to Robert Cecil in 1591.

13. This description is adapted from that of J. S. Cockburn, *A History of English Assizes from 1558 to 1714* (Cambridge: Cambridge University Press, 1972).

14. Sir Walter Raleigh, *The History of the World* (1634; London: G. Latham & R. Young), 153.

15. Edmund Burke, "Speech on the Petition of the Unitarians," *Works*, 9 vols. (London, 1854–57), 4:115.

16. Richard Hooker, "A Remedy against Sorrow and Fear," in *The English Sermon 1550–1650*, ed. Martin Seymour-Smith (Cheadle, England: Carcanet Press Ltd., 1976), 171.

17. Christopher Marlowe, *Doctor Faustus* (New York: W. W. Norton, 1965).

18. All quotations from Shakespeare's plays, unless otherwise indicated, are from individual volumes of the Arden Shakespeare. In this case, William Shakespeare, *Hamlet*, ed. Harold Jenkins (London: Methuen, 1982).

19. William Shakespeare, *Richard III*, ed. Antony Hammond (London: Methuen, 1981).

20. *A Facsimile of the 1560 Edition* (Madison, Wisc.: University of Wisconsin Press, 1969).

Chapter 1: Henry VI, Part 2:
Judgment in a Disintegrating Kingdom

In this chapter, all quotations from *King Henry VI, Part 2* are from the Arden edition, ed. Andrew Cairncross (London: Methuen, 1957), except those identified as coming from the First Quarto version (Q1), for which I will use *The First Part of the Contention of the Two Famous Houses of Yorke & Lancaster* (Oxford: Malone Society Reprints, 1985); I have modernized spellings.

Much of this chapter is adapted from my two articles "Treason in the Family: The Trial of Thumpe v. Horner," *Shakespeare Quarterly* 42 (1991): 44–54; and "Jack Cade's Legal Carnival," *Studies in English Literature, 1500–1800,* 42 (2002): 259–74.

1. Lily Bess Campbell, *Shakespeare's "Histories," Mirrors of Elizabethan Policy* (San Marino, Calif.: Huntington Library Press, 1947), 85. Campbell was one of the finest historical scholars of Shakespeare of the mid-twentieth century. The following presentation of Raleigh's view is based on her presentation, pp. 80–84.

2. William Baldwin, *A Myrroure for Magistrates* (London, 1559), fol. xlvii.

3. Sir Walter Raleigh, *Works* (New York: Burt Franklin, 1829), 2:x.

4. Ibid., x, xi.

5. There is some historical debate over whether Richard really did murder the boys in the Tower; Tudor historians, however, took it as a fact.

6 Raleigh, *Works*, 2:xiii.

7 Campbell, *Shakespeare's "Histories,"* 84.

8. In general, "folio" and "quarto" are printing terms. "Folio" refers to pages that are folded once, thus giving the printer four pages to print on, including front and back. "Quarto" refers to pages folded twice, giving the printer eight pages to print on, front and back. As a result, the pages in folio editions of books are larger than quartos. In Shakespeare studies, "folio" generally refers to the first collection of Shakespeare's plays, the First Folio, published in 1623 by the actors Hemmings and Condell. Quarto refers to editions of his plays that were published individually before the First Folio. Because quarto editions sometimes have significantly different texts (as in this case) than the folio, scholars argue about whether some quarto versions were truly Shakespeare's work. The counterargument is that Shakespeare may have revised his plays, and that the quartos are evidence of this. Whether the Quarto version of *2 Henry VI* is completely Shakespeare's work is a matter of some dispute.

9. Steven R. Smith, "The London Apprentices as Seventeenth-Century Adolescents," *Past and Present* 61 (1973): 149–61, esp. 151.

10. Ibid., 152; Smith lists the following apprentice guidebooks: William Vaughn's *The Golden Grove,* Lewis Bayly's *The Practice of Piety,* William Whately's *A Bride-Bush,* William Gouge's *Of Domestical Duties,* Thomas Carter's *Christian Commonwealth,* John Dod and Robert Cleaver's *A Godly Form of Household Government,* William Ames's *Conscience with the Power and Cases Thereof,* Thomas Hilder's *Conjugal Counsel,* Robert Abbot's *A Christian Family Builded by God,* and Richard Allestree's *The Whole Duty of Man* (pp. 151–52).

11. Smith, 150.

12. John Bellamy, *The Tudor Law of Treason: An Introduction* (London: Routledge and Kegan Paul, 1979), 12.

13. Lacey Baldwin Smith, *Treason in Tudor England: Politics and Paranoia* (Princeton, N.J.: Princeton University Press, 1986), 44.

14. Curt Breight, "'Treason doth never prosper': *The Tempest* and the Discourse of Treason," *Shakespeare Quarterly* 41 (1990): 13.

15. Jaspar Ridley, *Elizabeth I* (London: Constable, 1987), 28.

16. Ordeal was a method of trying to determine the guilt or innocence of a person by submitting them to a painful test; for instance, if an accused could carry hot iron a certain distance without dropping it—or worse yet, without being burned—divine intervention would be assumed and innocence declared.

    The invocation that was spoken at the beginning of an ordeal, as set forth in *the Formulae Merowingici et karolini aevi* also provides a good theoretical statement for the justification of trial by battle. In *Trial by Fire and Water: The Medieval Judicial Ordeal* (Oxford: Clarendon

Press, 1986), Robert Bartlett quotes the following passage from *Formulae Merowingici et karolini aevi* (ed. Karl Eeumer [Hanover, 1886], 700–701):

> O God, the just judge, who are the author of peace and give fair judgment, we humbly pray you to deign to bless and sanctify this fiery iron, which is used in the examination of doubtful issues. If this man is innocent of the charge from which he seeks to clear himself, he will take this fiery iron in his hand and appear unharmed; if he is guilty, let your most just power declare that truth in him, so that wickedness may not conquer justice but falsehood always be overcome by truth.

17. Bartlett, *Trial by Fire and Water*, 121.

18. Ibid., 118.

19. John Stow, *The Annales of England* (London, 1615), 385. Though Shakespeare did not use Stow as a source, Stow's version provides good information about contemporary expectations of how servants and apprentices ought to behave within the family.

20. Stow, Annales, 385.

21. In this instance, however, I have to wonder whether Shakespeare, early in his career, isn't simply playing to an audience that has a large number of apprentices. See my article, "Jack Cade's Legal Carnival" (referenced at the beginning of the notes for this chapter), in which I consider how Shakespeare may have designed his plays for a very heterogeneous audience.

22. Raleigh, *Works*, 2: xi.

23. A list of the courts functioning in Shakespeare's time would include the main central courts, King's (or Queen's) Bench for criminal matters; Common Pleas for civil matters; Chancery (Equity) for civil cases in which a remedy was not provided at law in Common Pleas; Requests, another court of equitable jurisdiction that handled relatively small claims; and Star Chamber, the judicial arm of the King's (or Queen's) Privy Council. Local justice was generally done by justices of the peace, or in manorial courts where customary law was applied. Assize sessions were held by circuit judges, who were essentially extensions of the central courts, and included both criminal and civil matters. Ecclestiastical courts dealt mainly with what today we might classify as domestic relations cases and sexual offenses.

24. R. L. Storey, *The End of the House of Lancaster* (London: Barrie and Rockcliff, 1966), 8.

25. The Jack Cade Rebellion was the first popular uprising in England in which the participants issued a written complaint to justify their actions, and it is strangely ahistorical that Shakespeare portrays the Cade rebels as if they were the anti-literate members of the 1381 Ball Rebellion. The entire complaint of the commons of Kent is contained in Rafael Holinshed, *Chronicles* (1577; London: J. Johnson, 1807–8; facsimile, New York: AMS Press, 1965), 3:222–23; and in John Stow, *The Chronicles of England* (London: Richard Tottle and Harry Binneman, 1580), 641–42.

26. Stow, *Chronicles,* 640.

27. Wilfrid R. Prest, *The Rise of the Barristers: A Social History of the English Bar 1590–1640* (Oxford: Clarendon Press, 1986). See chapter 9, "Law, Lawyers, and Litigants."

28. Ibid, 285.

29. Ibid, 287.

30. David Cressy, *Literacy and the Social Order: Reading and Writing in Tudor and Stuart England* (Cambridge: Cambridge University Press, 1980), 7.

31. Shakespeare used the Geneva Bible.

32. Cairncross, ed., *Henry VI,* 112, fn 86.

33. Ellen C. Caldwell, "Jack Cade and *Shakespeare's Henry VI, Part 2*," *Studies in Philology* 92 (1995): 59. Caldwell's article is an excellent historical review of the Cade Rebellion.

34. I suspect in this context "score and tally" refers to the method of keeping tab of drinks consumed at the local tavern in keeping with the satiric vein in which Shakespeare presents Cade. An example of similar use is "Score a pint of bastard in the Half-moon" in a tavern scene from *1 Henry IV,* 2.5.23–24. Cairncross, however, glosses "score and tally" more generally as "a stick with transverse notches or scores to mark accounts of money lent. . . . When split lengthwise, one half was kept by the debtor, the other by the creditor. The halves should thus correspond, or tally" (p. 124, fn 33).

35. *The Book of Common Prayer* (New York: The Church Hymnal Corporation, 1979), 872.

Chapter 2:
Hamlet and the Limits of Human Judgment

In this chapter, all quotations from *Hamlet* are from the Arden edition, ed. Harold Jenkins (London: Methuen, 1982).

1. Perhaps the first and best prophet of nihilism in the English Renaissance is Christopher Marlowe in his plays *Tamburlaine, Parts 1* and *2* and *The Jew of Malta*.

2. James I, *Daemonologie* (Edinburgh, 1597), 63–64.

3. Lewes Lavater, *Of Ghostes and Spirites Walking by Nyght* (London, 1572).

4. James I, *Daemonologie*, 41. ". . . the soule once parting from the bodie, cannot wander anie longer in the worlde, but to its owne resting place must it goe immediatlie, abiding the conjunction of the bodie againe, at the later day."

5. Eleanor Prosser, *Hamlet and Revenge* (Stanford, Calif.: Stanford University Press, 1967), 103. My discussion is much indebted to Prosser.

6. The belief that melancholics were especially susceptible to temptation was widespread among Shakespeare's audience, and who is more melancholy than Hamlet? These souls, weakened by some great loss or perceived dishonor, and hence on the verge of despair, were fertile ground for temptation.

7. Prosser, *Hamlet and Revenge*, 6, 7.

8. Rene Girard of Stanford in "Hamlet's Dull Revenge," *Literary Theory and Renaissance Texts*, ed. Patricia Parker and David Quint (Baltimore, Md.: Johns Hopkins, 1986), 291, makes the most trenchant comment about the hordes of critics, during the past century, who have assumed that Hamlet's cautiousness is unjustified:

> Why should a well-educated young man have second thoughts when it comes to killing a close relative who also happens to be the king of the land and the husband of his own mother? This is some enigma indeed and the problem is not that a satisfactory answer has never been found but that we should expect to find one after our *a priori* exclusion of the one sensible and obvious answer.
>
> Should our enormous critical literature on *Hamlet* fall some day into the hands of people otherwise ignorant of our mores, they could not fail to conclude that our academic tribe must have been a savage breed, indeed. After four

centuries of controversies, Hamlet's temporary reluctance to commit murder still looks so outlandish to us that more and more books are being written in an unsuccessful effort to solve that mystery. The only way to account for this curious body of literature is to suppose that, back in the twentieth century no more was needed than some ghost to ask for it, and the average professor of literature would massacre his entire household without batting an eyelash.

9. Harold Jenkins, ed., *Hamlet* (New York: Routledge, 1982), 274, fn 2.

10. David Lodge, *Small World* (Harmondsworth: Penguin, 1995). Lodge's fictional English professor, Morris Zapp, is a monster deconstructionist until he is nearly killed by Italian terrorists. Afterwards, one of his colleagues says, "I thought deconstructionists didn't believe in the individual." Zapp replies, "They don't. But death is the one concept you can't deconstruct. Work back from there and you end up with the old idea of an autonomous self. I can die, therefore I am. I realized that when those wop radicals threatened to deconstruct me."

11. See Homer, *The Odyssey*, trans. Robert Fagles (New York: Viking, 1996), 265. In Hades, Odysseus tells Achilles about the reputation he has left behind:

> 'But you, Achilles,
> there's not a man in the world more blest than you—
> there never has been, never will be one.
> Time was, when you were alive, we Argives
> Honored you as a god, and now down here, I see,
> You lord it over the dead in all your power.
> So grieve no more at dying, great Achilles.'
>
> I reassured the ghost, but he broke out, protesting,
> 'No winning words about death to *me*, shining Odysseus!
> By god, I'd rather slave on earth for another man—
> Some dirt-poor tenant farmer who scrapes to keep alive—
> Than rule down here over all the breathless dead.

12. Ralph Walker, *A Learned and Profitable Treatise on God's Providence* (London, 1608), D3v.

13. Peter Baro, *A Special Treatise of God's Providence* (London, 1602), chap. 2 (pages unnumbered).

14. Thomas Jackson, in *A Treatise of Divine Essence and Attributes* (1628), argues that while humans exercise free will in deciding whether or not to obey the will of God, the entire concatenation of human action, event,

and accident always works to fulfill God's purposes. At times Jackson
seems to describe Providence in a manner more appropriate to quantum
mechanics than theology. It is the state of the entire system that
determines outcomes, not that of one individual (or molecule), and God
controls the system:

> Man in respect to some objects, hath a *true freedome* of
> choyse or *Contingencie,* and is enabled by his Creator to
> make a varietie of antecedents in *thought, word* or *deede.*
> But the antecedents being once made by man, though not
> without cooperation; God alone allots the *consequents,*
> without any concurrence or *suffrage* in man. To repair to
> God's house or loyter at home, or in worse places on the
> Lords day, is left free unto us by the divine decree: but
> what *good* or *evil,* spiritual or temporall, shall befall us
> upon our better or worse choise, is intirely and meerely in
> the hands of God. (175)

Romeo and Juliet could serve as a fictional example in support of
Jackson, for though Friar Lawrence, Romeo, and Juliet seem to be
making decisions of their own free will, Romeo and Juliet nevertheless
remain "star-crossed lovers," for accident subverts all planning. Romeo's
attempt to stop the fight between Tybalt and Mercutio gets Mercutio
killed; Friar Lawrence's messenger is delayed by plague, so Romeo
never learns that Juliet has taken a drug to simulate death; Juliet wakes
only moments after Romeo drinks poison. These "accidents" are all
unforeseeable, unavoidable, beyond the ability of human control.
Likewise, the slaughter in *Hamlet*'s final scene is, as Horatio describes
it, the result "Of carnal, bloody, and unnatural acts, / Of accidental
judgments, casual [i.e., unplanned, chance] slaughters, . . . / And, in
this upshot, purposes mistook / Fall'n on th' inventors' head" (5.2.382–
86). Nothing falls out according to anyone's plan.

Current definitions of Providence differ little from those of
Renaissance England. According to Presbyterian James Montgomery
Boice in *Foundations of the Christian Faith* [(Downers Grove, Ill.:
InterVarsity Press, 1986), 179], "Providence means that God has not
abandoned the world that he created, but rather works within that
creation to manage all things according to the 'immutable counsel of
His own will' (Westminster Confession of Faith, V, I)." The Roman
Catholic definition is similar; *The Catechism of the Catholic Church*
(New York: Doubleday, 1995), section 321, provides: "Divine providence
consists of the dispositions by which God guides all his creatures with
wisdom and love to their ultimate end."

15. Boice, *Fundamentals*, 179.

16. Ibid., 183.

17. Hugh Latimer, *Sermons* (London: Everyman's Library, 1906), 352–53.

Chapter 3: *The Merchant of Venice:*
Judgment and the Essence of Love

In this chapter, all quotations from *The Merchant of Venice* are from the
Arden edition, ed. John Russell Brown (London: Methuen, 1955).

1.   Israel Gollancz, *Allegory and Mysticism in Shakespeare*, ed. A. W. Pollard
     (London, 1931) 13–68; Nevil Coghill, "The Theme of *The Merchant of
     Venice*," *Shakespeare Criticism 1935–60*, ed. Anne Ridler (London:
     Oxford University Press, 1963): 213–20; Frank Kermode, "Some
     Themes in *The Merchant of Venice*," *Stratford-upon-Avon Studies 3:
     Early Shakespeare*, ed. John Russell Brown and Bernard Harris (London:
     Edward Arnold Ltd., 1961): 221–24; Barbara K. Lewalski, "Biblical
     Allusion, and Allegory in *The Merchant of Venice*," *Shakespeare
     Quarterly* 13 (1962): 327–43. Many of these articles, in whole or in
     part, are included in Sylvan Barnet, ed., *Twentieth-Century
     Interpretations of "The Merchant of Venice"* (Englewood Cliffs, N.J.:
     Prentice-Hall, 1970).

2.   For a collection of current essays, see Martin Coyle, ed., *New Casebooks:
     "The Merchant of Venice"* (New York: St. Martin's Press, 1998).

3.   The "hermeneutics of suspicion" refers to a way of reading governed by
     the assumption that literature is a kind of propaganda used to mask
     and support political or cultural oppression. A hermeneutically
     suspicious reading of a play by Shakespeare would look for places in
     the text where the mask slips, revealing the power structure beneath.
     This method can be quite satisfying to critics who are less interested in
     studying Shakespeare's work than in using it as a platform for their own
     political views. It is incapable of saying and has said virtually nothing
     about the aesthetic dimension of Shakespeare's work.

4.   Though it is a matter of some theoretical debate whether a "correct"
     interpretation can ever be achieved, everyone being entitled to his or
     her own brilliancies, I do believe that, given the available relevant
     information, a best interpretation is possible, and that we already have
     it.

5.   There is plenty of fruitful ambiguity in Shakespeare, due mainly to the

fact that he offers virtually no stage directions or clues as to how the actors should deliver their lines or take entrances and exits. A play by George Bernard Shaw or Henrik Ibsen reads like a novel in comparison. Thus, when producing Shakespeare, a range of interpretation—but not a range without limits—is always possible. How an actor chooses to inflect the word "say" in this line by Antonio can send its meaning in different directions; it is therefore very difficult to pin down the exact emotional content Shakespeare and his fellow players had in mind.

6. For biblical statements about homosexuality, see Lev. 18:22, Rom. 1:26–27, 1 Cor. 6:9.

7. These verse are more potently translated—at least for us—in the New International Version as follows:

> Whoever loves money never has money enough:
> Whoever loves wealth is never satisfied with his income.
> This too is meaningless.
> I have seen a grievous evil under the sun:
> wealth hoarded to the harm of its owner.

8. Harold Bloom, *Shakespeare: The Invention of the Human* (New York: Riverhead Books, 1998).

9. John Russell Brown, introduction, *The Merchant of Venice,* xlvii.

10. In Renaissance psychology, one's temperament was determined by the mixture of "humors" in the body, four liquid substances: blood (sanguine), phlegm (phlegmatic), yellow bile (choleric), and black bile (melancholic). The predominance of any led to a personality dominated by the humor that was in excess. Morocco does not have the balance suitable to Portia. He is a brave warrior, but he is not a subtle thinker, and he is not polished; like Othello, his body chemistry pushes him in a choleric direction. omeone comparable to Cato's daughter deserves a Brutus, whom Mark Anthony (temperamentally similar to Morocco) described as a balanced individual: "His life was gentle, and the elements [humors] / So mixed in him that nature might stand up / And say to all the world 'This was a man.' (*Julius Caesar,* 5.5.72–74). While I am not saying that Bassanio is another Brutus, his temperament makes him a more natural companion for an Italian lady.

11. Barbara Kiefer Lewalski, "Biblical Allusion and Allegory in *The Merchant of Venice,*" *Twentieth Century Interpretations of "The Merchant of Venice,"* ed. Sylvan Barnet (Englewood Cliffs, N. J.: Prentice-Hall, 1970), 45–46.

12. Ibid., 44.

13. Brown, *The Merchant of Venice,* Appendix V, 174: Extracts from History 32 of *Gesta Romanorum,* trans. R. Robinson (London, 1595).

14. Ibid., 174. Lewalski also notes the caskets' meaning derives from James 5: 2–3: "Your riches are corrupt: and your garments are moth-eaten / Your golde and silver is cankred, and the rust of them shall be a witness against you."

15. John E. Booty, ed., *The Book of Common Prayer* (1559; Charlottesville: University Press of Virginia, 1976), 290.

16. See, for instance, Clara Claiborne Park, "As We Like It, How a Girl Can Be Smart and Still Popular, in *The Woman's Part*, ed. Carolyn Ruth Swift Lenz, Gayle Greene, and Carol Neely (Chicago: University of Illinois Press, 1980), 100–16, setting forth what she calls the "Shakespearean formula": "Invent a girl of charm and intellect, allow her ego a brief premarital flourishing; make clear that it is soon to subside into voluntarily assumed subordination; make sure that this is mediated by love" (p. 112), the implication being that Portia will be Bassanio's underling for the rest of her fictionally suggested life. This is absurd both with regard to character development and the vision of love set forth in the play. There is no indication—quite the contrary—that Portia would be less influential in her marriage than Bassanio. Rather, one would say, Bassanio has married a woman who is more than his "match." From the standpoint of love, there is a mutual subordination, made very clear by the play's ethic of sacrifice, which Park either does not understand or has chosen to ignore.

17. Nevill Coghill, "The Theme of *The Merchant of Venice*," in *Twentieth Century Interpretations of "The Merchant of Venice*," 110.

18. Rigorous adherence to the law has been one of the fundamental and continuing elements of Judaism, according to David Ariel, in *What Do Jews Believe?* (New York: Schocken, 1995), 20:

> The belief in the one, invisible God was the result of a belief in the possibility of the moral goodness of humanity. In a world governed by disregard for human life and by pessimism and defeatism, the biblical God was an assertion that humans are created in a divine image and, therefore, human life is worthwhile. The supernatural God has a presence in the daily lives of people when they act in a moral manner consistent with the image of God. The biblical belief in God is belief in an ideal of strict justice and morality which makes uncompromising demands upon human behavior. No human action escapes the scrutinizing eye of God and no immoral action can be hidden from Him. The introduction of morality into belief was the unique contribution of ancient Israel and has been the decisive feature of Judaism ever since.
>
> Strict adherence to the law was particularly important

to the Pharisees, who believed that this was the most
effective way of preserving the identity of the Jewish nation
during the Roman occupation. The Pharisees saw Jesus'
breaking of the Sabbath not in terms of a legalistic quibble
but as a threat to a nation in danger of being absorbed by
Rome.

19. Coghill, "The Theme of *The Merchant of Venice*," 110.

20. Lewalski, "Biblical Allusion and Allegory in *The Merchant of Venice*," 47.

21. William Perkins, *Exposition of the Lord's Prayer* (London,1605), 410.

22. One of the classic discussions of this problem, among others that occur when hard cases push judges to make bad law, is found in Lon Fuller's delightful "The Case of the Speluncean Explorers," 62 *Harvard Law Review* (1949): 616–45.

23. R. H. Tawney, introduction, *A Discourse Upon Usury,* by Thomas Wilson (New York: Augustus Kelley, 1963), 164.

24. Lewalski points out that in choosing to call herself "Balthasar," Portia has invested her function as judge with religious meaning:

When Portia gives judgment at first in Shylock's favor, he cries out, 'A Daniel come to judgment: yea, a Daniel! / O wise young judge,' in obvious reference to the apocryphal Book of Susanna, wherein the young Daniel confounded the accusers of Susanna, upholding thereby the justice of the Law. The name, Daniel, which means in Hebrew, 'The Judge of the Lord,' was glossed in the Elizabethan Bibles as 'The Judgment of God.' But the name carries other implications as well, which Shylock ironically forgets. Portia has assumed the name 'Balthasar' for the purposes of her disguise, and the name given to the prophet Daniel in the Book of Daniel is Baltassar–a similarity hardly accidental. According to Christian exegetes, Daniel in this book foreshadows the Christian tradition by his explicit denial of any claim upon God by righteousness, and his humble appeal for mercy: 'O my God, encline thyne eare, & hearken, open thyne eyes, beholde howe we be desolated . . . for we doo not present our prayers before thee in our owne righteousness, but in they great mercies' (Daniel ix.18)."

25. Ariel, *What Jews Believe*, 20.

26. Lewalski notes that both the Christian theological tradition and
    contemporary sermons made use of the metaphor that the Law was a
    school teacher:

> The law was our pedagogue in Christ . . . . So also did he
> [God] wish to give such a law as men by their own forces
> could not fulfill, so that, while presuming on their own
> powers, they might find themselves to be sinners, and, being
> humbled, might have recourse to the help of grace. Thomas
> Aquinas, *Summa Theologica*, II.I. Ques. 98. Art. 2, in *Basic
> Writings*, ed. Anton Pegis (New York, 1944), 809.

> Another use of the law is . . . to reveale unto a man
> his sinne, his blindnesse, his misery, his impietie,
> ignoraunce, hatred and contempt of God, death, hel, the
> judgment and deserved wrath of God to the end that God
> might bridle and beare down this monster and this madde
> beaste (I meane the presumption of mans own
> righteousnesse) . . . [and drive] them to Christ. Martin Luther,
> *A Commentarie of M. Doctor Martin Luther upon the Epistle
> of S. Paul to the Galathians* (London: Thomas Vautroullier,
> 1575).

> Some . . . from too much confidence either in their
> own strength or in their own righteousness, are unfit to
> receive the grace of Christ till they have first been stripped
> of every thing. The law, therefore, reduces them to humility
> by a knowledge of their own misery, that thus they may be
> prepared to pray for that of which they before supposed
> themselves not destitute. John Calvin, *Institutes of the
> Christian Religion,* II, chap. 7, trans. John Allen
> (Philadelphia, 1936), 1: 388.

> The law . . . was given because of transgression. . . .
> out of the which they might learn the will of God, what sin,
> right, or unright is; and to know themselves, to go into
> themselves, and to consider, how that the holy works which
> God requireth are not in their own power; for the which
> cause all the world have great need of a mediator. . . . Thus
> was the law our schoolmaster unto Christ. Myles Coverdale,
> "The Old Faith," trans. Myles Coverdale from H. Bullinger,
> *Writings and Translations,* ed. George Pearson (1547;
> Cambridge, 1844), 42–43.

> The law . . . shewes us our sinnes, and that without
> remedy: it shewes us the damnation that is due unto us:
> and by this meanes, it makes us despaire of salvation in
> respect of our selves: & thus it inforceth us to seeke for
> helpe out of our selves in Christ. The law is then our

schoolemaster not by the plaine teaching, but by stripes and corrections. William Perkins, *A Commentarie, or Exposition upon the First Five Chapters of the Epistle to the Galatians* (London, 1617), 200.

27. *The Merchant of Venice,* dir. Jack Gold, prod. Jonathan Miller. BBC TV Productions in association with Time-Life Television, 1980.

28. See D. M. Cohen, "The Jew and Shylock," *Shakespeare Quarterly* 31 (1980): 53–63; and Richard Levin, *Love and Society in Shakespearean Comedy* (Newark, Del.: University of Delaware Press, 1985), 30–52.

29. See Claude G. Montefiori, "Rabbinic Judaism and the Epistles of St. Paul," *Jewish Quarterly Review* 13 (1900–1901): 161–217, which began a century-long reconsideration of the Pharisees and their beliefs. For an example of the continuing effect of Montefiori's article on biblical scholarship, see Frank Thielman, *Paul and the Law: A Contextual Approach* (Downers Grove, Ill.: Intervarsity Press, 1994), esp. chapter 1. Thielman writes:

> The elevated place of the law in rabbinic religion, moreover, did not lead inevitably to hypocrisy or externalism. Over and over the rabbis emphasized that works are not to be done for external show but that intentions as well as actions are important. When the law went unfulfilled, a gracious and merciful God stood ready to forgive at the slightest movement of the offending party toward repentance, and if good deeds did not outweigh evil ones on the day of judgment, God could and would graciously forgive the sinner and open the gates of paradise. (27–28)

30. John Barton sees Tubal as the good Jew, Shylock's foil; I think it is quite a stretch to assert this as Shakespeare's intention, but for Barton's argument, see "Exploring a Character," a presentation of Films for the Humanities; an Arts International-London "Weekend Television Production; prod. Melvyn Bragg and Nick Evans; dir. John Carlaw. 1984. Both Patrick Stewart and David Suchet demonstrate their understanding of Shylock.

31. This is especially evident in the books of Daniel, Hosea, and Jonah; Shakespeare shares the typical Christian view of his time when he assumes the Pharisees represent the essence of Judaism.

32. Martin Luther, *Luther's Works,* vol. 47: The Christian in Society IV (Philadelphia: Fortress Press, 1971), 268–93.

33. E.g., see John Donne's poem, "Batter My Heart, Three Personed God," and George Herbert's "The Altar."

34. See Christopher Marlowe, *Tamburlaine the Great, Part II*, in which the double-crossing Christian leaders of Hungary and Bohemia, who negotiate a fake truce, are slaughtered by the followers of "Mahomet."

35. Lewalski, "Biblical Allusion and Allegory in *The Merchant of Venice*," 53–54.

Chapter 4: Measure for Measure:
Trial as Political Theater

In this chapter, all quotations from *Measure for Measure* are from the Arden edition, ed. J. W. Lever (London: Methuen, 1965). I have adapted some of the material in this chapter from my article "Staging Justice: James I and the Trial Scenes of *Measure for Measure*," *Studies in English Literature, 1500–1900* 32 (1992): 247–69.

1. J. W. Lever, introduction, *Measure for Measure*, pp. xlviii–li; Josephine Waters Bennett, *"Measure for Measure" as Royal Entertainment* (New York: Columbia University Press, 1966); David L. Stevenson, *The Achievement of Shakespeare's "Measure for Measure"* (Ithaca, N.Y.: Cornell University Press, 1966); Jonathan Goldberg, *James I and the Politics of Literature* (Baltimore, Md.: Johns Hopkins Press, 1983), 231–39; Leonard Tennenhouse, *Power on Display: The Politics of Shakespeare's Genres* (London: Methuen, 1986), 154–59; and Paul Hammond, "The Argument of *Measure for Measure*," *English Literary Renaissance* 16, 3 (1986): 496–519.

2. For instance, see Roy Battenhouse, *"Measure for Measure* and the Christian Doctrine of Atonement," *PMLA* 61 (1946): 1029–59; Roy Battenhouse, *"Measure for Measure* and King James," *CLIO* 7 (1978): 193–215; and also the Bennett and Stevenson articles cited in the previous note.

3. James I, *Basilikon Doron, The Political Works of James I*, intro. Charles McIlwain (Cambridge, Mass.: Harvard University Press, 1918), 43:

> It is a trew old saying, That a King is as one set on a stage, whose smallest actions and gestures, all the people gazingly doe behold and therefore although a King be never so praecise in the discharging of his Office, the people, who seeth but the outward part, will ever judge of the substance, by the circumstances and according to the outward appearance, if his behaviour bee light or dissolute, will conceive prae-occupied conceits of the Kings inward

intention, which although with time (the trier of all trewth), it will evanish, by the evidence of the contrary effects, yet *interim patitur iustus*; and prae-judged conceits will, in the meane time, breed contempt, the mother of rebellion and disorder.

Nicolo Machiavelli, *The Prince*, trans. Luigi Rici (New York: The New American Library, Inc., 1952), 112–13:

A prince must also show himself a lover of merit, give preferment to the able, and honour those who excel in every art. . . . He ought, at convenient seasons of the year, to keep the people occupied with festivals and shows; and as every city is divided either into guilds or into classes, he ought to pay attention to all these groups, mingle with them from time to time, and give them an example of his humanity and munificence, always upholding, however, the majesty of his dignity, which must never be allowed to fail in anything whatever.

4. See Robert Lacey, *Sir Walter Raleigh* (London: Weidenfeld and Nicolson, 1973), 281–82. Lacey's description of James I has more than a touch of meanness in it, but also has some informative value:

King James . . . was, like [Robert] Cecil, physically deformed, walking with a crablike waddle, often leaning on the arm of his favourites. And those favourites were invariably male, James doting on them with extravagance that astonished before it shocked, the king nibbling their cheeks and busying his hands in the most intimate places— in public.

5. Sir Francis Bacon, *The Essays or Counsels, Civill and Morall*, ed. Michael Kiernan (Oxford: Clarendon Press, 1985), 166–67.

6. William Perkins, *Exposition of Christs Sermon in the Mount* (Cambridge, 1608), 424. My source for this and the following quotations of Perkins is Elizabeth Marie Pope, "The Renaissance Background of *Measure for Measure*," in *Twentieth Century Interpretations of Measure for Measure*," ed. George L. Geckle (Englewood Cliffs, N. J.: Prentice-Hall, 1970), 50–71.

7. William Perkins, *Treatise on Christian Equity and Moderation* (Cambridge, 1604), 15–18.

8. Francis Bacon, "Of Judicature," *The Essays or Counsels, Civill and Morall,* ed. Michael Kiernan (Oxford: Clarendon Press, 1985), 167.

9. William W. Lawrence, "The Duke," from *"Measure for Measure" in Shakespeare's Problem Comedies* (New York: Macmillan, 1931), 102–04.

10. (London, 1603, C3r–C3v).

11. Henry Smith, *Magistrates Scripture* [1590], printed in *Sermons* (London, 1631), 339–40.

12. Mary Elizabeth Pope, "The Renaissance Background of *Measure for Measure,*" *Shakespeare Survey II* (Cambridge University Press, 1949): 66–82.

13. Ibid., 60, with a contained quotation of Willymat from *A Loyal Subjects Looking-Glasse* (London, 1604), 58–59.

14. Philip C. McGuire, *Speechless Dialect: Shakespeare's Open Silences* (Berkeley: University of California Press, 1985), 66: "In Keith Hack's 1974 production for the Royal Shakespeare Company, Barnardine was played as 'a belching, bare-bummed loon.' [Michael Billington, *Guardian* (London, Manchester), 5 September 1974, p. 10.] Summoned from his cell to be executed (IV.ii), that grossly fat Barnardine proceeded to frustrate the Duke's design to use his head to deceive Angelo and save Claudio. Refusing to accept that his time to die had come, Barnardine bared his buttocks to all on-stage and in the theater before defiantly returning, through the stage trapdoor, to his cell."

15. J. W. Lever, introduction, *Measure for Measure,* xxxi–xxxv. For information on the St. Stephen's Day performance see Roy Battenhouse, "*Measure for Measure* and King James," *CLIO* 7 (1978): 193–215.

16. "Topical interpretation" refers to interpretation that connects events in works of fiction to contemporaneous non-fictive events and persons. An example would be the recognition that Duke Vincentio resembles James I in certain important ways. See Leah Marcus, *Puzzling Shakespeare* (Berkeley: University of California Press, 1988), especially the first chapter, "Localization."

17. See Stephen Greenblatt, *Sir Walter Raleigh: The Renaissance Man and His Roles* (New Haven, Conn.: Yale University Press, 1973), 55–66, for some examples of popular reaction to Raleigh.

18. Robert Lacey, *Sir Walter Ralegh* (London: Weidenfeld and Nicolson, 1973), 291.

19. *Calendar of State Papers Domestic* (James I), IV, 76, quoted by Robert Lacey, 295.

20. Thomas Bayley Howell, ed., *Cobbett's Complete Collection of State Trials and Proceedings for High Treason and Other Crimes and Misdemeanors from the Earliest Period to the Present Time,* 12 vols. (London: R. Bagshaw, 1809), 2:10–11.

21. C. G. L. DuCann, *English Treason Trials* (London: Frederick Muller, 1964), 102. Cecil's words were "Sir, you are more peremptory than honest."

22. Ibid., 28–29.

23. Ibid., 31.

24. Greenblatt, *Sir Walter Raleigh*, 116.

25. Dudley Carleton's letter to John Chamberlain, dated Winchester, 27 November 1603, quoted by Stephen Greenblatt, *Sir Walter Raleigh*, 116.

26. Edward Edwards, *The Life of Sir Walter Raleigh* (London: Macmillan, 1868), 443–46. For another account of the trial, see S. R. Gardiner, *The History of England from the Accession of James I to the Outbreak of the Civil War 1603–1642*, 10 vols. (New York: AMS Press, 1965), 1:117–40.

27. Edwards, *Life of Sir Walter Raleigh*, 46; Gardiner, *History of England*, 139.

28. Stephen Greenblatt, *Shakespearean Negotiations: The Circulation of Social Energy in Renaissance England* (Berkeley: University of California Press, 1988), 136.

29. Thomas Birch, *The Court and Times of James I* (1849; reprint, New York: AMS Press, 1979), 31. This, from a letter by Dudley Carleton to John Chamberlain, is also noted by Greenblatt, *Shakespearean Negotiations*, 137.

30. Birch, *The Court and Times of James I*, 28.

31. Edwards, *Life of Sir Walter Raleigh*, 443. On the general theatricality of Renaissance life, see Stephen Greenblatt, *Renaissance Self-Fashioning: From More to Shakespeare* (Chicago: Univ. of Chicago Press, 1980) and also Greenblatt's *Sir Walter Raleigh*; the latter contains a very interesting examination of Raleigh's "role-playing" during his trial.

32. Edwards, *Life of Sir Walter Raleigh*, 443–44.

33. Ibid., 449.

34. Ibid., 452.

35. Ibid., 454.

36. Birch, *The Court and Times of James I*, 31, quoting Carleton letter of December 11.

37. See footnote 3.

38. See the introduction to this book.

39. H. L. A. Hart, *Punishment and Responsibility: Essays in the Law* (Oxford: Oxford University Press, 1968), 2–3.

40. Lon Fuller, *The Morality of Law* (New Haven, Conn.: Yale University

Press, 1964); Fuller describes the relationship of law to two moralities: the morality of duty and the morality of aspiration. On page 30, Fuller notes:

> In the morality of duty it is understandable that penalties should take precedence over rewards. We do not praise a man or confer honor on him, because he has conformed to the minimum conditions of social living. Instead we leave him unmolested and concentrate our attention on the man who has failed in that conformity, visiting on him our disapproval, if not some more tangible unpleasantness. Considerations of symmetry would suggest that in the morality of aspiration, which strives toward the superlative, reward and praise should play the role that punishment and disapproval do in the morality of duty. To some extent this mirror image maintains itself in practice. But perfect symmetry is marred by the fact that the closer a man comes to the highest reaches of human achievement, the less competent are others to appraise his performance.

41. The duke's proposal to Isabella has been taken as problematic by recent interpreters and directors, and Shakespeare's text is open enough on this point to support productions in which Isabella hesitates or even refuses to accept. The duke proposes to her twice and Isabella has no lines of acceptance. Here, she truly has a "prone and speechless dialect." On Shakespeare's stage, perhaps she showed surprise, astonishment, gratitude, or joy. In modern productions she often shows horror and even refusal. This cannot be dismissed, since from what we have in the text, Isabella's ambition throughout the play is to become a Clare, not marry. This is one case in which an ambivalent acceptance or even a refusal cannot be tossed off as feminist revisionism.

42. Coleridge commented that the play is "the most painful—say rather, the only painful—part of [Shakespeare's] genuine works. The comic and tragic parts equally border on the . . . disgusting [and] the horrible, and the pardon and marriage of Angelo not merely baffles the strong indignant claim of justice . . . but is likewise degrading to the character of women" (Samuel Taylor Coleridge, *The Complete Works of Samuel Taylor Coleridge*, ed. William Greenough Thayer Shedd, 7 vols. [New York: Harper and Brothers, 1853], 4:92). A. C. Bradley described Vincentio's marriage to Isabella as a "scandalous proceeding" (A. C. Bradley, *Shakespearean Tragedy* (New York: Macmillan, 1949], 78). Quiller-Couch found the character of Isabella to be repulsive and inconsistent (Sir Arthur Quiller-Couch, introduction, *Measure for Measure* [Cambridge: Cambridge University Press, 1922], xxx–xxxii).

And L. C. Knights questioned the wisdom of marrying Angelo and Mariana and the duke's seemingly wholesale pardon policy (L. C. Knights, "The Ambiguity of *Measure for Measure*," *Scrutiny* 10, 3 [January 1942]: 222–33). More recently directors have emphasized some of the features of the "comic" ending that make the play problematic: the duke's excessive and apparently indiscriminate use of the pardon power, the duke's possibly coercive and unwanted proposal to Isabella, and the efficacy of the imposed marriages at the end of the play; see Philip McGuire, *Speechless Dialect: Shakespeare's Open Silences* (Berkeley: University of California Press, 1985), 64–66, 74, and 164 for notes on the Robin Philips, John Barton, and Jonathan Miller productions.

Battenhouse and Stevenson (cited in notes 1 and 2); Nevill Coghill, "Comic Form in *Measure for Measure*," *Shakespeare Survey* (1955), 14–26; Francis Fergusson, *The Human Image in Dramatic Literature* (New York: Doubleday, 1957), 126–43; and G. Wilson Knight, *The Wheel of Fire* (Oxford: Oxford University Press, 1949), 80–106, all contend that much of the confusion in critical response comes from a lack of understanding of historical, philosophical, and religious context and of genre. This controversy results partly from the assumption that there must have been one "right" interpretation at the time of the first production and that this interpretation can be attained if one gets the context right; but as Leah Marcus in *Puzzling Shakespeare* and Rosalind Miles in *The Problem of "Measure for Measure": A Historical Investigation* argue, there is no good reason to suppose interpretative unanimity among the first audiences of the play. The characterization of *Measure for Measure* as a "problem play" may not be so ahistorical after all. On this score, see also Joel Altman, *The Tudor Play of Mind* (Berkeley: University of California Press, 1978), in which Altman argues that many Renaissance plays were "fictional questions" that did not necessarily yield one "answer" or interpretation but were designed, rather, to encourage debate. For that master of negative capability, Shakespeare, this would go double.

43. Northrop Frye states, in passing, that Isabella's speech is "full of obvious fallacies as a legal argument." If these fallacies exist, Frye does not point them out and I find them anything but obvious. See *Northrop Frye on Shakespeare* (New Haven, Conn.: Yale University Press, 1986), 152.

44. Sanford H. Kadish, Stephen J. Schulhofer, and Monrad G. Paulsen, *Criminal Law and Its Processes: Cases and Materials* (Boston: Little Brown, 1983), 257–58.

45. If you want to delve into these muddy waters, see Craig Bernthal, "Staging Justice: James I and the Trial Scenes of *Measure for Measure*," *Studies in English Literature 1500–1900*, 32 (1992): 259–61, and the

following: J. Birje-Patil, "Marriage Contracts in Shakespeare's *Measure for Measure*," *Shakespeare Studies* 5 (1969): 106–11; Harriett Hawkins, "What Kind of Pre-contract Had Angelo?" *College English* 36, 2 (October 1974): 173–79; Davis P. Harding, "Elizabethan Betrothals and *Measure for Measure*," *Journal of English and Germanic Philology* 49 (1950): 139–58; the chapter on *Measure for Measure* in William W. Lawrence, *Shakespeare's Problem Comedies* (New York: Frederick Ungar, 1931); S. Nagarajan, "*Measure for Measure* and Elizabethan Betrothals," *Shakespeare Quarterly* 14 (1963): 115–19; Ernst Schanzer, "The Marriage Contracts in *Measure for Measure*," *Shakespeare Studies* 13 (1962): 81–89; Karl P. Wentersdorf, "The Marriage Contracts in *Measure for Measure*: A Reconsideration," *Shakespeare Survey* 32 (1979): 129–44.

46. Edwards, *Life of Sir Walter Raleigh*, 454.

47. C. H. Rolph, *The Queen's Pardon* (London: Cassell, 1978), 21.

Chapter 5: Judgment and Grace:
Women in Court in *The Winter's Tale* and *Henry VIII*

In this chapter, all quotations from Shakespeare's plays are from the following Arden editions: *The Winter's Tale*, ed. J. H. P. Padford (London: Methuen, 1963); *Henry VIII*, ed. Gordon McMullan (London: Arden Shakespeare, 2000); *Much Ado About Nothing*, ed. A. R. Humphreys (London: Methuen, 1981); and *A Midsummer Night's Dream*, ed. Harold F. Brooks (London: Methuen, 1979).

1. These include, in order of composition, *Pericles* (1607–08), *The Winter's Tale* (1609), *Cymbeline* (ca. 1610), *The Tempest* (1611), and *Henry VIII* (1613).

2. Neville Coghill, "The Basis of Shakespearean Comedy," *English Association Essays and Studies* 3 (1950): 4.

3. Peter Hall, dir., *A Midsummer Night's Dream*, 1968.

4. William Blackstone, *Blackstone's Commentaries on the Laws of England* (1765; Chicago: University of Chicago Press, 1979), 1:430.

5. Timothy Stretton, *Women Waging Law in Elizabethan England* (Cambridge: Cambridge University Press, 1998), 32–33.

6. Blackstone, *Commentaries*, 1:433.

7. Stretton, *Women Waging Law in Elizabethan England*, 27.

8. John Baker, *Introduction to English Legal History* (London: Butterworth's, 1972), 652 n. 74.

9. Stretton in *Women Waging Law in Elizabethan England* discusses *Marie Puttenham v. Richard Puttenham,* 143–47.

10. Eileen Spring, *Law, Land & Family: Aristocratic Inheritance In England, 1300 to 1800* (Chapel Hill: University of North Carolina Press, 1993), 43–65; Stretton, *Women Waging Law in Elizabethan England,* 31, 32. Both Spring and Stretton discuss the male reaction to women's inheritance of real property, and how changes in the law after the Stuart period made it progressively *harder* for women to inherit. Aristocratic males, apparently, often preferred their property to go to brothers, nephews, even more distant male heirs, rather than allowing women to inherit. A literary example of this is the entailment in *Pride and Prejudice* that prevents the Bennet daughters from inheriting Longbourn; rather, the estate will go to their father's cousin, Mr. Collins.

11. Stretton, *Women Waging Law in Elizabethan England,* 32–33.

12. Ibid., 39.

13. Ibid., 41.

14. Ibid., 217.

15. John Hawarde, *Les Reportes del Cases in Camera Stellata 1593–1609,* ed. William Baildon (Privately printed, 1894), 39, 161; quoted by Stretton, 52.

16. Stretton, *Women Waging Law in Elizabethan England,* 52.

17. Chilton L. Powell, *English Domestic Relations 1487–1653* (1917; New York: Russell and Russell, 1972), 147.

18. Richard Hooker, *The Folger Library Edition of the Works of Richard Hooker* (Cambridge, Mass.: Harvard University Press, 1977), 2:403–04. This is from *Of the Laws of Ecclesiastical Polity,* book 5, section 73.5.

19. Thomas Smith, *The Commonwealth of England, and Manner of Government Thereof* (London, 1601), 28.

20. Juan Luis Vives, *A Very Fruteful and Pleasant Boke Callyd the Instruction of a Christen Woman,* Trans. Richard Hyrde (London, 1541), fol 99v., as cited by Stretton, *Women Waging Law in Elizabethan England,* 49.

21. Richard Braithwait, *The English Gentlewoman* (London, 1631), 111.

22. Stretton, *Women Waging Law in Elizabethan England,* 51.

23. Benedick's line, *Much Ado about Nothing,* 2.1.141, in reference to subjects and their leaders.

24. Shakespeare's geography apparently impressed Ben Jonson, who told Drummond of Hawthornden that "Shakespeare, in a play, brought in a

number of men saying they had suffered shipwreck in Bohemia, where there is no sea near by some 100 miles." Jonson has got the geography right, but not the plot, since there are no survivors of the shipwreck.

25. *Catechism of the Catholic Church,* 2d ed. (Washington, D.C.: United States Catholic Conference, 1994), sec. 1459–60, pp. 366–67.

26. Roy Battenhouse, *Shakespeare's Christian Dimension* (Bloomington: Indiana University Press), 233.

27. "Within two years England and France were at war. Henry VIII went directly from the Field of the Cloth of Gold to meet the Emperor Charles. Late in 1521 the King and Emperor signed a treaty of common cause against France. And in 1522 the Earl of Surrey was leading armed English raiders over the same green pastures in which they had embraced France's nobles—and a few of France's ladies—as sworn bosom friends." Robert Lacey, *The Life and Times of Henry VIII* (New York: Weidenfeld & Nicholson, 1972), 62.

28. Roy Battenhouse, "Shakespeare's *Henry VIII* Reconsidered in the Light of Boethian and Biblical Commonplaces," in *Shakespeare and the Christian Tradition,* ed. E. Beatrice Bateson (Lewiston, N.Y.: Edwin Mellon, 1994), 50–82.

29. Robert Lacey summarizes the problems with Henry's argument, p. 107: "A major difficulty was the fact that whatever Henry's two treasured texts from Leviticus said, they seemed at face value to be concerned with the way in which brothers should conduct themselves with sisters-in-law whose husbands were *still living,* and the proper attitude towards *dead* brothers' wives was set out in Deuteronomy chapter XV, verse 5: 'When bretheren dwell together, and one of them dieth without children, the wife of the deceased shall not marry to another; but his brother shall take her, and raise up seed for his brother.' Which was exactly what Henry had done . . . ." (italics added)

30. *Contra* Shakespeare, Henry actually made Anne *marquess* of Pembroke, so that she held the title in her own right.

31. Raphael Holinshed, *Chronicles* (1577; New York: AMS Press, 1965), 737–8.

32. Garrett Mattingly, *Catherine of Aragon* (Boston: Little, Brown, 1941), 286.

33. Ibid, 367.

Chapter 6: *The Tempest:*
Judgment and Divine Providence

In this chapter, all quotations from *The Tempest* are from the Arden edition,
ed. Frank Kermode, (London: Methuen, 1954).

1. For example, see Francis Barker and Peter Hume, "Discursive Con-
    Texts of *The Tempest*," in *Alternative Shakespeares*, ed. John Drakakis
    (London; New York: Methuen, 1985), 191–205: *The Tempest* is "a play
    imbricated within the discourse of colonialism"; Lorie Jerrell Leininger,
    "The Miranda Trap: Sexism and Racism in Shakespeare's *Tempest*," in
    The Woman's Part: Feminist Criticism of Shakespeare, ed. Carolyn R. S.
    Lenz, Gayle Greene, and Carol T. Neely (Urbana, Ill.: University of
    Illinois Press, 1980), 285–94, wherein the author provides us with the
    long verbal wail she feels Miranda ought to give at the end of the play,
    including the line "I cannot give assent to an ethical scheme that locates
    all virtue symbolically in one part of my anatomy"; Ann Thompson,
    "'Miranda, Where's Your Sister?': Reading Shakespeare's *The Tempest*,"
    in *Feminist Criticism: Theory and Practice*, ed. Susan Sellers (Toronto:
    University of Toronto Press, 1991), 45–55, wherein Thompson's
    rhetorical question indicates her evaluation of the play, "What kind of
    pleasure can a woman and a feminist take in this text beyond the rather
    grim one of mapping its various patterns of exploitation?"

2. For connections between *The Tempest* and the book of Revelation, see
    Steven Marx, *Shakespeare and the Bible* (Oxford: Oxford University
    Press, 2000), 125–46.

3. Harold Bloom, *Shakespeare: The Invention of the Human* (New York:
    Riverhead Books, 1998), 662.

4. *The Catechism of the Catholic Church* (New York: Doubleday, 1995),
    sec. 312, provides a basic definition of Providence that both
    Shakespeare's Protestant and Catholic contemporaries would have
    agreed upon: "Divine providence consists of the dispositions by which
    God guides all his creatures with wisdom and love to their ultimate
    end."

5. Derived from Aristotle's *Poetics* and revised by continental dramatists
    such as Corneille, the unities required a play to take place with about
    twenty-four hours at the outside, or as close to real time as possible, in
    one location, and with only one dramatic action, i.e., one plot line.

6. Bloom, *Shakespeare: The Invention of the Human*, 671.

7. Stephen Orgel, introduction, *The Tempest* (Oxford: Oxford University
    Press, 1987), 44.

8. Jane Austen, *Pride and Prejudice* (New York: Alfred A. Knopf, 1991),
    293.

9. *Catechism of the Catholic Church* (New York: Doubleday, 1995), sec. 2350.

10. Robert Gram Hunter, *Shakespeare and the Comedy of Forgiveness* (New York: Columbia University Press, 1965), 234.

11. "The Order for the Administration of the Lord's Supper, or Holy Communion," *The Book of Common Prayer, 1559* (Published for the Folger Shakespeare Library, Charlottesville: University Press of Virginia, 1976), 247.

12. *Certain Sermons or Homilies Appointed to Be Read in Churches in the Time of Queen Elizabeth I (1547–1571)*, (Facsimile of 1623; Gainesville, Fla.: Scholars' Facsimiles & Reprints, 1968), 264–70.

13. See *Henry V,* 4.1.181–82: "Every subject's duty is the king's, / But every subject's soul is his own."

Conclusion: "Is this the promised end?"

All quotations from *King Lear* are from the Arden edition, ed. R. A. Foakes (London: Thomas Nelson, 1997).

1. R. A. Foakes, introduction, *King Lear* (London: Thomas Nelson, 1997), 12, describes the play as "curiously disconnected from chronicled time."

2. A. C. Bradley, *Shakespearean Tragedy,* 3d ed. (1904; New York: St. Martin's Press, 1992), 224.

3. Nicholas Brooke, *Shakespeare: King Lear* (London: Edward Arnold Publishers, Ltd., 1963), 59.

4. Foakes, 386 n. 262.

5. This, of course, is the problem of theodicy, which inspired Milton to write *Paradise Lost,* to justify the ways of God to man. I prefer God's answer to Job's.

INDEX